The Persian Gulf triangle

Manchester University Press

IDENTITIES AND GEOPOLITICS IN THE MIDDLE EAST

Series editors: Simon Mabon, Edward Wastnidge and May Darwich

After the Arab Uprisings and the ensuing fragmentation of regime-society relations across the Middle East, identities and geopolitics have become increasingly contested, with serious implications for the ordering of political life at domestic, regional and international levels, best seen in conflicts in Syria and Yemen. The Middle East is the most militarised region in the world where geopolitical factors remain predominant factors in shaping political dynamics. Another common feature of the regional landscape is the continued degeneration of communal relations as societal actors retreat into sub-state identities, while difference becomes increasingly violent, spilling out beyond state borders. The power of religion – and trans-state nature of religious views and linkages – thus provides the means for regional actors (such as Saudi Arabia and Iran) to exert influence over a number of groups across the region and beyond. This series provides space for the engagement with these ideas and the broader political, legal and theological factors to create space for an intellectual re-imagining of socio-political life in the Middle East.

Originating from the SEPAD project (www.sepad.org.uk), this series facilitates the re-imagining of political ideas, identities and organisation across the Middle East, moving beyond the exclusionary and binary forms of identity to reveal the contingent factors that shape and order life across the region.

To buy or to find out more about the books currently available in this series, please go to: https://manchesteruniversitypress.co.uk/series/identities-and-geopolitics-in-the-middle-east/

The Persian Gulf triangle

Strategic relations between Iran, Saudi Arabia and the United States

Luíza Cerioli

MANCHESTER UNIVERSITY PRESS

Published by Manchester University Press
Oxford Road, Manchester, M13 9PL

www.manchesteruniversitypress.co.uk

British Library Cataloguing-in-Publication Data
A catalogue record for this book is available from the British
Library

ISBN 978 1 5261 7808 4 hardback

First published 2024

Typeset by Newgen Publishing UK

Contents

Figures

Acknowledgements

I want to express my gratitude to the many people who have supported me during the process of writing this book and to the institutions that have placed their trust in me. First and foremost, I am thankful to my parents, Rosana and Gleno, for always encouraging me to strive to be the best version of myself. Without the tireless support of my first mentors, I would not have left home and embarked on this journey. To my partner Martin, who has become my home, I am incredibly thankful.

I am also deeply grateful to my PhD supervisors, Rachid Ouaissa and Thomas Juneau, for guiding me through the entire process and providing invaluable feedback and direction. I also want to express my appreciation to many friends and colleagues from Kassel, Marburg, Brasília, Porto Alegre, and Bagé. Your presence has brought me comfort, presented me with challenges, and filled my life with joy and wonder.

I want to acknowledge the Brazilian Federal Agency for Support and Evaluation of Graduate Education for providing the resources that have allowed me to reach this point. Finally, I extend my thanks to the editors of the Identities and Geopolitics in the Middle East series, the reviewers, and all the staff at Manchester University Press.

I always had students in mind as my audience when writing this book. If this book inspires you to explore the fascinating realms of Middle East Studies and International Relations, then I feel like I have accomplished my goal.

Introduction

Iran and Saudi Arabia are the two most influential countries in the Persian Gulf today. They are rich in oil resources, with a significant geostrategic position, their regimes are relatively stable, and they invest considerably in military forces. Both are entangled in several Middle Eastern political affairs, often employing ideological or identitarian tools to boost their regional leverage while trying to lessen the other's influence. Moreover, their relationship has been intrinsically linked to the United States' (US) behaviour in the region. For decades, the US has proactively taken part in the Persian Gulf's political and military disputes under the clout of protecting the oil market and the regional order. Directly or indirectly, it was involved in all the contemporary wars that tainted the region: the 1980s Iran–Iraq war, the 1990 Gulf War, the 2003 Iraq invasion and subsequent civil war, and the 2014–2017 clash against the Islamic State.

This book calls the complex relationship between this extra-regional actor and the two regional nations a strategic triangle. A change in one side of a triangle forces the other two sides to react as they are all linked. Making an analogy to this geometric figure, the book challenges the scholarly tendency in International Relations, Security Studies, and Area Studies to examine state–state relations only at the bilateral level. What if three countries have such interconnected interactions that looking only at one bilateral relation would not suffice? If something happens to one side of a triangle (the ties between countries A and B), the other two sides (the relationships between A and C and C and B) respond and adjust. This book shows how, since the early 1970s, the decision-making process in the US, Saudi Arabia, and Iran concerning the Persian Gulf's geopolitics has been so interweaved that studying each bilateral relation separately is inadequate. A change in one side of this triangle (for example, the Iran–Saudi Arabia dyad) mostly forces a change in the other two (the US–Saudi Arabia and US–Iran dyads), impacting the Persian Gulf regional system.

The Persian Gulf is a body of water in Western Asia that extends the Indian Ocean through the Arabian Sea and touches seven countries: Iran,

Iraq, Saudi Arabia, Qatar, the United Arab Emirates (UAE), Bahrain, and Oman. This region has been vital for global history for centuries. Ancient empires repeatedly fought to take hold of land there; vibrant port cities connected the Middle East to India, East Africa, and Asia; European powers such as Portugal and the United Kingdom built protectorates there for strategic gains; and, since the first large oil field was discovered in 1908 in Persia (now Iran), the region's resources became essential to global capitalist markets. As expected, external intervention, military coups, revolutions, tribal rivalries, cultural blossoms, and many transnational identities permeated the region's political history.

If one were to take a snapshot of the Persian Gulf geopolitics today, they would immediately detect the prominence of Iran, Saudi Arabia, and the US. Iran has long promoted itself as a regional leader due to its size, population, and centuries-long history. Moreover, its convoluted relations with the West, controversial nuclear programme, and revolutionary rhetoric have often put the country in the spotlight of international discussions. In turn, Saudi Arabia has an immensurable cultural value to Muslim people worldwide as well as to the global markets. An oil powerhouse with the production capacity to alter prices according to its own interests, the country also has one of the world's most significant military expenditures. Moreover, it has boosted its geopolitical weight in the Middle East in the last decades by assuming a participative role in the politics and economy of Egypt, Syria, Yemen, Bahrain, and Lebanon.

In turn, the US still holds the most advanced military capabilities in the region and shares strategic ties with most local countries. As a result, it is an active player in the Persian Gulf's geopolitical game, behaving like an extraregional actor with specific interests, strategies, and a securitarian agenda. Whereas Saudi Arabia sustains positive and security-leaning relations with Washington, Iran, on the contrary, is outright against the US presence in the region. The ties between Saudi Arabia and Iran have oscillated between pragmatic cooperation and hostility and accusation, often reflecting their very different expectations concerning regional order. This book discusses these three relationships in depth, portraying them as multifaceted and often thorny, something that reflects divergent concerns, political natures, and ambitions.

The competition for hearts and minds between Iran and Saudi Arabia goes beyond traditional definitions of hegemony-seeking behaviour, as they capitalise on ideological, religious, and ethnic factors to elaborate their narratives of pre-eminence. They are, indeed, two almost mirrored-opposed, religious-run countries with vastly different leadership styles. Iran's political ethos is revolutionary, anti-status quo, and pan-Islamist. However, it diverges from most of its neighbours for being Shia and Persian and for not having working relations with Washington. Conversely, Saudi Arabia aims to maintain the regional status quo and good relations with the West. An Arab and Wahhabi monarchy, home to Mecca and Medina, Saudi Arabia holds dear for itself a position of distinction among the world's Muslim community.

The US' relationship with the two is complex and full of myths and oversimplified definitions. After the 1979 Islamic Revolution, Iran went from a strategic ally to the most prominent foe of the US in the Middle East. A series of hostilities, misunderstandings, and escalations produced an enmity discourse between the US Americans and Iranians that has been hard to overcome. As the US–Iranian ties crumbled in the 1980s, the friendship of convenience between Washington and Riyadh consolidated as one of the most reliable elements in regional geopolitics. Despite their very distinct political and social beliefs, their securitarian interests converged, as both sought to safeguard order, avoid disturbance to the oil markets, and check the rise of any local hegemony. This way, the US–Saudi Arabian bilateral relationship is portrayed in opposition to the US–Iranian one.

Nevertheless, Iran and Saudi Arabia have not always been rivals, having already collaborated at different moments. In the 1970s, Riyadh and Tehran aligned with the US' goal of checking the Soviet regional influence. From the 1990s until 2005, they shared a rapprochement momentum in which they worked together to construct a win-win scenario. After a decade of escalating tensions through the 2010s, the 2020s may be cautiously opening a space for a Saudi–Iranian reconciliation once more. Diplomatic ties between the two, broken in 2016, were restored in 2023.

This book showcases a certain level of pragmatism within the US–Iranian bilateral relation that is often hidden. Iran and the US had moments of limited strategic settlement despite not sharing diplomatic ties. Moreover, since the 1990s, several presidencies from both countries have attempted to reduce tensions at least once. Interestingly, some of these efforts, such as the 2001 Bonn conference, were supported by the Saudis, whereas others, such as the 2015 Joint Comprehensive Plan of Action (JCPOA), were not.

Despite a visible degree of interconnectivity between these three countries, the specialised literature remains concentrated only on studying the relations bilaterally. For example, most of those investigating the Iran–Saudi relationship include the US' role as a factor or a part of the contextualisation rather than an extra-regional actor actively playing the geopolitical game.[1] Others chose a 'US plus the region' approach, avoiding scrutinising the US at the same analytical level as the local states.[2] These works imply that Washington is an actor who does not need to have its ideologies, identities, leadership, or political affiliations examined. Only a few have mentioned the need to treat Washington as a member of the regional system that impacts and is impacted by local politics, but a model for this analysis is yet to be offered.[3] On the other hand, studies concerning Saudi–Iranian relations are mostly time-constrained – concentrating on moments of tension or approximation – avoiding discussions about patterns of change and fluctuation that become visible only in more prolonged time frames.[4]

For those reasons and more, this book explores the three countries' interactions together, replacing the dyadic analytical lens with a triangular one. Critical events within one dyad (a side of the triangle) are assumed to link with the other two dyads. For example, in the 1970s, when President Nixon (1969–1974) elaborated a strategy for the region, he included both Iran and Saudi Arabia, despite Iran being much stronger. President Clinton's (1993–2001) policy of isolating Iran obstructed the Saudi–Iranian rapprochement throughout the 1990s. Conversely, President Obama (2009–2017) pledged his support to Saudi Arabia in the 2015 Yemeni war to appease the monarchy while the JCPOA was being implemented. This list is not exhaustive and reveals a complexity between the three countries worth investigating.

Building the Persian Gulf triangle

This book employs a cohesive International Relations (IR) analytical framework to explore the relations between these three actors in the regional system. While much is written about the security-for-oil alliance between Riyadh and Washington, the rivalry between Tehran and Riyadh, and the enmity between the US Americans and Iranians, few consider how interconnected these three bilateral ties are. Therefore, the book demonstrates that much nuance, detail, and specification are gained by considering that these three countries are entangled in a strategic triangular relationship. This triangulation has shaped the Persian Gulf since its formation as a modern regional system in the 1970s. Thus, the study touches on regional order debates, complex relational patterns, geopolitics, power competition, and the role of extra-regional powers.

The Persian Gulf developed into a modern regional system when the British ended their protectorate on the eve of the 1970s, and the Trucial States became independent countries. Since then, Bahrain, Oman, Saudi Arabia, Iran, Iraq, the UAE, and Qatar have shared preoccupations with the local order, showing different projects and ambitions of how it should be orchestrated. Moreover, during this period, the US elaborated its first specific policy on the Persian Gulf, the Twin Pillar Diplomacy. Before, the region's security was under British responsibility in the Western agenda. A decade later, the Carter Doctrine replaced the Twin Pillar strategy and consolidated the region as a significant security priority for Washington. Since then, the US' involvement in the region only grew in scope and commitment.

At this point, it is essential to shed light on the term *strategic triangle*. Lowell Dittmer first conceptualised it to grasp the relations between the US, the Soviet Union, and China.[5] He argued that these countries shared highly interdependent relationship patterns in the sense that each actor would look into its ties with the other two before making geopolitical decisions. This way, Dittmer defines a strategic triangle as a tripartite relational arrangement that constrains or influences the three countries' international behaviour. First, to be in a strategic triangle, three countries must perceive each other as strategically salient for the system they operate in. That means each of them must acknowledge that the other two are crucial and influential geopolitical actors. Second, even if the three actors are asymmetric in terms of power, each must be recognised by the other two as autonomous players, not contesting the other's sovereignty.[6] Third, each bilateral relationship is liable for the other two participants' relationships. Suppose they satisfy these three demands, and it is detectable that the three countries assess their geopolitical environment and elaborate their international strategy with an awareness of one another. In that case, they are in a strategic triangle.

This analytical construct assumes that each bilateral relation composing the triangle can be valued as positive or negative. Positive means that collaboration tendencies outweigh conflictive ones and negative is the other way round. This way, there can be four patterns of triangulation between actors locked into a strategic triangle: (i) *ménage à trois*, where the three parts have positive relations; (ii) *romantic triangle*, where a country has positive relations with the other two parties, but the two have negative relations; (iii) *stable marriage*, where two countries have a stable positive relation but have a negative relationship with the third party; and (iv) *veto triangle*, where there is no positive relationship between them (Figure 0.1).

This book takes this analytical construct as an exploratory tool to generate hypotheses about what type of triangular relationship these three countries had shared since the eve of 1970. It discusses how, since then, five major regional events have shaken the Persian Gulf balance of power, creating new opportunities and threats for the actors and, in turn, altering the type of triangular relations the three countries shared. These events are the British Empire's departure from the region on the eve of the 1970s, the Iranian Islamic Revolution of 1979, the Iraq invasion of Kuwait in 1990, the 2003 US invasion of Iraq, and the Islamic State of Iraq and Syria's (ISIS) offensive in June 2014.

We see how these five events altered the environment in which states interact, provoking changes within the relational pattern between the

US, Iran, and Saudi Arabia. Based on Dittmer's typology, this book demonstrates five different triangulations these countries shared:

- The *ménage à trois* (from 1969 to 1979): after the British departed from the Persian Gulf, Riyadh, Tehran, and Washington shared positive relations and engaged to guarantee the regional order under the Twin Pillar strategy.
- The *stable marriage* (from 1979 to 1989): after the Iranian Revolution, the US–Saudi ties intensified as their relations with Iran deteriorated, isolating Tehran during the Iran–Iraq war.
- The *romantic triangle* (from 1989 to 2003): following the Cold War's end and the 1990 Kuwait invasion, Iran and Saudi Arabia improved ties in a rapprochement period, while the US remained hostile to Iran, hindering the Iran–Saudi rapprochement.
- The *rebooted stable marriage* (from 2003 to 2014): Iran and Saudi Arabia gained power with the US invasion of Iraq but ceased their rapprochement for disagreeing with the regional order. As a result, rivalry between Riyadh and Iran emerged. That is also linked to Riyadh being dissatisfied with the US' role in the region, which, in turn, sought to tackle Iran's nuclear programme.

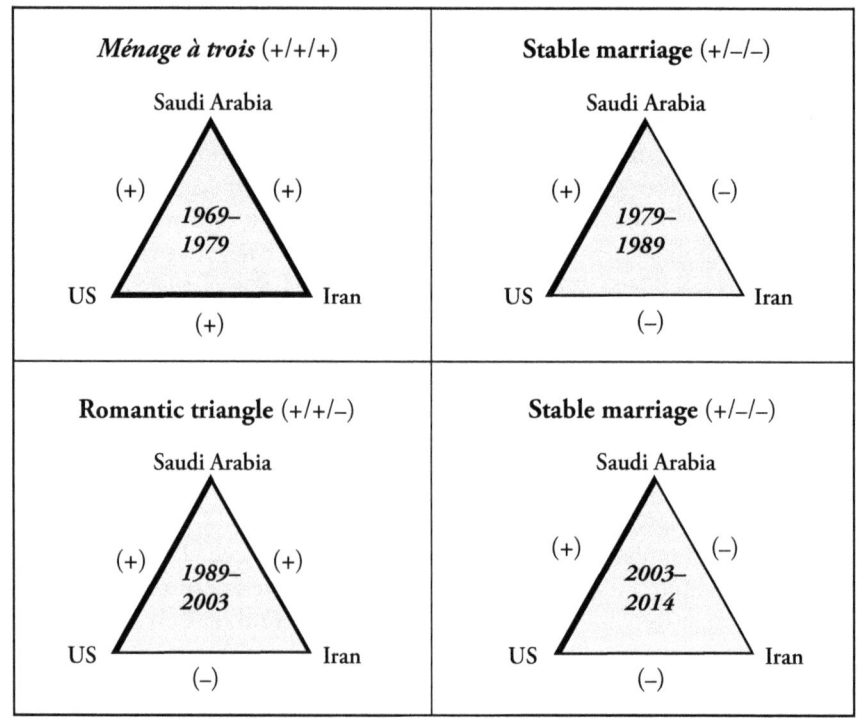

Figure 0.1 The four triangles

- The *ongoing triangle*: after the ISIS offensive on Mosul and Tikrit, Iran and the US sent troops to the region to check the expansion of the terrorist organisation. Simultaneously, Saudi Arabia has been conducting a war in Yemen to consolidate its role as a powerful regional actor. At the same time, other extra-regional powers, such as China and Russia, are increasing their political clout in the region. A definition of this triangulation remains elusive and is beyond the scope of this book.

Framing the triangles via Neoclassical Realism

While Dittmer's analytical construct enables more systematic thinking about triangular relationships, it does not provide a helpful theory to grasp how the three actors caught in this relationship pattern make decisions; nor does it show how this configuration may affect the regional system. For that, this book operationalises its argument through Neoclassical Realism (NCR), a strain of the Realist thought that brings contextualisation, history, and particularism to its analytical framework. Under NCR, the distribution of power between actors in the international system delineates the conditions for inter-state relations. Still, it does not determine the specificities of these relations, nor explain why states behave the way they do. For that, one must open the 'black box' of the state and examine the internal elements shaping and defining international behaviour.[7] Thus, NCR is a structural theory that seeks more explanative value, investigating political events as they are, not how they ought to be.

Such looser paradigmatic boundaries are welcome for studying the Middle East. The region provokes scholars to seek a middle ground between agency and structure, linking the system and the units. This book claims that NCR improves the standard eclecticism employed within International Relations of the Middle East (IRME) as it offers a deductive reasoning approach that elaborates synthetical, hierarchical, and replicable explanatory chains. In these chains, the international system is the independent variable creating conditions for action, while unit-level factors are intervening variables, meditating and redirecting signals into policies. For those reasons, NCR offers the tools for exploring relational patterns between three countries while providing an analytical model that can be reproduced.

The book works with an NCR framework that has the following explanatory chain: *contextualised power* (independent variable); *status satisfaction, state identity, and leadership preferences* (intervening variables); and *the strategic triangle* (dependent variable). Through this model, it shows that the triangulation between Iran, Saudi Arabia, and the US has a long-standing formation, learned and reproduced by ideational, cognitive, and leadership schemas.

This explanatory chain is applied in each period of regional power rebalancing (1969–1979; 1979–1990; 1990–2003; 2003–2014), which corresponds to the triangulations. Each analytical chapter first briefly discusses and contextualises the systemic event that altered the Persian Gulf's balance of power. These events provide the conditions for recalculating the explanatory chain as the countries assess new constraints and opportunities to orient their action. In other words, they set the analysis into motion. After the contextualisation, the analysis moves towards grasping the power (the independent variable) of the US, Iran, and Saudi Arabia throughout the period.

After discussing the power for each actor, the analysis explores how they are positioned in the Persian Gulf's power balance. It reviews each country's strengths and weaknesses, framing Iran, Saudi Arabia, and the US in the bigger picture of the regional system throughout the period. That allows for a broader perspective of the system's securitarian environment and includes, when necessary, other relevant actors.

The following step is the investigation of the intervening variables. First, *status satisfaction* determines if each country was revisionist or status quo during the period. Therefore, it concerns whether one's aspired position in the regional order corresponds to what others ascribe to it. Status satisfaction can vary positively (status aspiration corresponds to ascription; the actor is satisfied) or negatively (status aspirations do not correspond to ascription; the actor is revisionist). The second intervening variable is *state identity*, showcasing each country's cognitive roles projected to the region. This variable has a filtering effect, discarding available outcomes that do not correspond to a state's self-perceived image. The final intervening variable is *leadership preferences*, which explores the inclinations of those making international politics. For the US, the focus is on the presidents; for Saudi Arabia, it is on kings and crown princes; for Iran, the Pahlavi dynasty is in the first triangle, and the supreme leaders and the presidents are in the other triangles.[8]

The book has a *descriptive*, *interpretative*, and *explanative* focus, approaching historical events and official state narratives with critical lenses. It presents a qualitative research design, relying on primary and secondary literature about the Middle East, particularly that related to Iran, Saudi Arabia, or the US, as well as official documents, public statements, diplomatic cables, media outlets, memoirs, interviews, and speeches. In addition, declassified documents from the US administration provided by the Central Intelligence Agency's (CIA) website or the online presidential libraries were relevant. Finally, official documents from Iran and Saudi Arabia on their governmental websites were also valuable sources. The numbers for economic, demographic, and geographical factors are taken from the World Bank, Correlates of War, and other databases.

Finally, NCR's methodological preference is via case studies rich in qualitative data handled through process-tracing. This method consists of presenting detailed case studies to determine whether the hypothesis can be fulfilled and if the predicted causal effects of the chosen intervening variables are visible in the decision-making processes. Deductively, this methodology exposes which intervening events should have occurred within a case if the theory is an accurate explanation. Thus, process-tracing generates and analyses data on the causal mechanisms, linking putative causes to observed effects. It enables the book to identify and trace the connections between causes and observed phenomena via sequential processes.

The book's contribution

Beyond complementing the literature on Middle Eastern geopolitics, this book contributes to interlinked scholarly discussions. First, it engages with the Global IR movement, which aims to de-Westernise the discipline of IR to make it more reflective of the diverse realities outside the centre of knowledge production.[9] This disciplinary movement promotes dialogue between existing traditions to investigate how concepts are applied, modified, and expanded in the Global South. It suggests advancing the discipline by inclusion and reimagination, embracing academic power diffusion, and reducing intellectual barriers between the Global North and the Global South.

This book subscribes to the disciplinary pluralisation proposed by the Global IR initiative and seeks to displace knowledge production away from Western hegemony. For many decades, the Middle East has been kept away from most theory-building in IR because it was perceived as too unique to be compared to other regions.[10] Nevertheless, by producing an innovative, theoretically driven, and replicable analytical framework based on a regional empirical case that can be applied to other cases, this book rejects this ostracisation tendency. It brings the Middle East to the forefront of disciplinary discussions about rivalry, grand strategy, and relational patterns and contributes directly to IR progress.

Second, Realism has repeatedly been put in the spotlight for its Western bias, which dismisses other cases, actors, and voices outside the centre of knowledge production.[11] By employing an NCR framework for a Persian Gulf phenomenon, this book broadens the tradition's scope of inquiry and analytical horizons beyond the traditional Western cases. This exercise allows Realism to overcome its parochialist tendencies to marginalise non-Western ideas and cases, which is precisely what the Global IR initiative proposes. Therefore, this book presents itself as a path to reinvigorate and pluralise the Realist research programme by producing knowledge aligned with the reality outside the West.

Finally, the book promotes this de-Westernisation of the Realist tradition precisely by interacting with the Middle East Studies literature. Interdisciplinarity can bring scholars from different backgrounds closer to a transformative dialogue where one can find new cases, voices, and understandings. The book provides an extensive literature review that combines rich, in-depth knowledge about Iran, Saudi Arabia, and the US with IR concepts such as grand strategy, status, environmental restrictiveness, state identities, and balance of power. Thus, it works in both fields' interfaces, profiting from IR's cross-cutting theories and regional studies' valuable contextual analysis. Just like Global IR calls for Area Studies to be brought back to the discipline's theory-making, this book delivers a two-way conversation in which both fields learn from each other.

The outline of the book

Following this introduction, Chapter 1 explains the analytical boundaries and contextualises the study of the Persian Gulf as a regional system within the IRME. This chapter stresses the importance of regions to the IR discipline while narrowing the focus to the Persian Gulf as a subsystem within the Middle East. It points out the system's formation on the eve of the 1970s, characterising it as multipolar, heavily dependent on oil resources, and marked by transnational religious identities, militarisation, and US interventionism. The chapter also investigates how the literature has traditionally studied the three relational dyads – US–Iran, US–Saudi Arabia, and Saudi Arabia–Iran. This literature review is critical for outlining the intervening variables – thus providing the dialogue between area and discipline that starts the analysis.

Chapter 2 introduces the theoretical framework and has three parts. The first part reviews the IRME's theoretical inclinations to justify the choice of an NCR framework. This review shows how the field tends to tilt towards a middle ground between universalism and particularism, agency and structure, one that does not abandon Realism but insists on exploring characteristics of the state and other actors. The second part specifies NCR's added value concerning research agenda, rigour, and analytical replicability. The chapter concludes by displaying the variable selection and the research design.

Chapters 3, 4, 5, and 6 have the same structure and correspond to the four triangulations. Each chapter first describes the systemic change that ignited a modification in the balance of power. Then, in the sequence, there is an analysis of each country's power during each selected period. Here, first, power is dissected into several elements, material and non-material, and second, the Persian Gulf's balance of power is contextualised – emphasising Iran's, Saudi Arabia's, and the US' power projection capacities in the region. After evaluating the systemic change and the countries' power, each chapter explores the three intervening variables: status satisfaction, state identity, and leadership preferences. The chapters conclude by presenting the tendencies and main events of the respective strategic triangle.

In Chapter 3, the systemic change is the British departure from the Persian Gulf, inciting the Trucial States' independence and solidifying the region as a system. The first triangle's tendency was the *Twin Pillar Diplomacy*, in which the three countries worked together to maintain the status quo. The chapter shows how the US sought partners in strategic regions to guarantee Western interests without direct involvement. It argues that Iran capitalised on the Nixon Doctrine to boost the country's militarisation, modernisation, and regional ties. Conversely, the analysis shows how Saudi Arabia constructed a grand strategy that lasted for decades: assessing if Iran or Iraq were the most significant regional threat and balancing accordingly with the support of the US. Therefore, despite their differences in power, status ambitions, and state identities, each country shared threat perceptions and played roles that coexisted throughout the period, creating a collaborative security architecture.

In Chapter 4, the systemic change is the 1979 Iranian Revolution and the beginning of the Iran–Iraq war in 1980. The chapter shows how the Iranian state transformed, and, quite quickly, countries that once profited from Iranian protection started to support Saddam Hussein's war. Iran became the epitome of a revisionist country, promoting its form of Islamism as a tool for emancipation from Western imperialism. The chapter argues that these new characteristics drove the US and Saudi Arabia to seek political alternatives to maintain order. The Revolution pushed the triangle towards a 'stable marriage' type, in which the US–Saudi Arabia relationship grew strong due to a restrictive securitarian environment. At the same time, the other two relations became increasingly hostile. Nevertheless, the analysis shows how Iran's isolation was not immediate, with President Jimmy Carter and King Fahd attempting to reach out to Iran. However, the fear of Iran exporting its Revolution drove the eventual consolidation of the US–Saudi 'oil-for-security' alliance. That culminated in the Carter Doctrine, outlining an order protector role to the US.

Chapter 5 begins by describing the Gulf War in Kuwait as a systemic change. This chapter contends that the period from 1990 to 2003 was one of lost opportunities for the three countries to improve relations. They all shared the perception that Iraq was the most significant regional threat. However, that alone does not explain why the Saudi–Iranian rapprochement materialised in the 1990s, nor why Iran and the US failed to find a reconciliation path repeatedly. This chapter illustrates how domestic politics and ideas have played a crucial role in strategising in the three countries. For example, President Bill Clinton's Dual Containment strategy can be grasped as a product of ontological distress within US policymakers during the unipolar moment. The chapter concludes that the continued US–Iran hostility arguably weakened the ongoing Saudi–Iranian rapprochement.

The systemic change in Chapter 6 is the 2003 US invasion of Iraq, stressing how Iran, Saudi Arabia, and the US were beneficiated in terms of power with the fall of Saddam Hussein. The US expanded its military presence to unforeseeable levels and boosted security ties with the Gulf Cooperation Council (GCC); Iran's set of alliances was heightened with Shia groups' enfranchisement; and Saudi Arabia was relieved to see Saddam go. However, by the eve of the 2010s, the US Americans showed signs of war fatigue while growing sanctions ceased the Iranian empowerment moment. As a result, only Saudi Arabia retained steady growth and arrived at the end of the period with more power than it started with. This chapter explains why and how the triangle changed from a 'romantic triangle' to a 'rebooted stable marriage' with two tendencies: the gradual emergence of Saudi Arabia's regional power ambition, and the advance of nuclear negotiations between Iran and the US. It contends that Saudi Arabia's new role competed with Iran for regional leadership and responded to a growing dissatisfaction with the US, revealing, once again, how intertwined the triangle is.

The book concludes with some critical points on the current triangulation, which is analytically still under construction. After 2014, Washington and Tehran worried about containing the ISIS threat and increased their military and security cooperation with Iraq. As a result, Iran broadened its influence considerably over Iraqi and Syrian politics. The US, on the other hand, returned to Iraq with a military advisory role that translated into political clout. In parallel, Saudi Arabia has been trying to gain political-economic leverage in Iraq since it opened its embassy in Baghdad in 2016, after a twenty-five-year break. The conclusion does not employ the theoretical framework applied to the previous four triangles; nor does it aim to conclude with the tendencies, as it is impossible to make assumptions about something that is still going on. Therefore, the chapter concludes by stressing the theoretical and disciplinary contributions of the analysis as well as presenting some observations on the growing global multipolarity and its consequences to the Middle East and the Persian Gulf in particular.

Notes

1 Kim Ghattas, *Black wave: Saudi Arabia, Iran, and the forty-year rivalry that unraveled culture, religion, and collective memory in the Middle East* (New York: Henry Holt and Co, 2020); Dilip Hiro, *Cold War in the Islamic world: Saudi Arabia, Iran and the struggle for supremacy* (New York: Oxford University Press, 2018); Faisal b. S. al-Saud, *Iran, Saudi Arabia and the Gulf: Power politics in transition* (London, New York: I.B. Tauris, 2003).

2 Kenneth Pollack, *The Persian puzzle: The conflict between Iran and America* (Munich: Random House, 2005); Jeremy Pressman, Power without influence: The Bush administration's foreign policy failure in the Middle East. *International Security* 33: 4, 2009, pp. 149–179; Steven Hook, Hegemonic stability and American power, in Tim Niblock and Steven Hook (eds), *The United States and the Gulf: Shifting pressures, strategies and alignments* (Berlin: Gerlach Press, 2015), pp. 23–41.

3 Paul Aarts and Joris van Duijne, Saudi Arabia after the U.S.–Iranian détente: Left in the lurch?, *Middle East Policy* XVI: 3, 2009, pp. 64–78; Henner Fürtig, *Iran's rivalry with Saudi Arabia between the Gulf wars* (Reading: Ithaca Press, 2002); Banafsheh Keynoush, *Saudi Arabia and Iran: Friends or foes?* (New York: Palgrave Macmillan, 2016).

4 Shahram Chubin and Charles Tripp, *Iran–Saudi Arabia relations and regional order* (London: Oxford University Press, 1996); Gwenn Okruhlik, Saudi Arabian–Iranian relations: External rapprochement and internal consolidation, *Middle East Policy* 10: 2, 2003, pp. 113–125; Andrew W. Terrill, *The Saudi–Iranian rivalry and the future of Middle East security* (Carlisle: Strategic Studies Institute, US Army War College, 2011); Edward Wastnidge and Simon Mabon (eds), *Saudi Arabia and Iran: The struggle to shape the Middle East* (Manchester: Manchester University Press, 2022).

5 Lowell Dittmer, The strategic triangle: An elementary game-theoretical analysis, *World Politics* 33: 4, 1981, pp. 485–515.

6 Danielle F. Cohen, *Retracing the triangle: China's strategic perceptions of Japan in the post-Cold War era* (Contemporary Asian Studies No. 2) (Baltimore, MD: School of Law, 2005).

7 Michiel Foulon and Gustav Meibauer, Realist avenues to global International Relations. *European Journal of International Relations* 26: 4, 2020, pp. 1203–1229; Jennifer Sterling-Folker, Forward is as forward does: Assessing Neoclassical Realism from a traditions perspective, in Annette Freyberg-Inan, Ewan Harrison, and Patrick James (eds), *Rethinking Realism in International Relations* (Baltimore: Johns Hopkins University Press, 2009), pp. 192–218; Nicholas Kitchen, Neoclassical Realism and a theory of international politics, in Gustav Meibauer, Linde Desmaele, Tudor Onea, Nicholas Kitchen, Michiel Foulon, Alexander Reichwein, and Jennifer Sterling-Folker (eds), Forum: Rethinking Neoclassical Realism at theory's end. *International Studies Review* 23: 1, 2020, pp. 268–295; Steven Lobell, Jeffrey Taliaferro, and Norrin Ripsman (eds), *Neoclassical Realism, the state, and foreign policy* (New York: Cambridge University Press, 2009).

8 In sum, the book covers, for the US, the following administrations: Richard Nixon (1969–1974), Gerald Ford (1974–1977), Jimmy Carter (1977–1981), Ronald Reagan (1981–1989), George H. W. Bush (1989–1993), Bill Clinton (1993–2001), George Bush (2001–2009), and Barack Obama (2009–2021). For Saudi Arabia, it covers the kingdoms of: Faisal (1964–1975), Khalid (1975–1982), Fahd (1982–2005), and Abdullah (2005–2015). Finally, it covers for Iran the rule of the Shah Reza Pahlavi (1941–1979), the revolutionary consolidation (1979–1989), as well as the following presidencies of the second constitution: Akbar Hashemi Rafsanjani (1989–1997), Mohammad Khatami (1997–2005), Mahmoud Ahmadinejad (2005–2013), and Hassan Rouhani (2013–2021).

9 Amitav Acharya, Global International Relations (IR) and regional worlds, *International Studies Quarterly* 58: 4, 2014, pp. 647–659; Maiken Gelardi, Moving Global IR forward – a road map, *International Studies Review* 22: 4, 2020, pp. 830–852; Amitav Acharya and Barry Buzan, Why is there no non-Western international relations theory? An introduction, *International Relations of the Asia-Pacific* 7: 4, 2007, pp. 287–312.

10 Morten Valbjørn, Toward a 'Mesopotamian turn': Disciplinarily and the study of the International Relations of the Middle East, *Journal of Mediterranean Studies* 14: 1/2, 2004, pp. 47–75; Louise Fawcett, International Relations and the Middle East: Bringing Area Studies (back) in, in Contributor introduction: Does International Relations need Area Studies? *St Antony's International Review (STAIR)* 16, 2020, pp. 8–14.

11 Carlos Escudé, *Realismo periférico* (Buenos Aires: Planeta, 1992); Mohammed Ayoob, Inequality and theorizing in International Relations: The case for subaltern Realism, *International Studies Review* 4: 3, 2002, pp. 27–48; Pinar Bilgin, Thinking past Western IR, *Third World Quarterly* 29: 1, 2008, pp. 5–23; Turan Kayaoglu, Westphalian Eurocentrism in International Relations theory, *International Studies Review* 12: 2, 2010, pp. 193–217; David Blaney and Arlene B. Tickner, International Relations in the prison of colonial modernity, *International Relations* 31: 1, 2017, pp. 71–75.

1

The Persian Gulf regional system: Iran, Saudi Arabia, and the United States as regional actors

Regions and the Middle East

The concept of a regional system is frequently used within IR without a clear conceptualisation or definition. Briefly, there is an international system in which all the countries take part and interact. However, there are also other structures, some of them geographically bounded, into which states find themselves inserted and, due to it, have their politics, economy, and security dynamics affected. Under this logic, a region is a geographical cluster of units embedded in a larger international system but still with its own structure.[1] Regions help us narrow our focus to a feasible geospatial subject and explore the patterns of intrastate relations, politics, and securitarian concerns happening there. Countries in a particular region tend to share a similar historical path and general concerns, with or without a common ethnicity or identity. It is a broadly defined unit, without an actor quality, comprised of states tied together by political, economic, and cultural interactions.

However, what makes a region? There is no consensus on where one region starts and another ends, and nothing is natural or set in stone regarding the notion that there is a Middle East, a Latin America, or a Europe. In fact, these terms are geopolitical inventions to benefit those who held the most power in a particular territory at a specific moment in its history. Simply put, regions can have multiple meanings, which are fluid and indeterminate, often reflecting the interests of those who can lead the conversation. For example, US Captain Alfred Mahan first coined the term Middle East in an article for the *National Review* based on his own strategic-military conceptions.[2] Different interests led to the creation of other terms to describe that territory, broadening or narrowing its boundaries – the Arab region, the Muslim Middle East, the Mediterranean region, the Middle East and North Africa (MENA) region, and so forth. Thus, more often than not, the definition of a region as a distinctive area of operation depends more on the observer's point of view and geopolitical inclinations than on lines on a map.

Independent of how regions are defined, they do not have an actor quality – the Middle East does not act, but Middle Eastern countries do.

Regions are structures with their own arrangements of interrelationships while still hierarchically submitted to the global power distribution.[3] This way, it becomes possible to transfer concepts we use to understand the international system – such as order, the balance of power, structural patterns, polarity, anarchy, and so on – to the notion of a regional system. Therefore, from now on, we will talk about the Middle Eastern regional system and its subdivisions.

For Barry Buzan and Ole Wæver, a regional system consists of a set of states whose 'securitisation and desecuritization processes are so interlinked that their security cannot reasonably be analysed or resolved apart from one another'.[4] Accordingly, regional systems are marked by durable amity and enmity patterns, a shared history, and possibly, but not necessarily, common cultural, ethnic, or identitarian traits. Many authors have discussed the Middle East regional system.[5] They seem to agree that it began to be acknowledged as a modern state system during the late nineteenth and early twentieth centuries due to the region's relevance to the imperialist expansion of Great Britain, France, and Russia. From then on, it has been the stage for great power competition due to its strategic location, crucial trading routes, religious importance, and, more recently, oil resources.

European imperialism fragmented the region into many artificial states, often at odds with each other and dependent on external patrons to guarantee their security. Old and new states coexisted when the region was forced into this subjugated position in the international system, which simultaneously oppressed and enabled local leaders. This way, the postcolonial states emerged with high economic and securitarian dependence on external powers and under the rule of political elites that, more often than not, failed to install robust institutions or inclusive political participation mechanisms. Moreover, domestic and regional actors repeatedly contested these states' authority, leading to processes of militarisation, exclusion, cooption, or repression. This environment of lasting tension and conflict undermined most states' capacity to provide welfare to citizens, aggravating internal opposition and non-military threats.

Moreover, because many of these states were arbitrarily imposed by external actors at the expense of pre-existing identities, one cannot assume high congruence between nationality and state.[6] As a result, irredentist political movements, such as Arab nationalism and Islamism, and transnational ethnic or religious identities like Kurdish, Sunni, and Shia deeply inform politics in the Middle East. While by the 1980s, local elites managed to adopt their version of the Western state model, with the principles of sovereignty and autonomy becoming dominant, that does not mean precolonial elements stopped existing. Therefore, a national sense of belonging coexists with other – as crucial, or even more – senses of social identification. That means a national interest consensus cannot be assumed, and transnational sentiments and ideologies strongly mark this system. In this sense, national symbols and other social practices grew alongside the state.[7]

Notwithstanding their lack of efficiency and capacity to provide adequate public health, education, social justice, or economic development, Middle Eastern states proved themselves resilient.[8] However, like many other regions that struggle with colonialism, these states, while being sovereign, are submitted to an unequal interdependency towards the Global North and are vulnerable to many material and immaterial pressures and threats. The Cold War superpowers acted as heirs of the colonial era, continuing to interfere in many of the region's politics, security, and economics. US interventionism in the Middle East increased after the end of bipolarity. A case in point is the two wars against Iraq (1990 and 2003). Since the 2010s, we have seen an incipient re-emergence of great power competition, and actors such as China and Russia are not holding back from the opportunity to increase their presence and influence in the region.

Therefore, the Middle East regional system is a product of the local actors' interaction with great powers during the European imperialist era, the Second World War, and the Cold War. The story could – and probably should – have been different, as there were other securitarian relational patterns in this territory before its European invasion and domination. Nevertheless, the history of imperialism and colonialism and its pervasiveness created a profoundly penetrated regional system that exposed the disparate asymmetries of a core–periphery divided world. Thus, this collective experience led to the consolidation of states that differed from the Western model in terms of cohesiveness.

Interestingly, the system had not witnessed the emergence of a regional power in the sense of an actor whose power capabilities significantly outweighed others. Throughout history, many countries have tried to project a regional leadership image. Still, they eventually failed to acquire the needed material and ideological resources to influence geopolitics, obtain local legitimacy, and enforce a preferred institutional order. Several relatively powerful countries (such as Iran, Iraq, Egypt, Turkey, Israel, and Saudi Arabia) possessed some resources to proclaim leadership, but not enough to command the order configuration of the system. In short, the Middle East regional system is multipolar. In this multipolarity, states have frequently interfered in each other's political affairs in an environment that is more competitive than collaborative.[9]

All these characteristics made the Middle East a conflictual system, less prone to developing a collaborative agenda. That does not mean that organisations like the Arab League or the GCC have not had thriving moments throughout history. Nevertheless, the research agenda about the region has mainly revolved around territorial disputes, long-lasting conflicts, ideological battles, resource competition, power rivalry, and ethnic and religious divisions. Far from being a consequence of cultural peculiarities like Samuel P. Huntington's *Clash of civilizations* predicted,[10] these characteristics double back to the exogenous impositions of a global core–peripheric division. The legacy of colonialism, the often negative influence of external powers, overlapping transnational identities, and the absence of clear hierarchies between local countries shape the regional system.

*

If a structure can have substructures, a regional system can have subregional systems. In the same logic as before, subregions represent distinctive patterns of security interdependence caught up in a broader pattern that defines the system as a whole. The Middle East has three subregions or subcomplexes: the Levant, the Maghreb, and the Persian Gulf. Focusing on a subregion allows us to narrow even further our analytical lenses and, in this way, gain a deeper understanding of interstate dynamics and relational patterns. Now, let us enter the Persian Gulf subcomplex.

The Persian Gulf system

In ancient times, the Persian Gulf region was a crucial route for empires such as the Achaemenid, the Islamic, and the Ottoman. Moreover, its port cities were key for trading roads connecting the Middle East to India, East Africa, and Asia. During the European maritime expansion towards India, the region became remarkably attractive for strategic reasons, with the first Portuguese expedition to Hormuz dating 1507 and the Dutch and the British following suit. Therefore, for centuries, the port cities touching the Persian Gulf waters were a space for the interchange of commerce and peoples, establishing cosmopolitan, mercantile societies. Likewise, these maritime flows created robust migration and acculturation processes that flourished into a hybrid Arab–Persian culture that mixed and matched ethnicities, languages, and religions.

By the nineteenth century, increasing great power competition drove the British to formalise their dominance in the Persian Gulf to protect their Indian frontier. Their main goal was commercial, aiming to control piracy, take hold of commercial routes, as well as build alliances with local sheikhs or shahs. In 1908, the first large petroleum field was discovered in Persia and soon after in other neighbouring countries. The Anglo-Persian Company, founded in 1909, quickly became a major fuel supplier to the UK military. During most of the twentieth century,

Western private companies had long-term contracts that granted them exclusive rights to extract oil in the region. For example, in 1933, the Standard Oil Company of California (SoCal) secured the right to explore the Saudi Arabian Eastern oil province exclusively. By the 1940s, the Arabian American Oil Company (ARAMCO) extracted oil in massive commercial quantities.

Whereas Persia has never been under direct colonial rule, Iraq became independent from the British in October 1932. In the same year, Abdulaziz bin Abdul Rahman Al Saud founded the Kingdom of Saudi Arabia – the other small monarchies would only gain full autonomy in the 1960s and 1970s. Regardless of this, foreign interference remained constant, particularly during the Second World War. To check German expansion and secure the oilfields for military demand, the Allies' forces occupied most of the Persian Gulf. Thus, the region was inserted into global geopolitics as a crucial energy provider – particularly to the West. The US had to become more engaged in guaranteeing the oil flow to the West during the Cold War. The reconstruction of Western Europe and Japan after the Second World War was heavily reliant on oil at affordable prices. Hence, the US success in the bipolar competition was somewhat contingent on maintaining the Persian Gulf under Western influence.

In the first decades of the Cold War, the United Kingdom served as a Western surrogate that guaranteed order via its protectorates and ties with local leaders. London and Washington pressured the Soviets out of Iran and provided the latter aid packages, military training assistance, and armaments. Moreover, in 1953, they actively assisted Iran's Mohammad Reza Shah Pahlavi in the coup d'état that overthrew the nationalist Prime Minister Mohammad Mossadegh after he attempted to nationalise the oil. Until this period, the US involvement was still indirect, mostly non-military, and primarily through its oil companies operating in the region.[11] It centred its efforts in other parts of the Middle East, namely the Levant, while the British guaranteed Western interests in the Gulf. That would not, however, hold for much longer, as the UK slowly reckoned they were not the same powerful empire they once were.

The first blow to the British strategy came in 1967 when the People's Democratic Republic of Yemen, or South Yemen, separated and announced its independent Marxist republic. In 1968, a military coup in Iraq toppled the pro-British monarchy and brought the Arab Socialist *Baath* Party to power, which was closer to the Soviets. The following year, the British Labour Party finally announced its intention to end its protectorate over the Persian Gulf (Figure 1.1). A combination of domestic economic distress, unpopular colonial policies, and uprisings and contestations in the Middle East drove the

Figure 1.1 The Persian Gulf (Source: Google Maps)

decision. The Sultanate of Oman was reorganised in 1970, Bahrain and Qatar became independent in August and September of 1971, respectively, while the remaining seven sheikdoms that formed the Trucial States joined the new United Arab Emirates (UAE) in December 1971. The British transition was complete.

Hence, the eve of the 1970s marked the beginning of the Persian Gulf system, composed of independent actors that shared securitarian concerns. With Iraq signing a fifteen-year Treaty of Friendship and Cooperation with the Soviets in April 1972 and Saudi Arabia and Iran reaffirming their commitment to the Western powers by boosting their ties with the US, the system was immersed into the Cold War powerplay. After the end of the bipolar confrontation, the region continued to be penetrated by external powers' interests and local mistrust, embedded in the international power balance and interdependent with the global economy and general anxieties towards energy security. Hence, let us now discuss the central characteristics of this subsystem before we dive into this book's central concern.

Persian Gulf's asymmetry

One characteristic comes up when exploring the Persian Gulf regional system: there is a visible asymmetry of sheer size among the countries. On the one hand, Iran and Saudi Arabia are territorially vast countries, encompassing 1.64 million km² and 2.15 km² of land, respectively. Whereas Iran has a considerable population that is relatively well distributed throughout its territory, Saudi Arabia lies in an arid territory, with most of its population concentrated in some specific urban centres. On the other hand, Oman, Iraq, and Yemen are middle-sized countries, being 309,000 km², 438,000 km², and 527,900 km², respectively. However, Oman's population is much smaller than the other two and mainly concentrated in Muscat. Finally, there are four small monarchies: UAE (83,600 km²), Kuwait (17,800 km²), Qatar (11,500 km²), and Bahrain (760 km²). The population in these small states is very scarce, and only a parcel of it represents national citizens, as the countries rely on high migrant labour.

The geopolitical history of the regional system reflects these asymmetries. While it has remained chiefly without a regional hegemon, it always presented challengers or candidates to such a role. Throughout history, Iran and Iraq presented themselves as such candidates due to their ancient history, military might, and closer ties with the two opposing superpowers. Especially in the first decades of the Cold War, Iran and Iraq projected their ambitions of regional supremacy, frequently associating it with transnational ideologies such as Arabism or other exceptionalism linked to past glories. The other big player, Saudi Arabia, has not traditionally projected a hegemon's ambition, mainly due to a history of cautious foreign policy-making. However, it can also be listed as a regional power candidate due to its massive oil reserves, religious importance, and special ties with the US. Most importantly, its proactive behaviour since the 2010s suggests that it recognises this possibility. The other countries, however, primarily due to their geographical and demographical limitations, have not projected such hegemonic ambitions – which does not mean they are not crucial for understanding the system's dynamics.

For those reasons, some authors conclude that the Persian Gulf is tripolar because competition between Iran, Iraq, and Saudi Arabia shapes the regional balance of power.[12] This book tends to disagree with this interpretation for two main reasons. First, as discussed in more detail in other chapters, it is impossible to assume that Saudi Arabia competed with Iran and Iraq for regional leadership from 1971 until 2003. Second, this tripolar framework overlooks that, since the 1980s, the US has been a participative actor in the region's security-making processes. This book argues instead that the US became an extra-regional power with military capacities that overpassed local actors. In other words, understanding the Persian Gulf must include the US as a proactive – and highly asymmetric – actor in its construct rather than an element affecting outcomes passively.

Persian Gulf and religion

A second characteristic that becomes quickly distinctive when one explores the region is the importance of religion in local politics.[13] Decades of cultural interchange on the mercantile cities' shores meant people coexisted among many religions and sects.[14] By the nineteenth century, Shiism concentrated in the territories of what today we call Iraq, Iran, and Bahrain, while Sunnism overruled the Arabian Peninsula. Particularly in the Peninsula, the state formation processes did not detach themselves from Islam, and until today, the rulers' legitimacy depends much on their religious practice. Take, for example, Saudi Arabia: to build the country, the Al'Saud dynasty needed to develop an intimate association with the Wahhabi sect. Moreover, as hosts of two of the three main Islamic sacred cities, Medina and Mecca, they believe the country's politics must serve to protect and promote Islam worldwide.

The Iranian Revolution of 1979 added a second theocracy to the Persian Gulf, a republican and Shia one. The revolutionary *Ayatollahs* promoted their political awakening as a new Islamist model to be followed by Muslims everywhere.[15] This way, Iranian politics also sees their policymaking linked to the sponsorship of Islamist ideals in the region. The legitimacy of the other monarchies in Qatar, the UAE, Oman, and Bahrain also depends on their ties with local *ulama* (Muslim clerics) and the protection of sacred sites. Moreover, since the fall of Iraqi President Saddam Hussein's Baathist regime in 2003, sectarian disputes have increasingly permeated Iraq's politics.

For those reasons, some authors have focused on the Shia vs Sunni divide to explain the Persian Gulf's geopolitics.[16] Indeed, it is tempting to see the current tension between Saudi Arabia and Iran as oppositive sides of an identity divide. However, that is a false premise reflecting a somewhat short memory. As this book will extensively debate, the rivalry between Iran and Saudi Arabia is not permanent and is based on geopolitical and strategic matters. Moreover, while doctrinal differences exist between both sects, they do not, by definition, instigate a divide. Yes, political leaders can and do use identities to differentiate themselves, expand internal and external influence, and weaken a strategic competitor. Yet, they can also use these same identities to promote cooperation, integration, or consensus. Moreover, religious affiliations do not prevent someone from belonging to a country. Thus, such narratives on an inherent struggle between sects have little explanative value for international politics.

Persian Gulf and oil wealth

A third characteristic that emerges when one thinks about the region is hydrocarbon resources. Together, the region amounts to more than 47 per cent of the total proven oil reserves globally and 37.5 per cent of the world's total proven natural gas reserves. Saudi Arabia alone holds 11.8 per cent of the total oil exports, with its biggest markets being China, India, Japan, and Europe. The extraction and exportation of oil and gas have been essential to maintaining the global economy for decades. Aware of that from early on, Iran, Saudi Arabia, Iraq, and Kuwait joined Venezuela in Baghdad in 1960 to create the Organization of Petroleum Exporting Countries (OPEC). In the 1973 embargo, the organisation showed its power to interrupt the supplies and shift production, consumption, and pricing – exposing how dependent the Western world had become on such an energy resource. In the same decade, local leaders managed to take control of the oil production in their countries by nationalisation processes and revoking remaining foreign concessions.

The flow of oil rents enabled governments to consolidate their power, strengthen institutions, and construct sturdy alliances – often clientelist and patrimonial – with key social groups that could guarantee general stability.[17] Particularly in countries with small populations, the oil income was enough for the rulers to lift many of their subjects out of poverty, providing them with subsidies on energy, cheap water, and almost no taxes.[18] The citizens of the Gulf monarchies traditionally enjoy a large welfare state in which the government provides jobs, housing, and essential goods at the oil wealth costs.[19] The monarchs, on their turn, rule under relative political stability and with little opposition.

While abundant natural resources are a blessing, they can also be a curse. Many other Global Southern countries are locked in this position of provider of resources to the world and buyer of almost anything else. The predominance of extractivism creates specific types of state–society relations, societal patterns, and unequal interchanges that can hamper the consolidation of a sustainable and inclusive socioeconomic development. The rentier state literature has long stressed how these economies depend highly on oil price fluctuation, showing deep structural imbalances that hinder production diversification and are often more vulnerable to authoritarian setbacks, corruption, clientelism, and exclusions.[20] Even within the monarchies, growing population, rising consumption, and declining production underscore vulnerability and possible security problems in the long run. These problems have been visible in the Persian Gulf for a while already, and they tend to increase further with the growing consent that we need to shift away from nonrenewable resources to halt climate change.

Persian Gulf and militarisation

Interestingly, the availability of oil rents has traditionally led to a high level of militarisation in the region. Moreover, oil draws external actors into the region, creating border disputes or exacerbating existing conflicts – almost literally putting fuel into the fire. The specialised literature often stresses how tensions due to transnational ideologies, resource competition, bordering-settling, and nuclear proliferation have permeated the region, increasing instability and states' threat perceptions.[21] Only after the Second World War, there were four wars – the Iran–Iraq war from 1980 to 1988, the 1990 Gulf War after the Iraqi invasion of Kuwait in August 1990, the US invasion of Iraq in March 2003, and the ongoing 2014 Yemeni Civil War – two revolutions – the Iraqi in 1968 and the Iranian in 1979 – and several social unrests – such as the Siege of the Grand Mosque in 1979, the Iranian Green Movement in 2009, and the Bahraini Uprising in 2011.

Since its formation, the region has shown significant defence expenditures. During the 1970s, Iran invested extraordinarily in its military, buying expensive, state-of-the-art weaponry from the US and building an advanced air force. In the 1980s, Iraq boosted its army and navy, becoming the strongest military in the region with both Western powers and the Soviet Union's assistance. Meanwhile, Saudi Arabia gradually boosted its defence-spending, focusing on guaranteeing strong security relations with the US and keeping regional adversaries ashore. In the 2000s, it accelerated its militarisation process to unprecedented levels, reaching the status of having the third-biggest defence budget in the world in 2014. Qatar and the UAE followed through, especially after the 2011 Arab Uprisings, due to the risk of social unrest arriving at their doors. In the last decade, the Gulf monarchies have invested increasingly in military capabilities to safeguard themselves from other regional actors and possible domestic turmoil.

Persian Gulf and the US presence

A final characteristic of the Persian Gulf system is the long-standing US presence. Several factors, such as political stability and energy security, have placed the region prominently within Washington's national security calculations, something that will not change in any predictable short-term scenario. Its political involvement in the region developed gradually and even somewhat reluctantly, giving preference to surrogate actors to ensure its interests instead of direct involvement – first, the United Kingdom and later Iran. However, losing its main regional ally with the 1979 Iranian Revolution drove the US to build a more coherent, long-term strategy for the Persian Gulf. As we further discuss, the 1980s Carter Doctrine defined the tenants for the US' regional interests that remain until today: guarantee the stability of the oil market, protect traditional partners, sustain a Western-oriented order, and avoid the emergence of a local hegemon.

Fighting its first direct war against Iraq in 1990, Washington started sustaining a permanent military presence in the region to keep its interests – or, in their view, order and stability. This presence also scaled into increasingly complex diplomatic relations with local actors, the development of military–military relations, more robust economic ties, and security interdependence. For those reasons, we can describe Washington as an extra-regional power in the Persian Gulf system.[22] The US has the most advanced military capabilities deployable in the region and shares economic and strategic relations with most countries. In this sense, while not belonging geographically, the US is an extra-regional actor because it plays a crucial role in establishing and maintaining the regional order. It is far from being a neutral actor fostering stability but rather a partisan player in the geopolitical game. Therefore, its role should be studied as part of the systemic interplay, not an element only affecting it. That is precisely what this book proposes.

*

This section has stressed five characteristics that define the Persian Gulf regional system: the asymmetries between the countries, the importance of religion in policymaking, the predominance of oil rents, high militar-isation, and the direct presence of the US. The specialised literature indeed extensively discusses these points. However, there is another phenomenon that has not been discussed so far, which is the triangular relationship be-tween Iran, Saudi Arabia, and the US. As discussed, only Iran, Iraq, and Saudi Arabia have the potential capabilities (size, population, military, and ambition) to promote a role of regional power. While Iraq's projection was in principle detached from the US presence in the region – more often than not, they were linked with the anticolonial struggle, Arabism, and personal ambitions of Saddam Hussein – Iran and Saudi Arabia promoted their role in the association, positively or negatively, to the US behaviour in the region. This observation does not mean that the region is tripolar, nor that the Persian Gulf can be fully explained by this triangulation, which would be illogical, as there are many other members in the system. Nevertheless, it is a phenomenon worth understanding.

The following pages review how the literature has dealt with the three dyads that compose the triangle: US–Iran, US–Saudi Arabia, and Iran–Saudi Arabia. This review enables us to grasp which are the primary analytical sets of tools to understand these complex relations. More importantly, it sheds light on elements that authors have repeatedly stressed as crucial to understanding each relationship. This step is essential considering that this book presents an IR theoretically driven analysis that dialogues with – instead of only borrowing from – Area Studies. Consequently, the analyt-ical framework is presented in the next chapter only after pinpointing and categorising the key elements to understand the three bilateral relations.

The United States and Iran relations

The relationship between the US and Iran is, by far, the most debated one, being defined as dysfunctional, contentious, hostile, dogmatic, and even mythological.[23] From close partners in the 1960s and 1970s to enemies since the 1980s, they have taken each other permanently into account when developing their regional foreign policies.[24] In modern history, few inter-state relations have as much emotion, hostility, and ideological disputes as the US–Iranian one.

Although diplomatic relations were established only in 1883, the two countries had already signed a Treaty of Commerce and Friendship by the early 1850s, when Protestant US-American missionaries had set up a base in Persia. Back then, Great Britain and Russia occupied parts of Persia, which brought resentment to the locals and the ruling regime. The Qajar monarchy was much more sympathetic to the US, seeing it as a non-colonial and unselfish international actor because it managed to escape Britain's rule.[25] However, the relations were minimal, with Washington only vaguely supporting the Persian Constitutional Revolution (1905–1911). Maintaining its typical isolationism for the time, the US did not seek to challenge British or Russian imperialism in the region.

US Americans began to show genuine interest in Persia by the end of the First World War as oil rose to the status of the most strategic natural resource in the world. In 1919, Washington positioned itself against the Anglo-Persian Agreement, which would have given the United Kingdom exclusive rights over Persian oil. By the 1920s, the US Congress urged citizens to acquire oil properties abroad. From then on, the US involvement in Iran grew cautiously. It was neutral when the military Reza Shah did a coup against the Qajar dynasty in February 1921 and installed its own Pahlavi dynasty. Soon after, Reza Shah, focusing on his modernisation project, began to welcome the growing US interest in the region. Nevertheless, this did not result in close ties with Washington. When the Pahlavi ruler began to show many signals of sympathy for Nazi Germany (which included changing the country's name to Iran, the land of the Arian people), Washington supported the UK-Russian occupation of Iran in February 1941.

The 1941 occupation forced Reza Shah to abdicate power to his son, Mohammad Reza Pahlavi, who was very enthusiastic about the Americans. From the 1950s to 1979, the US–Iran ties transformed into a solid economic, political, and securitarian partnership.[26] A key turning point, however, was the US support for the overthrow of nationalist Prime Minister Mohammad Mossadegh in 1953, which quickly consolidated an absolute rule under the hands of the Shah Pahlavi. At this point, the perception among most Iranians that the US was an unselfish international actor was utterly crushed. A bitterness towards the Americans' deep association with the Pahlavi regime was visible in the 1979 Iranian Revolution. The revolutionaries framed these ties as one of the primary byproducts of oppression and wrongdoings the monarchy inflicted on Iranians.

The abrupt change from partners to enemies has been a topic of many investigations. Explanations address cultural and ideological dimensions, misinterpretations and miscommunication patterns, ideological and identitarian definitions, and political scheme-crafting. Unfortunately, much of this literature is harmed by this long-standing status of enmity, producing non-academically driven texts written from either one of the government's perspectives. Some authors are often politicised due to the high tension and friction between both countries. The ability to detect biased opinions and framing devices is an art to be mastered by anyone studying US–Iran relations.

Nevertheless, authors from both countries have managed to escape these predispositions and provide detailed and historically contextualised descriptions of the US–Iranian ties.[27] They have reported on the many sources of disagreements and their path-dependent effect on politics, presenting a more nuanced explanation of the mutual culture of mistrust between the countries rather than repeating misconceptions and prejudices. They argue that high mistrust generated distorted perceptions of one another that harmed rational decision-making. On the one hand, the US struggles to see Iran beyond the image of a revolution exporter, anti-US American, and untrusty actor. On the other hand, the idea that the US language is of threat, intimidation, and domination profoundly influences the Iranian government. These framing devices of enmity have become dogmas, where exaggerated narratives of the other are used to justify their own behaviour, perpetuating hostility.[28] This way, the discursive field in which the countries interact is permeated by memories of violence perpetrated by actors thriving on the antagonism.[29]

William Beeman calls the US–Iran relations a 'true postmodern culture conflict', as it centres not on a concrete conflict but on symbolic discourses constructed to fit the otherness as an idealised enemy.[30] To US Americans, the original sin that made them not trust Iran was the US embassy hostage crisis that followed the Revolution. The US media widely broadcast with utter disbelief how Iranian revolutionaries kept fifty-two captives for 444 days in Tehran. This event led Washington to break diplomatic ties in April 1980. Since then, Washington has stressed Iran's liaison with supposedly terrorist groups and its poor human rights record. Conversely, Iranians condemn the US participation in the 1953 coup against Mossadegh, its alliance with the Shah, and its support to Iraq against Iran in the 1980s war. These experiences established depreciative schemes and exaggerated stereotypes that prompted decision-makers to anticipate deception and to double-cross one another.[31]

There is a growing effort to dissect the complex field in which the relationship developed and how narratives and opposed identities work to set the countries apart. To Penelope Kinch, Iran and the US perceive for themselves a missionary quality in which it is their international duty to promote the ideals of their own revolutions elsewhere.[32] They have an expectation about how the system should be, and they intend to lead a change towards such an ideal, which leads to conflict rather than coexistence. All these exciting approaches warn us of how ideas, narratives, and identities matter in grasping these relations. However, these analyses sometimes obscure the weight of systemic inputs, direct or indirect threats, and power competitions. Much of the Iranian–US relations are defined by structural and material issues that cannot be explained only by identity or ideational elements.

A case in point concerns the nuclear issue, a topic often in discussions due to the growing international concern over the Iranian nuclear capacitation and its plans to enrich uranium. In a refreshing contribution, Jason Jones examines the Iranian and US-American discursive practices in government and press, reflecting on media and its function to normalise images that states make of one another.[33] Similarly, Andrew Prosser focuses on the sanctions, their socioeconomic effects, and the possibilities of reinserting Iran into the international community.[34] While purely material approaches are incomplete for ignoring crucial non-tangible elements, abandoning issues of power distribution and security altogether does not fix the problem. As James Bill insists, if stripped from all the patterns of hostility and animosity, much of the game these two countries play depends on the balance of power.[35]

A trend within the US–Iran literature is to focus on the role of leadership in a particular moment. Many authors emphasise the person in charge in each of the US or Iranian administrations and his preferred policies to explain foreign policy.[36] They emphasise how much policy decisions can alter from one president to another, implying that policymaking can shift outcomes in one direction despite the country's ideational ambitions and national identities. To argue this, they employ psychological profiling, thick descriptions of diplomatic meetings, official documents, speeches, and memoirs to stress such prominence.

In short, the literature is permeated by studies about rivalry, emotion, vilified images, antagonism, identities, and miscommunication. Authors have investigated this complex relation through lenses that include cognitive and ideational factors. A series of hostile interactions after 1979 created images of inherent antagonism that are tricky to transform or abandon. These images are ingrained in each country's political memory and constantly reproduced by their leaders, reinforcing mistrust among the political elite and the general public.[37] That underscores that we should include political narratives and identities to understand these bilateral relations. Others have stressed the importance of leadership while pinpointing the patterns of non-communication and expectations of deception that influence decision-making. Therefore, cognitive factors and leaders' skills to receive signals are also crucial elements for fully grasping the relationship.

The United States and Saudi Arabia relations

The US and Saudi Arabia share an enduring bond that has been called a special alliance, a paradox, a strategic partnership, and even an oxymoron.[38] All these labels describe a pragmatic relationship between two countries that do not have much in common but share crucial strategic interests. The US was among the first to recognise Saudi Arabia as independent in 1932. Already in 1933, the US-American Standard Oil for California (SoCal) was granted a concession to explore Saudi oil, thus beginning a relationship based on the importance of black gold and regional stability maintenance. In 1938, the California Arabian Standard Oil Company (CASOC), a subsidiary of SoCal, hit the jackpot in Dhahran, immediately producing more than 1,000 barrels daily; by 1940, the company produced around 20,000 barrels every day.[39] In 1944, the company changed its name to the Arabian American Oil Company (ARAMCO).

Thus, it is predictable that a chunk of the US–Saudi literature focuses on ARAMCO, the oil market dynamics, and the government–companies interactions. For example, Anthony C. Brown evaluates the private and public sectors' exchanges and oil politics, surveying the Saudi American oil diplomacy's historiography, while Parker Hart offers inside information, detailed personality profiles, and rich diplomatic stories.[40] Similar to the US–Iran case, there is a certain initial mystification of the benevolent role of the US in contrast with Britain's imperialism. ARAMCO was often seen as an exception among exploitative foreign enterprises. However, Robert Vitalis unveils how the company reproduced racial and exclusionary practices that impacted Saudi institutional development.[41] Indeed, much of the US–Saudi relation is a product of the US hegemonic interests, which shaped 'unique circumstances of Saudi state-building, enabling the ruling family to postpone crucial decisions about the division of power and wealth in the kingdom'.[42]

By the end of the Second World War, President Franklin Delano Roosevelt met King Abdulaziz on board the *United States Ship (USS) Quincy* naval cruiser. There, a strategic partnership, often dubbed an 'oil-for-security bargain', was conceived. In that meeting, the King sought a security partner in the US, while Roosevelt expected Saudi oil to reconstruct the European economy.[43] Successfully, Riyadh guaranteed a stable oil supply to the global market, and Washington retributed it by guaranteeing security, diplomatic support, and military protection.[44] Interestingly enough, by that time, the centrality of oil in the relationship was less related to US-American consumption than reconstructing Western economies.

Therefore, for both the US and Saudi Arabia, a top priority should have been to ensure that the system was orderly, stable, and collaborative with the flow of oil to the West. Border disputes, social instability, and local or regional protests could have threatened the stability of this oil-for-security arrangement. Similarly, the emergence of a regional hegemon that challenged the balance of power or another extra-regional actor that directly competed with the US interests was also a menace.[45] However, the partnership remained stable since its foundation, despite certain disagreements. Moreover, after the creation of the OPEC, Saudi Arabia boosted its strategic importance for the West as the leading oil nation that could swing prices and influence other producing countries within the organisation.[46]

Until as recently as 2011, the US has been Saudi Arabia's leading economic partner, and, as Robert Mason argues, there were more than enough geostrategic stimuli for both countries to keep a working, positive relationship.[47] However, there was, of course, divergence; as David Long puts it, there has always been a 'rocky road for collaboration', permeated by overlapping goals and conflictual interests.[48] Conflictual interests were visible in issues related to the Israel–Palestine conflict, questions about democratisation, and interference in internal affairs. Despite the long-standing strategic alignment and decades of investment in education and cultural interchange, some authors stress that a shallow understanding between societies is a potential source of tension.[49] That led some to say that the relations have been 'troubled since its birth at the summit on the Quincy' or, more pessimistically, trapped in a 'marriage from which there is no divorce'.[50]

Thus, if there were no pressuring economic or securitarian demands, Saudi Arabians and US Americans would lack the typical ideological, cultural, or societal proximity of allies. However, other authors have challenged this assessment. During the Cold War, strategic interests were combined with genuine anti-communist convictions.[51] Interestingly, Rachel Bronson stresses how, at that time, the two countries were also ideologically connected by conservativism.[52] Thus, religion provided an ideological and political layer to the partnership. Similarly, Deepa Kumar analyses how traditional English-speaking media sympathetically described Islam as a moderation source in opposition to Arab nationalism during the Cold War.[53] Hence, the authors highlight how both countries employed ideological and religious factors as tools to gain influence and satisfy their own interests.

In the last decade, Saudi Arabia has been diversifying its trading partners, and the US has been reducing its energy dependency. However, commitment to the regional order and the stability of the oil markets will probably continue to compel both countries not to jeopardise their close ties. There is, of course, an asymmetrical interdependency between them that cannot be ignored, as it is still a core–periphery type of relationship. In case a post-oil future eventually arises and, due to the energy transition, the world reduces its dependency on Saudi Arabian resources, the dynamic of this relationship will most certainly shift.

Moreover, despite shared interests concerning the balance of power, both countries can align ideologically when they share threats more broadly. This happened during the Cold War, but, as this book will show in detail, a fear of regional change has also intensified the alignment of preferences between leaders in both countries. As a result, the issue of perceptions – particularly concerning regional and domestic instability – is a crucial element in grasping the complexity of this bilateral relation. For example, factors such as Iran's regional influence, political Islamism, or the proliferation of nuclear capacities have been framed as multifactual sources of threat that cannot be explained alone through the material oil-for-security bargain framework. As Bronson argues, cognitive elements can work together with the security-for-oil frame as yet another layer bringing the countries together.[54]

Saudi Arabia and Iran relations

The Saudi–Iranian ties have been recently defined as an institutionalised competition, a not-so-hidden rivalry, a multifront Cold War or a struggle for supremacy.[55] Since the fall of Saddam Hussein in 2003 and particularly the 2011 Arab Uprisings, a sense of competition between Iran and Saudi Arabia has prompted many authors to explain how this rivalry has been shaping the region's politics.[56] However, that has not always been the case. Iran and Saudi Arabia shared collaborative moments throughout history, leaning towards cooperation in security, economics, and religious matters. They have experienced variations in the character of their ties, passing through periods of tension, conflict, de-escalation, rapprochement, and re-escalation.

The first diplomatic engagement between the Kingdom of Saudi Arabia and Persia was in August 1929, a Friendship Treaty that indicated the Shah's early support for the Al Saud dynasty. Initially, the relations were not too expansive and were mainly concerned with handling Iranian pilgrims travelling to Mecca and Medina.[57] Ties were even severed between 1943 and 1945 due to a death sentence for an Iranian pilgrim given by the Saudi monarchy. However, by the 1950s, a mutual perception of the potential threat coming from Egyptian President Gamal Abdel Nasser brought the two monarchies closer together. The ideals of pan-Arabism and republicanism were uncomfortable for the conservatives in Saudi Arabia and Iran. Moreover, both countries feared the growing Soviet presence in the Middle East due to its ties with Egypt and Yemen. Thus, the two started to converge their foreign policy positions regarding Egypt, Yemen, and other regional matters in the 1950s and 1960s.[58]

Moreover, they were two oil countries aligned with the West during the first decades of the Cold War. It was only natural that their relationship grew increasingly positive due to mutual interests in security and oil production. While the British departure produced some initial anxieties,

Chapter 5 shows how this was managed by crafty leaders who were aware of the benefits they could obtain from closer ties. Andrew S. Cooper and Faisal b. S. al-Saud provide exceptional historical analyses showing that the 1970s was the age of strategic collaboration between two outstanding negotiators, Saudi King Faisal bin Abdulaziz Al Saud and Shah Pahlavi.[59] That would crumble with the 1979 Iranian Revolution, building tensions between the two and eventually driving the severance of ties in 1987.

However, most of the literature we see today tends to lessen or even ignore this long-standing period (almost five decades) of positive ties and collaboration. Some of this literature also reduces the importance of the fact that, from 1991 to 2016, diplomatic ties were restored, and a constructive (but ultimately failed) rapprochement was built. The waves of literature production tend to reflect this variation in a limited fashion, often making temporal delimitations to their study to emphasise moments of rapprochement or hyper-hostility.[60] The current focus on the rivalry makes sense, but it should not be done at the cost of more longue durée investigations.

Some authors that seem to struggle with this longer historical perspective are those who have stressed that competition for religious leadership is the leading cause of the rivalry.[61] These works frame Iran as a promoter of Shia resistance globally, and Saudi Arabia as a monarchy anxious to conserve Sunni dominance. They focus on an inherently conflictual dichotomy that defines the relation's nature and plays a 'catalytic role' in directing policies towards each other. By affirming that 'religious, ideological and identity schism made them fated to be rivals', they draw near to determinism, overlooking the countries' history as well as the simple but powerful fact that Shias and Sunnis have coexisted for many decades without any innate conflict.[62]

This perception that sectarian differences are naturally a source of political conflict with an immutable nature is hugely problematic and, many times, can be borderline discriminatory. Some studies eventually present one side as the good one and the other as bad, one rational and the other irrational, reproducing stereotypes that are not at all constructive. As Edward Wastnidge and Simon Mabon rightly stress, this argument, which has gained traction in many political debates and journalistic articles, has little success among scholars because it reduces the two countries to embody their respective sects.[63] They correctly emphasise that religious identities, sectarian tension, and distortion of the realities have often been intertwined within the Saudi–Iranian rivalry, but they have not created it.

On the other end of the spectrum, some scholars explain the rivalry through a Realist understanding of the balance of power: Iran and Saudi Arabia would compete for territory, oil prices, and military hegemony.[64] These approaches argue that countries' threat perceptions increase or reduce according to the change in power distribution, leading to the fluctuating scenarios of rivalry and rapprochement. For example, Andrew W. Terrill and Gregory Gause claim that the current rivalry results from a regional balance shock after 2003, with Iraq becoming a space for others to gain influence.[65] Nevertheless, they adopt a broad understanding that includes political and societal expressions of (in)security beyond the military one. For these authors, the countries compete through accumulating capacities and alliances and by manipulating religious and identitarian factors to justify their expansive role and reduce the other's influence.[66]

Their main argument is that the balance of power explains the nature of the conflict. However, further investigation of different sources of threats is needed to assess the countries' mechanisms to increase power. In this sense, theological or ideological differences intensify conflict but do not generate it.[67] Moreover, ideational ambitions shaping Saudi–Iranian relations do not reduce themselves to religious matters. As Paul Aarts and Joris van Duijne stress, Saudi Arabia and Iran disagree about their expectations of how the regional system should be organised – particularly concerning the US role.[68] While the US plays an integral role in ensuring security for the Saudis, for Iranians, geopolitical arrangements should be left for those from the region.

Interestingly, Simon Mabon suggests that the rivalry plays in ideological and geopolitical spheres simultaneously.[69] Competing identities, such as ethnonational and religious ones, drive the first. The second sphere relates to Riyadh's and Tehran's claim for influence over the Persian Gulf, which became even more pertinent after the decline of Iraq as a regional power in 2003. Thus, they pay a delicate balance to preserve territorial integrity, ideological predominance, and political legitimacy. In addition, some scholars insist that economic competition should not be left from the equation, as they frequently disagree at OPEC about the oil production, mainly because they diverge on their goals and economic policy choices.[70]

Therefore, the literature is very eclectic in examining how ethnicity, religion, ideology, economy, and even tribal identities produce incongruences with ramifications for the Saudi–Iran dyad. Authors have found these bilateral relations a fruitful case to study threat perception, ideological competition, sectarianism, and geopolitical rivalry. Yet, they have diverged about the main driver of the competition – power or religion – and whether there is even one driver only or a mix of several. Thus, a larger temporal framework that includes material and non-material sources of competition is clearly needed if one wants to grasp this relationship by its full complexity.

*

This literature review was necessary not only to introduce the reader to the three dyads that compose the strategic triangle but also to inform how the theoretical framework is constructed. It shows three essential elements needed for a thick and inclusive analysis of the three dyads: *ideational* (perceptions and systemic expectations), *cognitive* (identities and self-perceptions), and *leadership* (the importance of those deciding on politics). The next chapter operationalises these findings into the Neoclassical Realist framework.

First, issues related to ambition, maintenance or revision of the regional order, revolutionary prospects, and leadership are relevant in the three bulks of the literature. For example, many specialists highlighted the disruptive connotation of Iran's revisionist behaviour to the other two countries or how much Saudi Arabia and the US are reliant on the status quo's continuity. Therefore, one category for intervening variables is ideational.

Second, self-images, roles, dogmas, and narratives of exceptionalism are frequent in the three dyads. While the hostility and antagonism characterise the US–Iran dyad, religion profoundly influences the Iran–Saudi one. Even for the US–Saudi case, authors diverge on the cultural chasm being a problematic issue or another political layer to their partnership. Identities are conditioners for deeper ties or prolonged disaffection in the dyads, indicating that cognitive factors should be a second category for the intervening variables.

Finally, leadership matters because it can give continuity to patterns or provoke changes. Many authors see kings, presidents, and other foreign policy executives as key in determining a country's international agenda. Their mindsets, preferences, political affiliations, experiences, and grievances should be analysed. Moreover, only by exploring leaders' behaviour and preferences can one detect the discursive field in which these cognitive and ideational images, enmities, rivalries, and friendships are repeated and reinforced. Thus, leadership should be a third category for intervening in the theoretical framework.

Notes

1 Barry Buzan and Ole Waever, *Regions and powers: The structure of international security* (New York: Cambridge University Press, 2003).
2 Clayton R. Koppes, Captain Mahan, General Gordon, and the origins of the term 'Middle East', *Middle Eastern Studies* 12: 1, 1972, pp. 95–98.
3 Douglas Lemke, *Regions of war and peace* (Cambridge, New York: Cambridge University Press, 2002).
4 Buzan and Waever, Regions and powers.

5 See, for example: Buzan and Waever, *Regions and powers*; Steven A. Yetiv, The Iraq War of 2003: Why did the United States decide to invade, in David Lesch and Mark Haas (eds), *The Middle East and the United States: History, politics, and ideologies* (New York: Taylor & Francis, 2018), pp. 253–274; Fawcett, International Relations and the Middle East; Bahgat Korany and Hillah Dessouki, *The foreign policies of Arab states: The challenge of globalization* (Cairo: American University of Cairo Press, 2008); Gregory Gause, *The international relations of the Persian Gulf* (Cambridge: Cambridge University Press, 2010); Raymond Hinnebusch and Anousharivan Ehteshami (eds), *The foreign policies of the Middle East states* (Boulder, CO: Lynne Rienner, 2014).

6 Raymond Hinnebusch, *The international politics of the Middle East* (New York: Manchester University Press, 2003); Simon Mabon, *Saudi Arabia and Iran: Power and rivalry in the Middle East* (London: I.B. Tauris, 2015).

7 Gause, *The international relations of the Persian Gulf*.

8 Tareq Ismael, *International relations of the contemporary Middle East: A study in world politics* (Syracuse, New York: Syracuse University Press, 1986); Louise Fawcett, Alliances and regionalism in the Middle East, in Louise Fawcett (ed.), *International relations of the Middle East* (London: Oxford University Press, 2016), pp. 196–218.

9 Fred Halliday, The Middle East and conceptions of 'international society', in Barry Buzan and Ana Gonzales-Pelaez (eds), *International society and the Middle East: English school theory at the regional level* (New York: Palgrave Macmillan, 2009), pp. 1–24; Martin Beck, The concept of regional power as applied to the Middle East, in Henner Fürtig (ed.), *Regional powers in the Middle East: New constellations after the Arab revolts* (New York: Palgrave Macmillan, 2014), pp. 1–23.

10 Samuel P. Huntington, *The clash of civilizations and the remaking of world order* (New York: Simon & Schuster, 1996).

11 William Taylor Fain, *American ascendance and British retreat in the Persian Gulf region* (New York: Palgrave Macmillan, 2008).

12 Fürtig, Iran's rivalry with Saudi Arabia between the Gulf wars; Aarts and van Duijne, Saudi Arabia after the U.S.–Iranian détente; Gause, *The international relations of the Persian Gulf*.

13 Mabon, Saudi Arabia and Iran; Ghattas, Black Wave; Vali Nasr, *The Shia revival: How conflicts within Islam will shape the future* (New York: W.W. Norton & Company, 2007).

14 Lawrence Potter (ed.), *The Persian Gulf in history* (New York: Palgrave Macmillan, 2009).

15 Ervand Abrahamian, *A history of modern Iran* (New York: Cambridge University Press, 2008).

16 Mahan Abedin, Iran *resurgent: The rise and rise of the Shia state* (London: Hurst & Company, 2019); Nasr, The Shia revival.

17 Hossein Mahdavy, Patterns and problems of economic development in rentier states: The case of Iran, in M. A. Cook (ed.), *Studies in the economic history of the Middle East: From the rise of Islam to the present day* (New York: Oxford

University Press, 1970), pp. 428–468; Steffen Hertog, The 'rentier mentality', 30 years on: Evidence from survey data, *British Journal of Middle Eastern Studies* 47: 1, 2020, pp. 6–23.

18 Jim Krane, *Energy kingdoms: Oil and political survival in the Persian Gulf* (New York: Columbia University Press, 2019).

19 Jill Crystal, Coalitions in oil monarchies: Kuwait and Qatar, *Comparative Politics* 32: 4, 1989, pp. 427–443.

20 Michael L. Ross, *The oil curse: How petroleum wealth shapes the development of nations* (Princeton: Princeton University Press, 2012).

21 Fred Halliday, *The Middle East in international relations: Power, politics and ideology* (Cambridge: Cambridge University Press, 2005); Gause, The international relations of the Persian Gulf; Kristen C. Ulrichsen, *Insecure Gulf: The end of certainty and the transition to the post-oil era* (New York: Oxford University Press, 2015).

22 Thomas Juneau, U.S. power in the Middle East: Not declining, *Middle East Policy* XXI: 2, 2014, pp. 40–52; Hook, Hegemonic stability and American power; Christopher Layne, *The peace of illusions: American grand strategy from 1940 to the present* (Ithaca, London: Cornell University Press, 2006).

23 Alethia H. Cook and Jalīl Rawshandil, *The United States and Iran: Policy challenges and opportunities* (New York: Palgrave Macmillan, 2009); Joseph St. Marie and Shahdad Naghshpour, *Revolutionary Iran and the United States: Low-intensity conflict in the Persian Gulf* (Farnham, Burlington: Ashgate, 2011); Hossein Musavian, *Iran and the United States: An insider's view on the failed past and the road to peace* (New York: Bloomsbury, 2014); William Beeman, *The 'Great Satan' vs. the 'Mad Mullahs': How the United States and Iran demonize each other* (Westport, London: Greenwood, 2005).

24 Arshin Adib-Moghaddam, Discourse and violence: The friend–enemy conjunction in contemporary Iranian–American relations, in Anoushiravan Ehteshami and Reza Molavi (eds), *Iran and the international system* (London, New York: Routledge, 2012), pp. 150–163.

25 Kamyar Ghaneabassiri, U.S. foreign policy and Persia, 1856–1921, *Iranian Studies* 35: 1, 2002, pp. 145–175.

26 Tore Petersen, *Richard Nixon, Great Britain and the Anglo-American alignment in the Persian Gulf and Arabian Peninsula: Making allies out of clients* (Sussex: Sussex Academic Press, 2011).

27 James Bill, *The eagle and the lion: The tragedy of American–Iranian relations* (New Haven, London: Yale University Press, 1998); Cook and Rawshandil, *The United States and Iran*; Musavian, *Iran and the United States*; Ofira Seliktar, *Navigating Iran: From Carter to Obama* (New York: Palgrave Macmillan, 2012); Pollack, The Persian puzzle.

28 Musavian, *Iran and the United States*.

29 Adib-Moghaddam, Discourse and violence.

30 Beeman, *The 'Great Satan' vs. the 'Mad Mullahs'*.

31 James Blight, Janet Lang, Banai Hussain, Malcon Byrne, and John Tirman, *Becoming enemies: US–Iran relations and the Iran–Iraq War, 1979–1988* (Plymouth: Rowman & Littlefield, 2012).

32 Penelope Kinch, *The US–Iran relationship: The impact of political identity on foreign policy* (London, New York: I.B. Tauris, 2016).

33 Jason Jones, *American rhetorical construction of the Iranian nuclear threat* (London, New York: Continuum International Publishing Group, 2011).

34 Andrew Prosser, Much ado about nothing? Status ambitions and Iranian nuclear reversal, *Strategic Studies Quarterly* 11: 3, 2017, pp. 26–81.

35 James Bill, The politics of hegemony: the United States and Iran, *Middle East Policy* VIII: 3, 2001, pp. 89–100.

36 Babak Ganji, *Politics of confrontation: The foreign policy of the USA and revolutionary Iran* (New York: Palgrave Macmillan, 2006); Mohamed El-Khawas, Obama's engagement strategy with Iran: Limited results, *Mediterranean Quarterly* 22: 1, 2011, pp. 93–113; Karim Sadjadpour, *Reading Khamenei: The world view of Iran's most powerful leader* (Washington, DC: Carnegie Endowment of International Peace, 2009); Roham Alvandi, Nixon, Kissinger, and the Shah: The origins of Iranian primacy in the Persian Gulf, *Diplomatic History* 36: 2, 2012, pp. 337–372.

37 Adib-Moghaddam, Discourse and violence.

38 Robert Vitalis, *America's kingdom: Mythmaking on the Saudi oil frontier* (Stanford, CA: Stanford University Press, 2007); Bruce Riedel, *Kings and presidents: Saudi Arabia and the United States since FDR* (Washington, DC: Brookings Institution, 2018); Anthony H. Cordesman, *Saudi Arabia and the United States: Common interests and continuing sources of tension* (Washington, DC: Center for Strategic and International Studies, 2016); Felicia Grey, How oil twists the hegemon's arm: The case of the United States and Saudi Arabia and their ambivalent partnership, *Digest of Middle East Studies* 26: 2, 2017, pp. 320–339.

39 Steven R. Ward, *Immortal: A military history of Iran and its armed forces* (Washington, DC: Georgetown University Press, 2009).

40 Anthony C. Brown, *Oil, God and gold: The story of Aramco and the Saudi kings* (Boston, MA: Houghton Mifflin Harcourt, 1999); Parker Hart, *Saudi Arabia and the United States: Birth of a security partnership* (Bloomington, IN: Indiana University Press, 1998).

41 Vitalis, *America's kingdom.*

42 Nathan Citino, *From Arab nationalism to OPEC: Eisenhower, King Saud, and the making of US–Saudi relations* (Indianapolis, IN: Indiana University Press, 2002).

43 Riedel, *Kings and presidents.*

44 David Long, US–Saudi relations: Evolution, current conditions, and future prospects, *Mediterranean Quarterly* 15: 3, 2004, pp. 24–37; Neil Partrick, *Saudi Arabian foreign policy? Conflict and cooperation* (New York: I.B. Tauris, 2016).

45 Partrick, *Saudi Arabian foreign policy?*

46 Grey, How oil twists the hegemon's arm.

47 Robert Mason, Back to realism for an enduring US–Saudi relationship, *Middle East Policy* XXI, 2014, pp. 32–44.

48 David Long, *The United States and Saudi Arabia: Ambivalent allies* (Boulder, CO, London: Westview Press, 1985).

49 Gregory Gause, Saudi Arabia's regional security strategy, in Mehran Kamrava (ed.), *International politics of the Persian Gulf* (Syracuse, New York: Syracuse University Press, 2011), pp. 169–183.

50 Riedel, *Kings and presidents*, p. 184; Long, US–Saudi relations.

51 Partrick, *Saudi Arabian foreign policy?*; Josh Pollack, Saudi Arabia and the United States, 1931–2002, *Middle East Review of International Affairs* 6: 3, 2002, pp. 77–102.

52 Rachel Bronson, *Thicker than oil: America's uneasy partnership with Saudi Arabia* (Oxford, New York: Oxford University Press, 2006).

53 Deepa Kumar, The right kind of 'Islam', *Journalism Studies* 19: 8, 2018, pp. 1079–1097.

54 Bronson, *Thicker than oil*.

55 Partrick, *Saudi Arabian foreign policy?*; Hossein Sadegui and Hassan Ahmadian, Iran–Saudi relations: Past pattern, future outlook, *Iranian Review of Foreign Affairs* 1: 4, 2011, pp. 115–148; Hiro, Cold War in the Islamic *w*orld; Simon Mabon, *The Struggle for Supremacy in the Middle East* (Cambridge: Cambridge University Press, 2023).

56 Wastnidge and Mabon (eds), Saudi Arabia and Iran.

57 Keynoush, Saudi Arabia and Iran.

58 Saeed M. Badeeb, *Saudi–Iranian relations 1932–1982* (London: Centre for Arab and Iranian Studies and Echoes, 1993).

59 Andrew S. Cooper, *The oil kings: How the U.S., Iran and Saudi Arabia changed the balance of power in the Middle East* (New York: Simon & Schuster Paperbacks, 2012); Al-Saud, Iran, Saudi Arabia and the Gulf.

60 Gawdat Bahgat, Iranian–Saudi rapprochement: Prospects and implications, *World Affairs* 162: 3, 2000, pp. 108–115; Okruhlik, Saudi Arabian–Iranian relations; Gregory Gause, *Beyond sectarianism: The new Middle East Cold War* (Washington, DC, Doha: Brookings Doha Center, 2014); Terrill, *The Saudi–Iranian rivalry and the future of Middle East security*; Frederic M. Wehrey, Theodore Karasik, Alireza Nader, Jeremy Ghez, Lydia Hansell, and Robert Guffey, *Saudi–Iranian relations since the fall of Saddam: Rivalry, cooperation, and implications for U.S. policy* (Santa Monica, CA: RAND Security Research Division, 2009).

61 Shokrollah K. Majin, Iranian and Saudi cultural and religious identities: Constructivist perspective, *Open Journal of Political Science* 7: 1, 2017, pp. 65–81; Hiro, Cold War in the Islamic *w*orld; Sadegui and Ahmadian, Iran–Saudi relations.

62 Hassan Ahmadian, Iran and Saudi Arabia in the age of Trump, *Survival* 60: 2, 2018, pp. 133–150, p. 133.

63 Wastnidge and Mabon (eds), Saudi Arabia and Iran.

64 Henner Fürtig (ed.), *Regional powers in the Middle East: New constellations after the Arab revolts* (New York: Palgrave Macmillan, 2014).

65 Terrill, The Saudi–Iranian rivalry and the future of Middle East security; Gause, *Beyond sectarianism*.

66 Chubin and Tripp, Iran–Saudi Arabia relations and regional order; Fürtig, Iran's rivalry with Saudi Arabia between the Gulf *w*ars; Keynoush, Saudi Arabia and Iran.

67 Anoushiravan Ehteshami, Iran and its immediate neighbourhood, in Anoushiravan Ehteshami and Mahjoob Zweiri (eds), *Iran's foreign policy from Khatami to Ahmadinejad* (New York: Ithaca Press, 2008), pp. 129–130.
68 Aarts and van Duijne, Saudi Arabia after the U.S.–Iranian détente.
69 Mabon, Saudi Arabia and Iran.
70 Timothy Luke, Dependent development and the OPEC states: State formation in Saudi Arabia and Iran under the international energy regime, *Studies in Comparative International Development* 20, 1985, pp. 31–54; Bahgat, Iranian–Saudi rapprochement; Mason, Back to realism for an enduring US–Saudi relationship.

2

Neoclassical Realism and the Iran–US–Saudi Arabia triangle

Producing IR *from* and *for* the Middle East

The disciplinary field of IR, as one knows it today, emerged as a function of great power competition, permeated by the normative objective of explaining how wars happen and how to prevent them.[1] For a long time, producing IR knowledge meant creating concepts and approaches that reflected the experiences of these great powers and their geopolitical game, while the 'rest' remained mostly excluded from theorisation. The Western experiences were taken as universal and transformed into parsimonious theories that could be applied elsewhere to explain all international political patterns. Conversely, regions devastated by colonialism and other not-so-powerful countries were the subjects of Area Studies and Cultural Studies, which, more often than not, created and reproduced discriminatory representations of non-Western nations to serve imperialist activities, something Edward Said famously denounces.[2] Originated as a Western enterprise to produce knowledge about 'exotic people' and 'exceptional countries', Middle East Studies (MES) was no exception to this rule, and, for decades, it overemphasised the cultural, political, and religious particularities of the region, turning it into something beyond comparison.[3]

As the US Social Sciences moved towards rationalist epistemologies and methodological behaviourism, the bulk of IR followed suit, consolidating an artificial divide between Area Studies and the field of international politics. Social Sciences were to be a problem-solving discipline, producing generalisations and applicable concepts, while Area Studies were to produce rich, practical, and contextual work on regions.[4] Decades of forcefully differentiating these fields created an artificial division of labour between them, hampering intellectual exchange. While area specialists should cover the uncouth and exotic regions, IR academics should reject particularism in favour of generalising theories and approaches that aim to produce universalising science.

As the US academic system became dominant within the discipline's politics during the Cold War, it consolidated itself into what Stanley Hoffman calls an 'American Science'.[5] The urge to maintain the US political domination relegated a significant part of the world to a peripherical position in disciplinary knowledge production.[6] Area Studies departments conflated with government interests, feeding information about relevant regions to the geopolitical game, a legacy that still lingers today. Thus, inequalities within the power distribution among nations were replicated in how IR knowledge was produced and consumed.[7] Mainstream IR became mostly West-dominated, ignoring or silencing the experience and agency from the Global South and struggling to include what is thought outside of the West. Moreover, these regions were not seen as knowledge producers but as consumers, as well as gas stations that provided empirical fuel for Western scholars.[8]

Conversely, many Area Studies specialists showed problematic tendencies towards cultural essentialism and an inability to grasp structural conditions within international politics. For example, after the 9/11 attacks, many MES scholars began to stress regional particularities and cultural differences as causes of political conflict or failures to implement Western-like democracy.[9] While it is crucial to understand how different actors ascribe meaning to their actions concerning their culture, history, and politics, one must be suspicious of culturalist accounts when looking for explanations for international behaviour. When a particular culture is the cause of an international event, the concepts and ideas developed for that analysis cannot be applied in any other case, reducing the study's general relevance. More often than not, Area Studies scholars have overemphasised the idiosyncrasies of one region or case, injecting more parochialism and cultural inwardness in the field and retreating from comparisons or systemic-level explanations. Hence, they have contributed to the Global South's permanence in the periphery of IR theory-building.[10]

For these reasons, producing IR knowledge for and from a non-Western region has been an arduous task. A question is always posed: do regions essentially differentiate themselves from one another, or are patterns of international politics equal everywhere? This provocation to opt between universalism and particularism has challenged any IR scholar specialising in a region, being in the Middle East, Africa, Latin America, or South Asia. They must work in the interface of IR and Area Studies, combining the first's cross-cutting theories with the second's plentiful contextual analysis, a delicate balancing act.[11] If the discipline's object of inquiry is the interaction between actors in a supranational context, one expects different regions to produce different traditions for understanding reality. However, if these traditions cannot find any common standing, they might as well be called another thing, not IR. For producing content that contributes to the discipline's progress, some level of scholarly agreement is needed on the nature of the international structure, the patterns of relations between states, and how a diverse set of actors tends to behave when faced with certain types of stimuli.

IR knowledge produced in non-Western regions should be capable of recalibrating the discipline by including and connecting various academic communities, embracing and promoting academic diffusion. Here, it is interesting to think that there is an 'academic world market' in which concepts, theories, and approaches are projected and sold – some are bought, others not. They then travel, being adapted, adjusted, and twisted to explain local realities. A basis for good IR practice is to think critically about how ideas, traditions, and theories travel worldwide and discuss these travails, connecting and comparing them. These tradeable goods can also influence other disciplinary fields, contesting and transforming scholarly power relations and knowledge production's boundaries.

Most IR done in the Global South has gone shopping in that market of ideas, picked one theory or approach, and adapted it to fit their cases better.[12] Using strategies of hybridisation, denationalisation of ideas, and mimicry, Global South scholars have inserted themselves into the IR debates by subscribing to one paradigm and simultaneously pinpointing its flaws, using local experience and data to advance on alternatives to these pitfalls.[13] They employed the strategy of analytical eclecticism, mixing and matching ideas from different paradigms. When well employed, these strategies have demonstrated not only disciplinarity originality but, most importantly, an ability to tackle interdisciplinarity, balancing IR and Area Studies.

On the eve of the 2000s, some scholars raised awareness about an intellectual divide permeating IRME and keeping it at a suboptimal development level.[14] They argued that while regional particularities blinded MES scholars, IR researchers were blinded to idiosyncrasies not visible in the West. On the one hand, MES tended to escape universalistic discussions, preferring detailed analyses of the local. On the other hand, IR avoided selecting Middle Eastern countries because they were too unique. After almost two decades of these discussions, many outstanding works combining in-depth knowledge about the region and IR theories and concepts emerged.[15] They applied an eclectic combination of theories and concepts to better cope with regional particularities. One way or the other, these eclectic analyses highlighted the international system's cruciality in tandem with domestic elements, finding a middle ground between agency and structure.

However, this evolution is still far from its potential. First, a not insignificant part of the scholar community still insists on an eristic dialogue, interacting with Area Studies only to attest they are correct. Some insist on cultural essentialism to explain Middle Eastern political events, whereas others keep fitting the region into Western-made concepts and theories without any adaption. Second, a part of this dialogue is still hierarchical, in the sense that IR scholars see MES as a shop providing local empirical data for them to apply a theory, not a space for dialoguing, intellectual exchange, or paradigmatic change.[16] This book, however, aims at a transformative dialogue between the fields by moulding its theoretical framework after the knowledge from Area Studies discussed in the previous chapter. But before that, let us delve quickly into the literature of IRME to grasp its current state better.

IRME today

First, it is important to stress that many excellent works from MES scholars about regional international politics exist. Nevertheless, many of those often paid lip service to IR disciplinary concerns towards methods, theoretical subscription, or paradigmatic coherence, preferring descriptive explanations for what happened instead of seeking behaviour patterns. However, those that attempt to employ an IR analytical framework to the region tend to swing from employing Realism to Constructivism, or mixing both traditions eclectically.

From the many strands of Realism out there, Neorealism consolidated itself as the theory of studying war, security, and competition.[17] Self-help impetus, the inability to know the other's motivations, and the eagerness to survive drive states to seek the maximisation of their gains in a system where power is distributed unequally, there is no superior authority, and information is not plenty. These restrictive conditions seem to fit well into the Middle Eastern geopolitical context and its many interstate wars, the constant sense of threat, the low level of cooperation, the high degree of militarisation, and several foreign interventions. Nevertheless, most works in the region do not employ Neorealism in its sheer form but adapt it to local particularities.

For example, Stephen Walt challenges Neorealism's reliance on power as the sole determinant of international politics, arguing that states also balance threats according to others' aggressive intent.[18] Many others advanced this balance of threats theory, opening the state's black box to explore how intention and threats influence decision-making in international politics, investigating factors such as identity, religion, ideology, and transnationalism.[19] For instance, Raymond Hinnebusch argues that the high level of incongruence between states, the many transnational identities, and the deep infiltration of foreign actors made the system subordinated, and leaders must make decisions under a much more restrictive scenario.[20] Similarly, Gregory Gause argued that systemic analysis should not be divorced from the ideological map influencing leaders in their decision-making process.[21] In her turn, May Darwich combined the balance of power framework with onto-logical security to grasp under which circumstances ideational factors are more relevant to threat perception than material ones.[22]

Therefore, these works called for a Realist course correction. The Realist tradition is alluring to IRME because it explains conflicts by the logic of anarchy and mistrust. Nonetheless, the structure alone cannot account for the region's particularities; therefore, Noerealism inevitably produces misrepresented and incomplete interpretations of reality.[23] Aware of that, IRME authors tend to emphasise the overbearing effect of the international structure on state–state relations while offering different toolsets to investigate the impacts of domestic and transnational factors shaping decisions and perceptions. They agree that concepts such as anarchy, state centrality, and security dilemma are crucial. Nevertheless, they mimetically accuse Neorealism of being incapable of accounting for the region's complexity. By mixing and matching some Neorealist tenets with domestic and regional elements, they tackle the critiques about materialist simplification while providing essential in-depth analysis with rich explanatory and practical value.

Unsurprisingly, this awareness of Neorealism's limitations drove other IRME scholars to Constructivism, which grasps the international system as an intersubjective and constant interaction between agency and structure over social norms, practices, and ideas.[24] Often presented as an alternative to Realism, Constructivism expanded IR topics, bringing light to crucial yet undervalued, non-material factors, such as beliefs, ideas, culture, ideology, and identity. In his landmark *Dialogues in Arab Politics*, Michael Barnett shows how transnational identities such as Arabism justify choices and alter foreign policy orientations and alliance-making.[25] Some authors followed this exercise of putting unit-level factors at the analytical centre without structural pre-constraints. For example, Marc Lynch explores how the Jordanian national identity guided its foreign policy's inconsistencies.[26] In turn, Arshin Adib-Moghaddam presents a cultural genealogic investigation of anarchy to explain the historical cycles of violence that permeated the Persian Gulf, bringing to light the importance of language, manufactured images, and conflictive experiences.[27]

Within IRME, Constructivism became a starting point for weighting discourses, rhetoric, language, symbols, and images as key non-material elements influencing politics. However, it is interesting to notice that, just like there are few orthodox Neorealist works within IRME, there are also relatively few works inextricably grounded on the idea that the social world is co-constitutive on the basis of how actors give meaning to reality. Instead, a more flexible synthesis of the Constructive perspective, the Copenhagen School, is preferred. Prominent authors such as Mehran Kamrava, Kristian Coates Ulrichsen, and Simon Mabon find in securitisation – the idea that a plethora of themes can receive the status of threat by a leader in a particular social context of framing – a valuable tool to grasp how Middle Eastern countries manipulate identity to gain political support.[28] This way, the Copenhagen School can also be seen as an eclectic move combining elements, finding a middle ground between structure determinants, parsimony, agency, and particularism.

The main problem of all these eclectic analytical studies is that, by making so many different combinations of traditions and theoretical perspectives, they have so far not arrived at a clear and sustained theoretical progress within IR.[29] Moreover, many of these analyses patchworked different theories in isolation, so each theory explains one part of the analysis. Like that, they risk degeneration (everything can matter) and overdetermination (making it impossible to isolate each factor's causal impact). This way, a reproducible research design becomes mostly inexistent, and there are few possibilities for intellectual cross-fertilisation.

That can be strategically problematic for de-Westernising the disciplinary field. While IRME's eclecticism is responding to the call of theoretical pluralism by seizing the middle ground between particularism and parsimony, its value added to discipline is blurry because it offers different combinations that incorporate factors in an ad hoc manner. As a collective, they have made only tentative contributions to IR's progress by not proposing analytical models that can be used even beyond the Middle East in a consistent manner, showing generalisable causal mechanisms and testing mechanisms under specific scopes and conditions. So far, most of what they proposed is not supposed to travel to other regions. As a result, they, most likely inadvertently, maintain the region in the periphery of disciplinary theory-building, not dialoguing with cases outside the Middle East.

As part of the Global South, the Middle East poses exciting perspectives on international relations that can contribute to the discipline's pluralisation. As a region that came late in the international system and had its borders and politics dictated by others for a long time, it offers unique insights into nationalism, statecraft, global asymmetries, regionalism, and alliance-making, among others. Moreover, colonialism, imperialism, and the current context of immense socioeconomic and development inequality between states are not particular to the Middle East but are part of a hegemonic project. In this sense, the region is not an exception but an inseparable part of global development with its own twists and turns. For these reasons, IRME should provide much space for cross-regional and transregional comparisons.

However, IRME's contributions to globalising IR are still far from potential. While the literature provides needed selectivity, sophistication, and expertise, it still struggles to see the Middle East as part of the Global South. By not attempting to create models and arguments that can travel to other regions and instigate comparisons, IRME has missed the opportunity to participate in the de-Westernisation of IR – or, at least, to take a central role. A pathway to improve the contribution of IRME to the general state of IR should be, therefore, via a more precise definition of available analytical tools, predictable capability, and methodological rigour that manages to escape excessive culturalism or particularism. This book argues that NCR, although initially created in the Global North, can offer a better route for inserting IRME into this project via a reflexive and transformative dialogue.

NCR as a Realist course correction

NCR scholars are those who, while keeping core Realist assumptions about the international system, have included unit-level variables to explain why states act differently upon the same systemic stimuli.[30] While they adhere to the logic that international relations are driven first and foremost by a country's place in systemic power distribution, they insist that the anarchical structure is insufficient to explain why and how states deliberate policies. Therefore, they look inside the states to investigate how unit-level variables influence the decision-making process in international politics.[31] In other words, the structure only tells half of the story. The international system creates conditions but does not have complete control over the outcomes.

As a philosophical tradition, what unites all Realists is a pessimistic view of the human condition and the prospects for change and cooperation in human behaviour. This idea can be traced back to Thucydides, Sun Tzu, Machiavelli, and Clausewitz. For a long time, Neorealists have been discussing whether a state seeks power accumulation for defence or offensive reasons. Instead, NCR proposes that states are influence maximisers, meaning that the more they perceive their power increases, the more control over the environment they want. Therefore, while anarchy defines the system, actors can perceive the environment in which they interact as more or less permissive. Under a permissive environment, where state survival is less endangered, decision-makers can have the 'luxury' of seeking other international goals beyond security. Hence, NCR creates space for the discussion of different motivations when it comes to international relations. To explain these different motivations, it opens the black box of the state.

For NCR, policymakers interpret pressures and opportunities coming from the system (inputs) differently and elaborate policies (outputs) according to what they interpret as the best option for securing their state's interest. The key word here is perception. As systemic anarchy is indeterminate and information is never always clear or plenty, it is up to leaders – with all their bias, ambiguity, and delays – to interpret how permissive or restrictive the environment is to them.[32] Therefore, exploring internal characteristics of the states is essential to explain why similar actors can perceive systemic stimuli and mobilise resources differently.

The principle is that states receive systemic inputs, and intervening variables (domestic factors) filter these signals to create meaning for policy-making. These elements are added not because NCR understands reality as socially constructed but because the states fall back in perception to comprehend reality. Therefore, these factors receive the second position in the analytical chain, as domestic variables cannot transcend the systemic structure's limits. Ideas, perceptions, and ideologies remain anchored in individual action, meaning that they help the decision-maker detect interests amid uncertainty.

Most importantly, intervening variables explain how some outcomes are discarded during decision-making, and others are preferred. Thus, it allows the investigation of motivations, political elites, regime endurance, multinational identities, and leadership preferences. That permits research that includes the particularities the IRME scholars argue are crucial for understanding the region. For example, ideational factors are essential to grasp why revisionist states and non-state actors, such as Iran and Hezbollah, continue their uncompromising behaviour despite systemic punishment. They also explain why the GCC countries aligned with Iraq against Iran in the 1980s despite Iraq being the most prominent military threat.

Finally, NCR is pluralistic and epistemologically diverse, offering various contributions that expand the Realist tradition's scope and topics. Despite this flexibility, NCR scholars still share attributes that assemble them into the Realist scholarly community, such as research interests, methodology, and ontology.[33] The main difference between NCR and IRME's eclecticism lies in this ambition to consolidate a coherent approach for studying international behaviour variance within the Realist tradition. All NCR scholars agree on a predefined hierarchical arrangement of variables: on its analytical chain, unit-level variables are subsequential to systemic-level variables. Agency is possible within a structurally determined perimeter of options that the balance of power defines. This way, intervening variables fill the gap between systemic stimuli and concrete policies – they are hierarchically below systemic variables. This acquiescence of domestic variables into the analytical chain as an influence on decision-making avoids overdetermination because it provides a straightforward, predefined research design.

Thus, NCR's primary added value to IRME is enabling creative research designs that combine the knowledge produced by MES specialists while still seeking to build a cohesive framework grounded in IR. That is because there is a consensus on what independent, intervening, and dependent variables can be and their explanative function. Conversely, NCR can embrace different works touching Realist themes due to its loose paradigmatic boundaries, broadening the intellectual tradition.[34] Thus, it stands in the halfway of IR-theorising, between systemic determinism and domestic determinism, dodging the extremes of parsimony and particularism.[35] This position allows research with similar diagnostic precision and political relevancy as that from IRME, while it does not lose theoretical replicability and methodological rigour. This way, by applying NCR to Middle Eastern cases, one can build upon the in-depth and complex analysis and theoretical frameworks that can travel to other cases and regions, advancing IRME and contributing to the de-Westernisation of the IR discipline.

An NCR model for the triangular relationship

The NCR framework is set: the independent variable is power, the intervening variables are a set of domestic factors that influence decision-making (which can vary according to the case selected), and the dependent variable is a foreign policy change, a grand strategy adjustment, or another pattern of international behaviour. The dependent variable is, therefore, what we want to study, while the intervening variables must be selected carefully and grounded on an in-depth case evaluation. These intervening variables allow the researcher to conceptually narrow the band of policy choices available, with each newly added variable having a filtering impact over these options.

The previous chapter investigated which elements MES scholars have explored as crucial to grasping the three dyads that compose our Persian Gulf triangle (Iran–Saudi Arabia, US–Iran, and US–Saudi Arabia). As a result, the review highlighted ideational, cognitive, and leadership categories. For these reasons, the three intervening variables this book explores are: status satisfaction (ideational factor), state identity (cognitive factor), and leaders' preferences (leadership factor). These variables are displayed in the analytical chain in order of comprehensiveness. Status satisfaction *shifts* the policy parameters towards revisionism or continuity, state identity *narrows* the band of possible action, and leaders *tilt* the outcomes to the direction of their preferences, interests, and interpretations. The dependable variable is the strategic triangle, which contains the three countries' processes of grand strategising for the region.

Significant events can disrupt the distribution of power within the regional system (*structural changes*), provoking a new set of systemic constraints and opportunities (*inputs*) and affecting the results (*outputs*) in the causal chain. Figure 2.1 shows how intervening variables translate

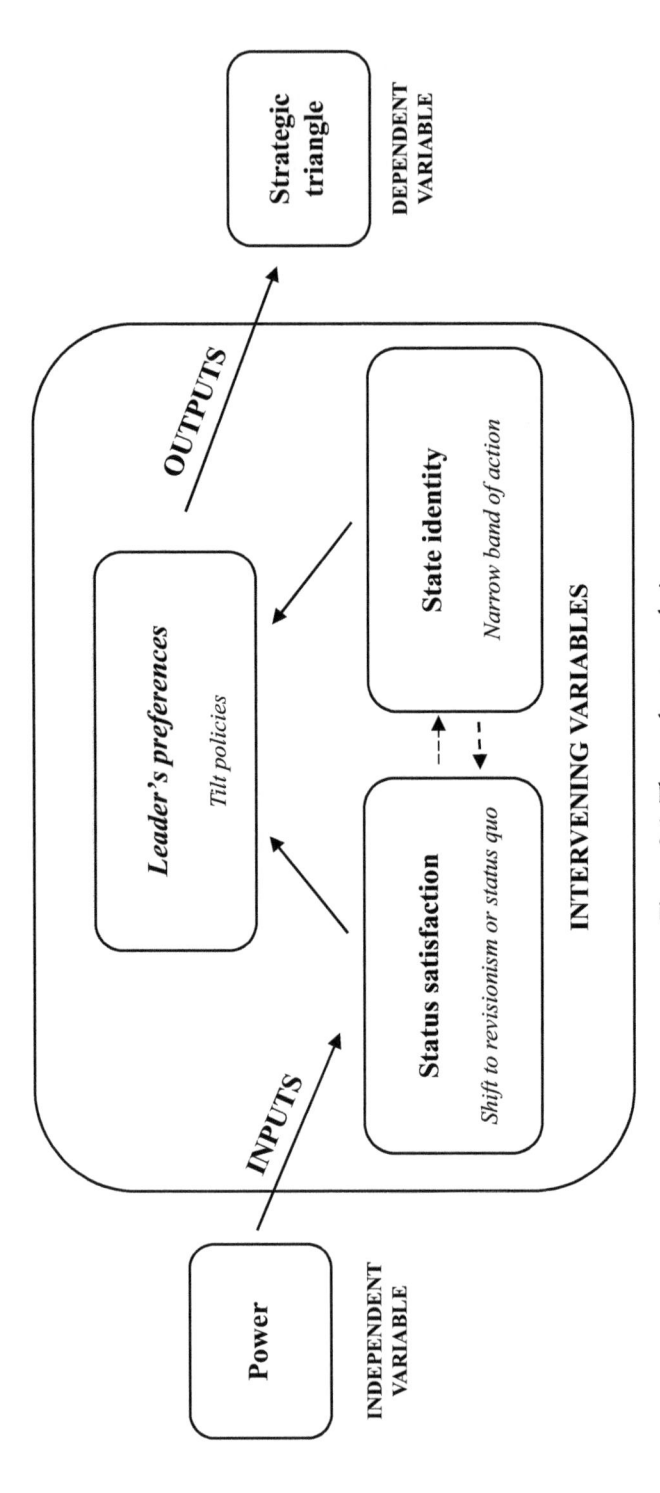

Figure 2.1 The explanatory chain

Strategic triangle

DEPENDENT VARIABLE

OUTPUTS

Leader's preferences

Tilt policies

State identity

Narrow band of action

INTERVENING VARIABLES

Status satisfaction

Shift to revisionism or status quo

INPUTS

Power

INDEPENDENT VARIABLE

systemic inputs, narrowing the outputs available. For example, a country receives a systemic input X. The status satisfaction shifts feasible foreign policy options towards revisionism or continuity while the state identity filters the options, offering the leaders the possible policies A, B, or C. Analysing the leadership variable will explain why a country chooses policy B and not A or C.

Figure 2.1 shows how outcomes are ultimately bound to the leaders and how they perceive environmental restrictiveness, interpret cognitive functions, and calculate risks and opportunities. That is why the first two intervening variables, status satisfaction and state identity, are at the same level, whereas the leaders are on top. It is also important to stress that identities can have an ideational character and vice versa, meaning it is inviable to separate identity from status entirely. For this reason, there is a dotted arrow between both variables, indicating their interconnection. It is possible, nonetheless, to identify their distinct function in the analytical chain. While status satisfaction tilts options towards revisionism or status quo, state identity filters out policies that do not fit into the cognitive lenses available. Let us now dive into each variable more thoroughly.

Contextualising power

Like Neorealism, NCR understands power as the possession of assets or capabilities and a means to an end. However, like Classic Realists, it claims that power shapes interests and is divisible into different elements. Classical Realists such as Hans J. Morgenthau, Reinhold Niebuhr, and Edward H. Carr explained that power-seeking behaviour is inherent in human nature and that political actors use material and immaterial assets to induce international politics in their favour.[36] For example, Morgenthau distinguished between two element types that contributed to a state's power: stable ones and those subject to unexpected change.[37] The stable elements were quantitative, such as geography, natural resources, military capability, demography, and industry. The changeable elements were qualitative, referring to non-material features such as national morale, quality of government, influence, leadership, and diplomacy.

Similarly, NCR calls for a detailed conceptualisation of power incorporating material and non-material components at the state's disposal.[38] That enables a more complex understanding of power shifts as well as giving more context to the elements that a state can capitalise on for doing politics. This book explores the assets and capabilities that the US, Iran, and Saudi Arabia can project into the region through these stable and changeable categories.

In this study, power comprises geographical and demographical assets, economic capabilities, government stability, and military capacities. First, geography is relevant regarding size and access to resources, particularly in cases where a country lies over profitable or strategic raw materials or, on the contrary, lacks essential resources such as water or energy. Moreover, a country can be strategic or isolated based on location; its borders can provide natural protection and sea access or spark territorial conflicts. Conversely, demography relates to a country's potential to be defined as a great, regional, or small power, as a significant population is necessary for ever-growing economic and military demands.

Similarly, economic strength matters as an enabler of other power components. Impoverished countries cannot guarantee the modernisation of their defence and industrial apparatus. They are also susceptible to protests, political instabilities, and acute socioeconomic crises that hamper the country's ability to accumulate resources. Moreover, economic mismanagement, unemployment, and inflation can weaken a state by making it vulnerable to domestic and international contestation. Political stability is also crucial, mainly considering that mobilisation and decision-making depend on the institutional and governmental organisation. For example, regimes that perceive themselves in a volatile domestic position might turn inward-looking regarding their choices. In contrast, those with visible popular support and strong institutions tend to expand their international exposure and influence.

Under a Realist framework, the cruciality of military capabilities is undeniable in defining how powerful a country is. In a scenario of insecurity and lack of information, states often find themselves in security dilemmas, which instigate capacity accumulation and militarisation for offensive or defensive reasons. A country with enough military capabilities can impose its will by coercion, threat of force deployment, or precise operations. From a broader perspective, forces can be conventional or asymmetrical, organised for defence, deterrence, or offensive aims. A stable and relatively high defence budget and an adequate ratio between the reserve and regular troops allow for greater political and securitarian exertion. While quantity is crucial, quality is also paramount, as well as policy, doctrine, organisation, and training.

The changeable power category comprises non-material sources – like alliances, diplomatic ties, political reputation, and regional appeal – which can improve a country's ability to shape others' opinions or preferences.[39] These elements can vary depending on the political environment and the state's mobilisation capacities. Alliances and long-standing partnerships are efficient strategies a state can use to combine resources with like-minded countries and boost their interests. Also, alliances and membership in securitarian blocs such as the North Atlantic Treaty Organization (NATO) or the

Association of Southeast Asian Nations (ASEAN) can provide deterrence capabilities. It is undeniable that a country is stronger if it has more friends than enemies and if these friends collaborate in economic or securitarian terms. Moreover, alliances and partnerships provide political and diplomatic support, legitimacy, leverage, strategic depth, and bargaining authority.

Morgenthau gave special attention to diplomatic skills in his understanding of power, as 'the conduct of a nation's foreign affairs by its diplomats is for national power in peace what military strategy and tactics by its military leaders are for national power in war'.[40] Moreover, a country's political reputation is important for international prestige and status, high-ranking political meetings, diplomatic visits, participation in summits, and bilateral or international deals. Finally, it is crucial to stress that actors can gain power by sharing identitarian or religious affiliations with transnational communities beyond the frontiers of a state.

Status satisfaction

While the international system is anarchical because there is no superior authority beyond the states, power is unequally distributed, meaning different countries have different positionalities, limiting who has access to what.[41] International relations, therefore, operate under the underlying condition of power inequality that leads to different power configurations, polarities, and statuses such as superpower, middle power, weak state, or even failed state.[42] In this book, status satisfaction is an ideational variable that takes stock of whether a state's assigned status corresponds to its own expectations about its position in the international system.

Status is positional, social, and subjective.[43] Positional because it refers to a scarce, relative, and limited ranking: if everybody could have the same status, that would mean there was no inequality, and this concept would be useless. A position within a ranking can go up or down because of internal factors (a country gains or loses power) or external factors (another country can get more or less powerful, pushing others up or down on the ranking). Status is also social because it depends on how others in a peer group attest to this position.[44] No one can assign a status to itself. For a country to have a status of great power, it needs to get recognition via status markers, such as membership in selective assemblies like the Group of 7 (G7) or the United Nations Security Council (UNSC), leadership positions in international operations, hosting global events, among others. Finally, status is subjective as it cannot be quantified or empirically tested. It depends on the collective perception of power distribution.

This way, status per se is not a domestic factor; it belongs to the sphere in which states interact, the system. Nevertheless, how satisfied a country is with its perceived status is indeed a domestic factor, one that will determine if this country is interested in maintaining the current state of affairs or changing it. Status satisfaction, therefore, refers to the perceptual biases about positionality that can push a country towards accommodation (status quo actor) or nonconformity (revisionist actor) goals. This variable shows the country's ambitions towards the system and whether other states support or deny it. States will be discontent with their status when they perceive that they are being ascribed a lower status among their peer competitors than they think they deserve.

The relationship between aspiration and ascription provides two scenarios: when there is congruence or when the ascribed exceeds the expectations, the state is satisfied with the status quo; when the ascribed status is lesser than the aspirations, the state is dissatisfied with the order and favours revisionism.[45] This variable can also point to when states are anxious towards possible changes within the status quo, indicating if they perceive the international system as more restrictive or more open to other motivations beyond state survival.

In practical terms, this variable shows policy orientation within the analytical model: status quo or revisionist. While a revisionist actor disagrees with the existing power distribution or finds current interstate relations unfair, a status quo actor finds the current system legitimate, defending the power distribution and political order as it is.

State identity

In the simplest use of the term, identity is the state of being like something and different from another.[46] Identities are cognitive constructs providing self-schemas that organise what we are and are not, thus compiling and organising a massive amount of information about our experiences, acquired knowledge, and beliefs. Therefore, they cover representations one has about oneself and what they stand for, overcoming memory shortages and other information storage processes, and helping to cope with complex situations and reduce uncertainty.[47] They are the product of our continuous socialisation, usually durable and resistant to change, and combine material, social, historical, and cultural elements.

Most importantly, identity is a relational concept that involves creating boundaries that separate what you are from what others are that you are not. This means that for an understanding of a *self* to exist, it is necessary to have a differentiation relating to an *other*. Groupism is a foundational tenant of the Realist ontology: to survive several threats in an environment lacking clarity, actors build collective identities that distinguish in-groups from out-groups.[48] Groupism and fragmentation are immutable aspects of the human condition and political life, as humans cannot survive in an anarchical environment as individuals alone but as members of a larger group.[49] To ensure who belongs, actors construct these self-schemes that guarantee ontological distinctiveness to the group. This relational element is essential. When one group loses the uniqueness that separates it from others, it gets ontologically threatened, triggering the search for new differentiation mechanisms that can, once again, produce ontological security.

Now, let us bring these ideas to the leading group in which international politics have operated: states. Just like we have a notion of what we are and are not, states consolidate themselves through processes of collective identity formation – some more natural, others more artificial – that give ontological meaning to themselves. State identity can be broad or narrow, inclusive or exclusive, primarily reflecting the historical, cultural, and normative narratives promoted by the elite in power and transmitted through the government's bureaucratic body. These narratives represent traditionally powerful images of what their country should be. They are firmly rooted in the history of the state formation, cultural, religious, and ethnic intricacies, its experience with nation-building, and the path-dependent trajectory of the country's development and foreign relations.

In politics, identity serves to give an actor a sense of uniqueness in the environment in which one interacts with others.[50] Moreover, in anarchy, where chaos and security dilemmas lurk, these identities make state interaction more predictable and less random. This way, units have a familiar cognitive scheme that facilitates recognising competing threats, relating means to ends, and acting. Thus, states enable identitarian constructs that provide cognitive lenses from which policymakers can interpret their country's ontological purpose. In other words, state identities are filters limiting available action options. Being constructs that describe and prescribe how an actor should act, this intervening variable excludes some policies, despite their feasibility, reducing the universe of possible actions to a smaller set of conceivable ones. This way, state identity further specifies the causal chain.

Leadership preferences

The final variable asks about the individual preferences and mindsets of those making the policy. Leadership preferences show how individuals can tilt outcomes to their favour and interests. This variable refers to the people who occupy critical leadership positions in a country and are responsible for continuing or modifying foreign policy, long-term strategic planning, and elaborating responses to unpredictable situations. It includes the president, the prime minister, the king, the supreme leader, key cabinet members, ministers, and advisors.

Many NCR scholars have stressed the importance of a leader's beliefs, personality, and images in their analyses.[51] Leaders are in a privileged position in receiving the systemic inputs, accessing information about available resources and intelligence reports that will allow them to assess what needs to be done much before other actors. Undoubtedly, this assessment will be shaped by their own interpretation of the situation, their fears and ambitions, and their personal political projects. Indeed, people do not make decisions in an intellectual or contextual vacuum, being influenced by their beliefs, intellectual biases, motivations, and preferences.[52]

In short, to grasp if a country is a revisionist or status quo actor and to understand how state identity limits action, we need to check how leaders process these elements. This final intervening variable assesses environment restrictiveness, evaluates space for promoting ambitious behaviour, and selects the cognitive lenses to interpret a country's role. Therefore, while status satisfaction tilts the outcome towards one or another direction and the state identity limits action, leaders will ultimately make the decision, possibly mixing and matching different cognitive lenses and linking action to their own political agenda and beliefs.

It is important to note that there is no clear-cut division between the international and the domestic spheres of action when one wants to understand why a leader made a particular choice and not a different one. This variable has a Janus-faced characteristic: it can act internationally for domestic reasons or domestically for international purposes. It explains why some leaders chose one of the already filtered options and not others, tilting policy in their favour. In the end, it is up to those in charge of policymaking to perceive and interpret the inputs and define the outputs.

The strategic triangle

This book shows that, since 1969, the US, Saudi Arabia, and Iran have shared a triangular relationship in which the three dyads (bilateral relations) are highly interconnected. That means that whenever there is a change in one bilateral relationship concerning the Persian Gulf, the other two bilateral dyads will most probably be affected. This triangulation's long-standing patterns, learned and reproduced by each country's ideational, cognitive, and leadership schemas, has conditioned much of the countries' policies in the region (Figure 2.2).

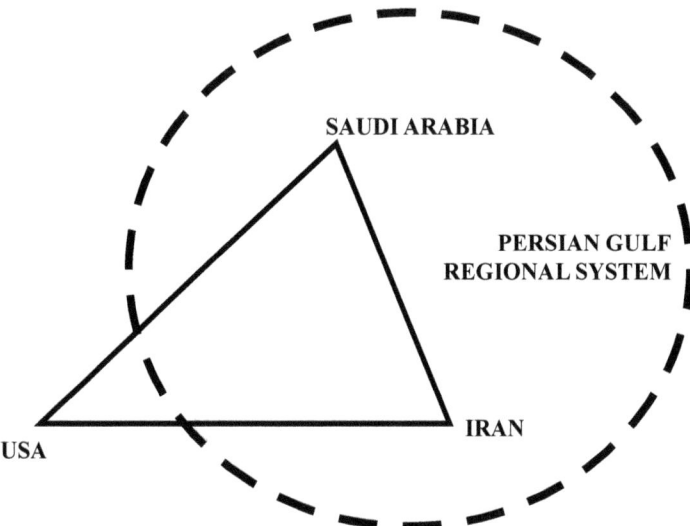

Figure 2.2 The dependent variable

As mentioned in the introduction, the concept of a strategic triangle in IR comes from Dittmer's work on the relations between China, the United States, and the Soviet Union.[53] He used game theory to explain the interconnection between the three bilateral relations inside the triangle and defined each 'side' as positive or negative. However, he considered that all actors had the same access to information, defined their policy via transitional costs, and overlooked the securitarian prioritisation of national interests. Thus, he did not open the state's black box. Instead, this book advances our understanding of how strategic triangles work by framing it through NCR. It borrows Dittmer's typology and lexicon for constructing hypotheses. Still, it goes beyond by including ideational, cognitive, and leadership variables that intervene in the decision-making process.

The following four chapters present this analytical framework in motion. Each of these chapters begins with contextualising a structural event that altered the power balance in the Persian Gulf. These events provoked a significant shift within the power distribution among all actors of the region. Moreover, they represented a new set of systemic constraints and opportunities and, consequently, offered conditions for the three actors to recalculate and reassess their regional strategies. As the chapters show, these recalculations eventually changed the dynamics within the strategic triangle.

Each of the following chapters focuses on one period (1969–1979; 1979–1989; 1989–2003; 2003–2014). After contextualising the events and exploring how the three actors are positioned in the Persian Gulf's power balance, the NCR framework is applied (independent variable–intervening variables–the strategic triangle). The triangulation is presented throughout the selected period, tracing its main tendencies. While the dependent variable does not discuss all events that happened between the three countries during the selected time, it stresses how they played out interdependently within the regional system.

Notes

1 Barry Buzan and Amitav Acharya, *The making of global international relations: Origins and evolution of IR at its centenary* (Cambridge: Cambridge University Press, 2019).

2 Edward Said, *Orientalism* (New York: Vintage Books, 1978).

3 Andrea Teti, Bridging the gap: IR, Middle East studies and the disciplinary politics of the Area Studies controversy, *European Journal of International Relations* 13: 1, 2007, pp. 117–145; Morten Valbjørn, 'Culture blind and culture blinded': Images of Middle Eastern conflicts in international relations, in Dietrich Jung (ed.), *The Middle East and Palestine: Global politics and regional conflict* (New York: Palgrave Macmillan US, 2004), pp. 39–78.

4 Seteney K. Shami and Cynthia Miller-Idriss (eds), *Middle East studies for the new millennium: Infrastructures of knowledge* (New York: New York University Press, 2016); Stephen Aris, International vs. area? The disciplinary-politics of knowledge-exchange between IR and Area Studies, *International Theory* 13: 3, 2020, pp. 1–32.

5 Stanley Hoffman, An American social science: International relations, *Daedalus* 106: 3, 1977, pp. 41–60.

6 Barry Buzan and George Lawson, *The global transformation: History, modernity and the making of international relations* (Cambridge: Cambridge University Press, 2015).

7 Christian Bueger, From epistemology to practice: A sociology of science for international relations, *Journal of International Relations and Development* 15: 1, 2012, pp. 97–109; Melody Fonseca, Global IR and Western dominance: Moving forward or Eurocentric entrapment?, *Millennium: Journal of International Studies* 48: 1, 2019, pp. 45–59.

8 Bilgin, Thinking past Western IR.

9 Lisa Wedeen, Scientific knowledge, liberalism, and empire: American political science in the modern Middle East, in Shami and Miller-Idriss (eds), *Middle East studies for the new millennium.*

10 Pinar Bilgin, One model of engagement between MES and IR, in *International Relations theory and a changing Middle East* (Washington, DC: Project on Middle East Political Science, 2015), pp. 6–12.

11 Fawcett, International Relations and the Middle East.

12 Arlene B. Tickner and Ole Wæver, Introduction, in Arlene B. Tickner and Ole Wæver (eds), *International Relations scholarship around the world* (Abingdon, Oxon, New York: Routledge, 2009); Bilgin, Thinking past Western IR.

13 Helen L. Turton and Lucas G. Freire, Peripheral possibilities: Revealing originality and encouraging dialogue through a reconsideration of 'marginal' IR scholarship, *Journal of International Relations and Development* 19: 4, 2016, pp. 534–557; Ersel Azdinli and Gonca Biltekin, A typology of home-grown theorizing, in Ersel Aydınlı and Gonca Biltekin (eds), *Widening the world of international relations* (London, New York: Routledge, 2018), pp. 15–40.

14 Gregory Gause, Systemic approaches to Middle East International Relations, *International Studies Review* 1, 1999, pp. 11–31; Fawaz Gerges, The study of Middle East International Relations: A critique, *British Journal of Middle Eastern Studies* 18: 2, 1991, pp. 208–220; Mark Tessler (ed.), *Area Studies and social science: Strategies for understanding Middle East politics* (Bloomington, IN: Indiana University Press, 1999); Teti, Bridging the gap; Valbjørn, 'Culture blind and culture blinded'.

15 Gause, The international relations of the Persian Gulf; Hinnebusch, The international politics of the Middle East; Mabon, Saudi Arabia and Iran; Lawrence Rubin, *Islam in the balance* (Stanford, CA: Stanford University Press, 2017); Ulrichsen, *Insecure Gulf*; May Darwich, *Threats and alliances in the Middle East* (Cambridge: Cambridge University Press, 2019).

16 May Darwich and Juliet Kaarbo, IR in the Middle East: Foreign policy analysis in theoretical approaches, *International Relations* 34: 2, 2020, pp. 225–245.

17 Kenneth Waltz, *A theory of international politics* (New York: Random House, 1979); Stephen van Evera, *Causes of war: Power and the roots of conflict* (Ithaca, New York: Cornell University Press, 1999); John Mearsheimer, *The tragedy of great power politics* (New York: Norton, 2001).

18 Stephen Walt, *The origin of alliances* (New York: Cornell University Press, 1987).

19 Gregory Gause, Balancing what? Threat perception and alliance choice in the Gulf, *Security Studies* 13: 2, 2003, pp. 273–305; Gerd Nonemman, *Analyzing Middle East foreign policies: The relationship with Europe* (New York: Routledge, 2005); Rubin, *Islam in the balance*; Darwich, *Threats and alliances in the Middle East*; Shibley Telhami, *Power and leadership in international bargaining: The path to the Camp David Accords* (New York: Columbia University Press, 1992).

20 Hinnebusch, *The international politics of the Middle East*.

21 Gause, *The international relations of the Persian Gulf*.

22 Darwich, *Threats and alliances in the Middle East*.

23 Halliday, *The Middle East in International Relations*.

24 Alexander Wendt, Anarchy is what states make of it: The social construction of power politics, *International Organization* 46, 1992, pp. 391–425; Ted Hopf, The promise of constructivism in International Relations theory, *International Security* 23: 1, 1998, pp. 171–200.

25 Michael Barnett, *Dialogues in Arab Politics: Negotiations in the regional order* (New York: Columbia University Press, 1998).

26 Marc Lynch, *State interests and public spheres: The international politics of Jordan's identity* (New York: Columbia University Press, 1999).

27 Arshin Adib-Moghaddam, *The international politics of the Persian Gulf: A cultural genealogy* (London: Routledge, 2006).

28 Mehran Kamrava (ed.), *International politics of the Persian Gulf* (Syracuse, New York: Syracuse University Press, 2011); Mabon, *Saudi Arabia and Iran*; Ulrichsen, *Insecure Gulf*.

29 Darwich and Kaarbo, IR in the Middle East; Fawcett, International Relations and the Middle East.

30 Lobell, Taliaferro, and Ripsman (eds), Neoclassical Realism, the state, and foreign policy; Gustav Meibauer, Linde Desmaele, Tudor Onea, Nicholas Kitchen, Michiel Foulon, Alexander Reichwein, and Jennifer Sterling-Folker (eds), Forum: Rethinking Neoclassical Realism at theory's end, special issue, *International Studies Review* 23: 1, 2020, pp. 268–295; Norrin Ripsman, Jeffrey Taliaferro, and Steven Lobell, *Neoclassical Realist theory of international politics* (New York: Oxford University Press, 2016); Thomas Juneau, *Squandered opportunity: Neoclassical Realism and Iranian foreign policy* (Stanford, CA: Stanford University Press, 2015).

31 Michiel Foulon, Neoclassical Realism: Challengers and bridging identities, *International Studies Review* 17, 2015, pp. 635–661; Layne, *The peace of illusions*.

32 Gustav Meibauer, Interests, ideas, and the study of state behaviour in neoclassical realism, *Review of International Studies* 46: 1, 2020, pp. 20–36; Brian Rathbun, A rose by any other name: Neoclassical realism as the logical and necessary extension of structural realism, *Security Studies* 17: 2, 2008, pp. 294–321.

33 Meibauer, Interests, ideas, and the study of state behaviour in neoclassical realism.

34 Foulon and Meibauer, Realist avenues to global International Relations.

35 Ripsman, Taliaferro, and Lobell, *Neoclassical Realist theory of international politics*.

36 Brian Schmidt, Realism and facets of power in international relations, in Felix Berenskoetter and M. K. Williams (eds), *Power in world politics* (New York: Routledge, 2007), pp. 43–64.

37 Hans J. Morgenthau, *Politics among nations* (Chicago, IL: University of Chicago Press, 1954).

38 Juneau, *Squandered opportunity*; Ripsman, Taliaferro, and Lobell, *Neoclassical Realist theory of international politics*.

39 David Sobek and Joe Clare, Me, myself, and allies: Understanding the external sources of power, *Journal of Peace Research* 50: 4, 2013, pp. 469–478; Schmidt, Realism and facets of power in international relations.

40 Morgenthau, *Politics among nations*.

41 Fred Halliday, *Rethinking International Relations* (New York: Red Globe Press, 1994); Alexander Anievas and Kerem Nişancıoğlu, *How the West came to rule: The geopolitical origins of capitalism* (London: Pluto Press, 2015); John Agnew, The new global economy: Time–space compression, geopolitics, and global uneven development, *Journal of World-Systems Research* 7: 2, 2001, pp. 133–154.

42 Thomas J. Volgy, Renato Corbetta, Keith Grant, and Ryan G. Baird (eds), *Major powers and the quest for status in international politics: Global and regional perspectives* (New York: Palgrave Macmillan, 2011); Kalevi Holsti, *The state, war and the state of war* (Cambridge: Cambridge University Press, 1996).

43 Jonathan Renshon, *Fighting for status: Hierarchy and conflict in world politics* (Princeton, NJ: Princeton University Press, 2017).

44 T. V. Paul, Deborah W. Larson, and William Wohlforth, Status and world order, in T. V. Paul, Deborah W. Larson, and William Wohlforth (eds), *Status in world politics* (New York: Cambridge University Press, 2014).

45 Juneau, *Squandered opportunity*.

46 Barnett, *Dialogues in Arab Politics*; Glenn Chafetz, Michael Spirtas, and Benjamin Frankel, Introduction: Tracing the influence of identity on foreign policy, *Security Studies* 8: 2–3, 1998, pp. 7–22.

47 Anthony Giddens, *Modernity and self-identity* (New York: Polity Press, 1991); Jennifer Mitzen, Ontological security in world politics: State identity and the security dilemma, *European Journal of International Relations* 12: 3, 2006, pp. 341–370.

48 Jennifer Sterling-Folker, Neoclassical Realism and identity: Peril despite profit across the Taiwan Strait, in Lobell, Taliaferro, and Ripsman (eds), Neoclassical Realism, the state, and foreign policy, pp. 99–139.

49 Steven Lobell, Jeffrey Taliaferro, and Norrin Ripsman, Introduction: Neoclassical Realism, the state, and foreign policy, in Lobell, Taliaferro, and Ripsman (eds), Neoclassical Realism, the state, and foreign policy, pp. 1–42.

50 Shibley Telhami and Michael Barnett, *Identity and foreign policy in the Middle East* (London: Cornell University Press, 2002); Rubin, *Islam in the balance*.

51 Juneau, *Squandered opportunity*; William Wohlforth, *The elusive balance: Power and perceptions during the Cold War* (Ithaca, New York: Cornell University Press, 1993); Jeffrey Taliaferro, *Balancing risks: Great power intervention in the periphery* (Ithaca, New York: Cornell University Press, 2004).

52 Foulon, Neoclassical Realism; Meibauer, Interests, ideas, and the study of state behaviour in neoclassical realism.

53 Dittmer, The strategic triangle.

3

The *ménage à trois* triangle (1969–1979): The Twin Pillar Diplomacy revisited

From the middle of the nineteenth century until the eve of the 1970s, the United Kingdom was the Persian Gulf's political arbiter. During the first decades of the Cold War, it assumed a surrogate position within the US grand strategy, guaranteeing that the region's oil would reconstruct European and Japanese economies. In other words, London's imperial role worked as a gatekeeper of Western interests in the Persian Gulf, keeping a check on interference. In this scenario, Washington played only a secondary role, mainly via private oil companies and their ties with local producers. The Pax Britannica prevented conflict between the small sheikdoms and discouraged the larger countries – Iran, Iraq, and Saudi Arabia – from hegemonic expansion.

However, it became increasingly difficult for the British government to keep justifying this role by the 1960s. Local dissatisfaction and protests rose in many UK colonies, particularly with the 1956 Suez crisis in Egypt. Thus, in January 1968, a combination of financial weakness, political overstretch, and nationalist sentiment in the remaining colonies led the UK Labour Party to announce its retraction from the Persian Gulf by 1971. This meant that the Trucial States, Bahrain, and Qatar needed to brace themselves for independence.

This decision presented a challenge for the US, as it could open a power vacuum in the Persian Gulf for the Soviets to take advantage of. From 1969 to 1971, there were intense consultations between the British and the Americans about the region's future to avoid an abrupt political change that would harm Western interests. They worried about possible local turmoil after the withdrawal and worked together to identify and neutralise sources of instability and avoid general disturbance in the oil markets. It is important to stress that, by then, the British authority was quite flexible, and most local leaders had some level of independence, facilitating the power transition.

Evidently, the most immediate consequence was the end of the British protectorate system. In 1971, Bahrain and Qatar became independent countries, and the six emirates unified to form the UAE.[1] Nevertheless, the departure also altered the region's power distribution despite being an essentially smooth transition. On the one hand, the removal of the extra-regional actor increased the regional countries in number and importance. On the other hand, a power vacuum emerged: who would guarantee the order and how? In the context of the Cold War, would the Persian Gulf remain under the Western sphere of influence, assume a neutral standing, or turn towards the Soviet Union?

It is in this context that the strategic triangular relationship between the US, Iran, and Saudi Arabia emerged. The British withdrawal led to the local empowerment of Iran and Saudi Arabia while simultaneously inserting the Persian Gulf into the US strategic agenda. The following pages first discuss how power was distributed among the three countries, to then delve into how the intervening variables shaped the establishment of the Twin Pillar Diplomacy from 1969 to 1979.

The US power: a readjusting superpower

The end of the Second World War consolidated the US as a great power. Being the third-largest country in the world and with a well-distributed and large population that grew steadily, the country had the obvious conditions to assume a leading global position. Geography gives the US a high level of security. It has access to both the Pacific and the Atlantic Oceans, which work as natural border shields, and it shares territorial frontiers only with Canada and Mexico, two long-standing partners – and much weaker in terms of military forces. Concerning resources, it has abundant agricultural land and a diverse set of natural resources, including oil and the world's largest coal reserves. Finally, its political system has been stable since the 1860s Civil War, making it the longest democracy alive.

Throughout the Cold War, the US held the status of the most powerful country in the world. The 1950s and 1960s represented a remarkable economic and military expansion period: the so-called Golden Age of US-American capitalism was defined by exponentially rising GDP, consumption expansion, high wages, low unemployment, and elevated government-spending. In terms of security, Washington invested in enlarging its strategic forces via high procurements, improving training, and developing high-tech weaponry. Nevertheless, the 1970s represented a deceleration moment: the GDP grew slower than before, sometimes at a negative rate.[2] Most Western economies were affected by the 1973 oil crisis and the crumbling of the Bretton Woods system, which led to the stock market crash and stagflation. Simultaneously, a new wave of industrialised countries was catching up, increasing competition and reducing the production gap between the US and other industrial nations.

A similar tendency of deceleration is detected in military terms. During the 1950s and the 1960s, military expansion aimed towards establishing an overwhelming advantage (defence and offence) over the Soviet Union. While it still had the most distinguished military power in the world in terms of traditional capabilities and technological innovation, the Soviet Union was starting to catch up in the 1970s. Moreover, domestic dissent over the Vietnam War and the economic recession compromised the state's ability to allocate resources for international conflicts, stimulating a reorientation of budgetary preferences.[3] Thus, whereas in 1969, military expenditure accounted for 8.2 per cent of the total GDP, it reduced to 4.7 per cent in 1979, and military personnel also reduced.[4]

Therefore, while still being the most powerful country globally, the 1970s represented a relative retreat of the US. Nonetheless, it continued to be the Western superpower, with an unmatched powerful position capable of influencing most of the outcomes within the capitalist bloc. Moreover, it was profiting from the détente with the Soviet Union that began in the 1960s, which reduced the fear of unwanted escalation between the superpowers. This meant that, in political and diplomatic terms, the environment was not restrictive for Washington to develop a strategic agenda that relied on diplomacy and reduced direct intervention.

US' changeable power

The US has been politically involved in the Middle East since the 1957 Eisenhower Doctrine, which aimed to check the spread of communism in the region through financial and military assistance. During the 1950s and 1960s, Washington was close to the conservative Arab countries as they shunned communism. The backbone of the US interests in the region was the Central Treaty Organization (Iran, Pakistan, Turkey, the US, and the United Kingdom), founded in 1955. However, the strength of this organisation was put into question in 1959 when Iraq left it.

In the Persian Gulf, the Pax Britannica had, so far, guaranteed Western interests. By the eve of the 1970s, the US military footprint in the region was small, mostly made of a token naval presence at Jufayr, Bahrain, which relied on British hospitality since 1947.[5] After the withdrawal, Washington built the Naval Communication Station at Diego Garcia Island, where it coordinated operations with partners. However, this station could not project military power directly into the region.

Regarding relations, Washington had working ties with most countries in the Persian Gulf, apart from Iraq – which was under the Soviet umbrella. It quickly recognised the Trucial States' independence and initiated diplomatic ties. As this chapter shows, relations with Iran and Saudi Arabia evolved swiftly: Iran became a crucial ally, while Saudi Arabia followed next. In fact, Washington developed a shared securitarian agenda for the region with the two monarchies, which stayed aligned within the Western bloc. Moreover, both countries became loyal buyers of US weaponry and kept being trusted oil providers despite the 1973 crisis.[6] Therefore, while the US had little capacity to project power in the region directly, there were few restrictions towards its influence; instead, most local actors indicated openness to it.

Iran's power: a regional power in the making

Iran has significant potential to be a regional power, considering its size, population, location, and natural resources. Geographically, it is the second-largest Middle Eastern country with a highly strategic position, accessing the Caspian Sea and the Arabian Sea via the Persian Gulf and sharing borders with seven states.[7] Moreover, its chains of mountains and central wastelands make it a difficult country to conquer if invaded. Most importantly, it has the fourth-largest oil reserves globally (behind Venezuela, Saudi Arabia, and Canada) and shares with Qatar the largest natural gas field in the world, the South Pars/North Dome, which holds approximately 1,800 trillion cubic feet of natural gas. Also, it has a demographic advantage compared to other Persian Gulf countries, with a much larger and well-distributed population.

During the 1970s, the Pahlavi dynasty ruled the country – a monarchical regime with sultanic undertones, secular and aligned to the Western bloc. It was inaugurated in 1925 by General Reza Shah, who was replaced by his son, Mohammad Reza Pahlavi, in 1941. In 1963, the Shah launched the White Revolution, a top-down development programme that brought about land reforms and a modest industrial build-up, transforming the demography and modernising the economy. That gave the Shah the tools to start converting Iran into a regional powerhouse. Still, contradictorily, it also started eroding the regime's legitimacy and capacity to respond to social demands, eventually leading to the 1979 Islamic Revolution.

Economically, Iran is a rentier state, highly dependent on oil exportation incomes. In 1971, the Tehran Agreement granted the OPEC members – of which Iran is a founding member – monopolistic control over oil production, increasing their economic power and ability to allocate rents domestically. Hence, in only one year, oil revenues in Iran increased from US$ 885 million in 1971 to US$ 1.6 billion in 1972. Like other oil countries, Iran profited substantially from the 1973 oil embargo, skyrocketing barrel prices. As a result, the GDP increased from US$ 9.7 billion in 1969 to US$ 90.39 billion in 1979.[8] Moreover, the number of small and medium-sized factories increased, and trade expanded regionally. There was also an urbanisation boom and rural evasion, with more than half the population living in metropolitan centres.[9]

However, the economic growth outdid Iran's infrastructure and available labour force, resulting in bottlenecks, congestion, and economic malpractices. Channelling the oil revenues into social benefits became a challenge aggravated by growing corruption, abuse of power, and out-of-control spending. Thus, in the second half of the 1970s, the economy became overheated, and consumer price inflation rose to almost 30 per cent of the GDP.[10] In short, the economic expansion did not meet expectations and created inflationary bubbles that increased living costs. Wealth was stuck within the elite, and social inequality rose fast. Almost 70 per cent of the adult population remained illiterate on the eve of the Revolution, the agricultural economy collapsed, and new urban underclasses emerged daily.[11]

Concerning military power, the oil boom liberated capital for investment. Throughout the 1970s, Tehran was given access to virtually any conventional US weapon system and technology it wanted. As a result, military expenses rose from US$ 566 million in 1969 to US$ 8.1 billion in 1978.[12] While military expenditure amounted to only 5.9 per cent of the GDP in 1969, it almost doubled, reaching 11.1 per cent in 1978.[13] The Shah focused on modernisation, especially the naval and air forces, buying F-14 Tomcats, modern destroyers, tankers, submarines, and fighter planes. With Washington's assistance, Iran bought a vast array of defence and offence missiles and invested in nuclear power infrastructure. Thus, it became one of the most powerful countries in the Middle East, and its army was the fifth-largest globally.[14] Also, it built a sophisticated air force, larger than those in France or West Germany, and a decisive naval force that could ensure dominance over all of the Persian Gulf's littoral.[15]

Nonetheless, the military displayed signs of malfunction, such as difficulties in absorbing the purchased technologies, struggles with operational ranges, shortages of training facilities, decentralised logistical systems, weak communication networks, and a lack of skilled personnel. A 1997 US report found that Iran depended heavily on US-American assistance despite having available material and technology.[16] Moreover, the Shah channelled all military communications to his office, penalised officers for the tiniest mistakes, and continuously rearranged the forces' structures according to his personal wishes, driving the army to politicisation and lethargy. Hence, like the political regime, the Shah's military was inflexible and unprepared to deal with the growing sociopolitical crisis that led to the Revolution.

Iran's changeable power

Iran is the odd one out in the Persian Gulf regarding ethnic and religious affiliation. While most countries in the region have Arab majorities and subscribe to the Sunni tradition, Iran's population is Persian and Shia. This distinct identity meant fewer natural allies. While other Arab nations did not have hostile relations with Iran, there was no natural convergence either. By the beginning of the 1970s, Iran had territorial disputes with Saudi Arabia, Iraq, and the Ras al-Kayma and Sharjah emirates. Likewise, local leaders rejected Pahlavi's territorial claims over Bahrain and other smaller islands near the UAE. Finally, the Shah had a hostile relationship with the Iraqi President Saddam Hussein, particularly concerning their territorial dispute over the Shatt al-Arab waterway.

Instead of trying to minimise this picture of being different, the Shah instead capitalised on cultural differentiation to project proximity to the West, showcasing Iran as the only modern enough country in the region. Indeed, Iran's diplomatic and military ties with the West improved immensely during the 1970s, participating in several international meetings and hosting high-level official visits in Tehran.[17] For example, it signed a defence agreement with the US in 1959, becoming, by the early 1970s, the largest recipient of US aid outside NATO.[18] An important status marker was when the Shah received many top international authorities in October 1971 to celebrate the 2,500th anniversary of the Persian Empire.

Therefore, Iran's international status improved with the British departure. Western countries seemed to agree that Tehran was the only country in the region powerful enough to take over, at least partially, London's role. Iran was committed to anti-communist operations in Pakistan, Iraqi Kurdistan, Jordan, and others throughout the decade. In 1971, while in Tehran, US President Richard Nixon famously told the Shah, 'protect me', insisting that Iran had a crucial position in the struggle against the USSR.[19]

But first, Iran needed to improve its ties with the other Persian Gulf countries to have the needed legitimacy to assume the regional protector role entirely. Therefore, the Shah ended a dispute with Saudi Arabia over shelf boundaries, abandoned its claim over Bahrain in March 1970, and eventually signed the 1975 Algiers Agreement to settle a border dispute with Iraq. Iran also signed agreements with Kuwait in 1970 and with Bahrain in 1971 and agreed to a joint patrolling operation with Oman in the Strait of Hormuz.[20] Thus, by 1975, it had diplomatic representation in almost all of the region except for South Yemen and Iraq.[21] While its regional role continued to provoke suspicion among the other Arab and Shia countries, Iran's capacity to project power in the Persian Gulf and guarantee local support for its actions improved immensely during the decade.

Saudi Arabia's power: a wary actor

Geography is crucial to grasp Saudi Arabia's capacities as it lays out its advantages and shortcomings. On one hand, it is the largest Middle Eastern country, extending for around 2.1 million km^2. It has abundant energy resources, amounting to the second-largest proven reserve of crude oil (266.2 billion bbl.) and the fourth-largest proven reserve of natural gas (8.6 trillion cubic metres). Its location is extremely strategic because it has maritime access to the Persian Gulf and the Red Sea while bordering seven countries by land.[22] On the other hand, it is a desert country, depleted of underground water resources or other permanent river bodies. The population is poorly distributed, concentrated in a few areas surrounding urban conurbations, and chunks of its territory are still uninhabited. By 1969, the Saudi population was 5.6 million, while, for comparison, Iran's was 27.7 million, and Iraq's was 9.58 million. Nevertheless, during the 1970s, it had one of the most significant growth rates in the Middle East, which meant that, in 1979, there were already 9.1 million inhabitants.[23]

The Al Saud dynasty founded Saudi Arabia in 1932 and has ruled it ever since.[24] The unification of the Arab Peninsula's tribes by Abdulaziz Al Saud was possible due to a powerful religious-military alliance with the Wahhabi clergy of Najd, which gave legitimacy to their political expansion. Additionally, the discovery of oil in the late 1930s provided the young monarchy with financial security, leading to the gradual strengthening of the political authority via redistributing oil rents to the population.[25] Thus, the Al Sauds guaranteed their political legitimacy by securing a rentier social contract and an allegiance towards Wahhabism. In this sense, the monarchy has held itself on top of two pillars: oil production and the Islamic practice's safeguard.

The substantial economic boost that oil countries received with the formation of OPEC and the first oil embargo represented a general increase in power to Riyadh in the 1970s. King Faisal bin Abdulaziz Al Saud (1964–1975) successfully centralised the rule and consolidated the state power by building strong institutions, elevating Saudi Arabia's foreign relations, and strengthening the domestic bureaucracy. The waves of incoming petrodollars after 1973 provided capital for investment, development plans, modernisation, and defence build-up. Quickly, the country became the world's top oil producer, with enough production capacity to have the final say on settling global prices within OPEC.

The oil boom liberated the government from fiscal restraint, and the GDP growth rate went from 6 per cent in 1969 to 11.9 per cent in 1979.[26] Moreover, in 1974, Riyadh assumed the majority ownership of ARAMCO.

Domestically, Faisal consolidated a welfare system in which the oil rents were distributed through services and public goods, and there was minimal taxation. At the same time, he used the oil rents to strengthen institutions and infrastructure that engendered social and political harmony among key groups of interest.[27]

Nevertheless, when the British announced their departure, Saudi Arabia did not have the military capabilities or personnel to guarantee regional order.[28] Traditionally, the monarchy was highly suspicious of military dissent and, for that matter, avoided administrative centralisation within the forces. Moreover, there was never a regulation of conscription, resulting in a weaker military culture within the society.[29] Likewise, the imperative of balancing tribal ascendancies within the country's chains of command as a way to keep elite loyalty to the king turned the forces into less professional, more clientelist institutions.[30] Thus, achieving military competency and sophistication was more problematic compared to countries like Iran and Iraq.

Therefore, by the time the regional balance of power was changing, Saudi Arabia had not yet effectively translated its new economic power into military clout due to human, technical, and physical constraints. Moreover, much of the defence expenditure was allocated to constructing military centres, training contracts, and other essential first-step capacitation. Hence, in case of a foreign threat, Riyadh would still need outside support to guarantee its protection. Thus, the departure of the British, even if that meant more autonomy, showcased Saudi Arabia's limitations.

Either way, the oil rents boom opened a window for military investment. There was progress in institutionalising and modernising the defence and security apparatus in the second half of the 1970s. As a result, military expenses skyrocketed, going from US$ 429.3 million in 1969 to US$ 17.6 billion in 1979.[31] Moreover, the Saudis gradually developed a strategic conception for their defence that included acquisitions for the three regular forces with the focus of making it costly for others to attack them. Particular emphasis was given to the Royal Saudi Air Force (RSAF). Incredibly, in 1978, Saudi Arabia had caught up and surmounted the Iranians in military-spending. By the end of the decade, Saudi Arabia's growing economic and military capacities could not be ignored in the Persian Gulf.

Saudi Arabia's changeable power

Unlike Iran, Saudi Arabia has ethnic and religious characteristics that naturally bring it closer to other Persian Gulf actors. Its population is mostly Arabic and Sunni, except for the Shia minority in the Eastern province. It is also home to two of the three Muslim sacred cities, Mecca and Medina, the latter where the *Hajj*, a massive Islamic pilgrimage, happens yearly. These elements give the Saudis an outstanding position within the global Muslim community (the *ummah*). During the 1950s and 1960s, Saudi Arabia was in the conservative camp against Nasserism and Arabism, as it worried about the damage the ideology could cause to the Islamic nations. As Nasserism's popularity decreased in the 1960s, Riyadh's conservative model began to gain a more positive reputation within the Arab world.

Since the beginning of the Cold War, Saudi Arabia has been aligned with the West, rejecting communism and socialism vehemently. Relations with the US have been positive since Roosevelt and Abdulaziz met on the *USS Quincy* in 1945, and, in June 1974, Nixon became the first US President to visit Riyadh. The Saudis also shared working relations with most European countries. By the mid-1970s, they had substantial reserves in Western banking institutions and representatives in many economic chamber councils.[32]

Moreover, during the 1970s, Saudi Arabia shared good relations with virtually all Middle Eastern countries except for South Yemen and Iraq. It endorsed partnerships and alliances across the Middle East with other conservative countries, providing economic assistance to Islamic organisations and supporting charities worldwide. Likewise, it sponsored anti-communist movements in Angola, Afghanistan, and Ethiopia. It is estimated that Riyadh spent an average of US$ 5 billion on foreign aid only in 1978.[33]

Finally, Riyadh promoted itself as a successful model of monarchy to the newly independent countries in the Persian Gulf, which eventually emulated similar regimes. To promote regional stability, Saudi Arabia assisted these countries, guaranteeing a privileged friendship among them. Moreover, it settled an ongoing border dispute about the Buraimi oasis with the UAE in 1974 and signed defence agreements for military cooperation and non-aggression pacts with all the other monarchies. This way, Saudi Arabia had a very convenient position within the Persian Gulf regarding its diplomatic and political influence. It had working ties with Iran, and after the 1975 Algiers Agreement, it gradually improved relations with Iraq. Thus, by the end of the 1970s, Saudi Arabia shared a strong regional influence endorsed by religion, monarchical interests, and Western alignment.

The Persian Gulf's power balance in the 1970s

The British departure was a systemic change because it removed the extra-regional power capable of maintaining the Persian Gulf under the Western political clout during the Cold War. Simultaneously, it enabled the independence of new countries. In this context, some conservative actors feared that revolutionary and communist-leaning ideologies in South Yemen or Iraq could inspire the new countries. Among those interested in maintaining the status quo as it was were Iran, Saudi Arabia, and the US.

During the 1970s, the regional system had no evident regional power. However, Iran and Iraq were much stronger in military terms than Saudi Arabia and shared the ambition of becoming a regional hegemon, projecting their influence to seek leadership. This dynamic mirrored the Cold War: whereas Hussein saw himself as a new Nasser and ruled under slogans of pan-Arabism and socialism, the Shah promoted himself as a solid Western ally in the Middle East. Iraq was the leading partner of the Soviets in the Middle East, while Iran was the stronghold of the US interests, receiving massive amounts of weaponry and training every year. Nevertheless, a country needs recognition and subscription from others to become a hegemon. Throughout the period, Iran and Iraq lacked the needed cultural, ideological, or political elements to be considered as such.

In its turn, Saudi Arabia is a Sunni, dynastic monarchy with huge cultural capital. It zealously assisted the smaller Gulf monarchies in their independence process, ensuring they were under its political clout. It also invested in Islamic solidarity, aiding, financing, and supporting Muslim institutions worldwide. Equally important was Riyadh's economic empowerment after the 1973 oil crisis. The decade consolidated Saudi Arabia as a financial force in the Middle East and strengthened its regime via rent redistribution. Nonetheless, despite huge investments, it could not strengthen its military during the period. For this reason, it is impossible to equate Riyadh with Tehran or Baghdad in terms of military power.

While the 1970s represented empowerment for Saudi Arabia and Iran, the US maintained virtually no direct military projection within the Persian Gulf. Nevertheless, it enhanced relations with Saudi Arabia and Iran throughout the decade, established diplomatic ties with the new monarchies and boosted military transactions to fortify its partners' defence. However, it did not assume the British role, nor consolidate a physical presence in the region. With Iran's visibly growing military superiority over Iraq, the threat of the Soviets filling the UK's power vacuum was reduced.

When looking only at the balance of power, we cannot explain the US' decision to elaborate a specific strategy for the Persian Gulf that included Saudi Arabia and not only Iran. Neither can we explain Saudi Arabia's alignment with Iran, considering it became clear that it was Tehran, not Baghdad, which was the most powerful country in the region with the hegemonic potential. Therefore, it becomes crucial to evaluate the factors influencing their decision-making processes that led to the Twin Pillar Diplomacy – the first strategic triangle. Let us, therefore, open the black box of the state and explore the three intervening variables: status satisfaction, state identity, and leadership preferences.

US status satisfaction: looking for a new surrogate

During the Cold War, the US promoted itself as the Western bloc's leader, seeing itself as the capitalist frontrunner against the Soviet project. Thus, it expected the Western hemisphere to emulate its socioeconomic model (based on liberalism, capitalism, democracy, and individualism), guaranteeing its political predominance and restricting the expansion of Soviet influence.[34] Since 1945, its position as a superpower has been unmatched, and no other actor has attempted to compete with it. The West embraced Washington's predominant position, expecting, in return, protection. In President Nixon's words: 'We are neither boastful of our power, nor apologetic about it. We recognise that it exists, and that, as well as conferring certain advantages, it also implies upon us certain obligations.'[35]

These responsibilities included providing guarantees that the Persian Gulf's oil would keep flowing to the capitalist economies, something that had been done so far by London. Thus, the UK's decision to exit the region represented a risk to the US' interests, generating anxiety. If not the British, who would guarantee the Western interests in the region? Therefore, it was necessary to find a new strategy. As one memorandum from the Secretary of the Department of State disclosed, Washington needed to show an 'interest in keeping the strategic territory out of Soviet hands and in using it for our own strategic purposes'.[36]

One option would be the US assuming the British role. However, that would demand a rapid and massive deployment to the region, as it had little military presence there. Moreover, that would go against the tendency of reducing military investment that was going on in the 1970s and probably could be met with some resistance domestically, as protests against military overstretch proliferated in the US. A letter from the Under Secretary of State for Political Affairs clearly stated: 'we have no intention of replacing the British in the Persian Gulf'.[37]

A second option was replacing London with another surrogate actor. That depended on finding an actor capable of doing so. Most regional actors, including Iran and Saudi Arabia, were already aligned with the West and showed interest in maintaining the status quo. Thus, while there was a need to replace the United Kingdom, the scenario was not perceived as too critical. An interdepartmental paper evaluated that the

US' situation in 1969 was 'neither as bad as the Cassandras claim nor as unshakeable as their detractors insist. Our position [in the Persian Gulf] is still significant, but it is probably vulnerable to the erosion of time'.[38] Therefore, they assessed that the regional environment on the eve of the 1970s needed revision but was not highly restrictive.

The status satisfaction variable indicates how much the US perceived its aspired status to be approved by its status community. It also shows how much the regional environment provoked anxiety in the actors. Considering that two of the three largest countries in the Persian Gulf expected Washington to keep the order as it was, the US perceived the environment as permissive enough to transfer the British role to local actors instead of assuming the role itself. While there was initial anxiety towards the possibility of Soviet interference, that lessened steadily throughout the period. For that, it was significant that the new regional monarchies emulated Saudi Arabia and pushed themselves away from Iraqi or Soviet influence.

In short, except for Iraq, all regional countries approved the US ambition of maintaining the Persian Gulf under the Western zone of influence and anticipated more security ties with Washington. Thus, the US was satisfied with its ascribed status in the Gulf. In the words of US President Jimmy Carter's national security advisor, Zbigniew Brzezinski, 'our present situation in the area is basically favourable, and realistically we would have no grounds to be dissatisfied if our position four years from now was essentially the same'.[39]

Iran's status satisfaction: authorised to lead

The Pahlavi regime was fundamentally ambitious, headed by leaders who aimed to transform the country into one of the most dominant forces in the Middle East. Thus, Iran perceived the UK departure as an opportunity to improve its position within the regional order and assume leadership. It is crucial to note that the Pahlavi dynasty rejected the communist model as unfavourable to its development plans.[40] Besides, a history of conflict and tensions between Iranians and the Russians pushed Iran towards the West. Thus, realising that it had the endorsement from the US, Iran saw the moment as a window of opportunity to promote itself as a new possible superintendent in the Middle East, which would guarantee the West-oriented order.[41]

As the identity variable further discusses, Iran's ancient history as a cultural cradle with considerable value for humankind determined much of this ambition for greatness. Throughout the Pahlavi dynasty, Iran seemed 'engaged in an endless and restless search for glory and status'.[42] This status-seeking be-haviour had two core manifestations. First, Iran linked itself to the West via a narrative of similar modernisation and liberal goals. It also presented itself as a token of anti-communism in the Middle East. In the Shah's words:

> In 20 or 25 years, I want it [Iran] to be ahead of the greatest nations in the world, we will have 60 million people in 25 years. With that number of people, we can be the most advanced country and do better than any other country.[43]
> If all our efforts continue as at present, and if no foreseeable situation outside our control arises, we shall construct during the next 12 years a solid indus-trial, agricultural and technological substructure for the country's develop-ment and will reach the present level of progress of Western Europe.[44]

Second, the Shah promoted a qualitative differentiation between Iran and the rest of the Arab world. The other Persian Gulf countries were seen as too vulnerable and incapable of guaranteeing regional order. He would often say that Iran's neighbours were susceptible to Soviet influence, and, for that matter, he was the only one capable of guaranteeing regional order – if he received more and more Western military support.[45] Hence, he connected this status ambition with the need to obtain more military capacities. Only then could Iran rise to the occasion, replace the British, and act as a stability guarantor.

Considering it did not perceive that its status community was rejecting its ambition, Iran's status-seeking behaviour should be considered promo-tional rather than revisionist. Throughout the 1970s, Tehran assumed that it received the needed international support to become a regional power. The Shah was 'widely regarded [in the West] as a force of stability, a cham-pion of progressive reform, and the bold leader'.[46] As a result, Iran felt valued as a trusted US partner and, during official meetings and bilateral communications, the US assured the Shah that his opinions about the region were highly appreciated.[47]

Hence, by taking the leading position as the US' partner, Iran seemed to be heading towards regional leadership with few barriers to achieving its aspired status. This perception became even more accentuated with the gradual improvement of relations with the other local actors and the cessation of conflict with Iraq. Therefore, the decade represented a moment of environmental openness for the country's ambitions. Rather than anxiety, the environment worked as an incentive to the Shah's grandeur ambitions.

Saudi Arabia's status satisfaction: cautiously adapting

The first thing we need to assess concerning Saudi Arabia's status satis-faction is that it did not have the ambition to be a regional power or a hegemon back then. It was acutely aware of its demographic and military vulnerabilities and that, if invaded, it lacked the capacity to resist or fight back. Simultaneously, it relied on a stable regional order so that no conflict threatened the steady income of oil rents, and no other local actor attempted to assume a hegemonic position. Hence, the British departure boosted Saudi Arabia's anxiety towards the regional order: who could ensure that Iran and Iraq would not assume a hegemonic position or that the Soviet Union would not interfere in local politics?

Saudi Arabia perceived the proliferation of secular ideological projects in the Middle East as detrimental to Muslim unity. In short, they were against all the 'isms' that could threaten Islamic religious predominance as the principal anchor in the region: communism, radical nationalism, Zionism, and Arabism.[48] It has hence promoted its conservative Islamism as an alternative to the pan-Arabism movement. As mentioned, some Western leaders have welcomed the Saudi type of Islamism as an ideological force against communism, frequently referring to the religious bond that united Christian and Muslim nations.[49] Some US officials called the Saudi King the 'Islamic pope' – giving the Saudis a sense that the West agreed with their overall dread of letting the region fall under the hands of communism.

Right after the UK announced its departure, Riyadh worried that the recently independent countries could adopt the Soviet model or even instigate expansionist desires in Iran or Iraq. Saudi Arabia expected the US to assume the British role as regional protector – it was, after all, the most powerful country in the West and already shared good ties with most of the actors in the Persian Gulf. In short, it anticipated that the US would 'play a more positive and helpful role' and 'do more to support conservative and pro-Western forces' after 1969.[50]

The new countries' decision to follow the monarchical model reduced Saudi Arabia's anxiety as they did not fall prey to the Soviet Union, Iran, or Iraq. Moreover, this anxiety significantly decreased as the US authorised more weaponry sales to Saudi Arabia. During the 1970s, while the Saudis kept their suspicions towards the Shah's expansionist ambitions, they perceived the US' regional policy as a gesture that Washington would not allow Iran to threaten the weaker monarchies. Finally, the 1973 oil boom worked in the kingdom's interests by improving its importance to the Western economies. It also made more money available for Riyadh to boost its donations to Islamic institutions all over the world and increase its regional approval.

In conclusion, Saudi Arabia wanted to be seen as a guardian of the Islamic faith and a partner of the West. It did not compete for regional supremacy or antagonise the status quo. It was satisfied as long as the US checked the emergence of any regional hegemon and the expansion of communism, and other non-Islamic ideologies. Thus, after an initial moment of anxiety towards the status quo, the country cautiously adapted to the new scenario. Indeed, Saudi Arabia's status ambition and ascription matched because it perceived that Iran and the US were willing to cooperate to preserve the order.

US state identity: liberal exceptionalism and limited liability

The US foundational myth is that the first settlers had a predestined mission in the 'city upon the hill', where they would inaugurate the 'New World' in opposition to the old European one.[51] The first Calvinist settlers believed their physical isolation from Europe was a virtue that enabled them to emphasise individual freedom and Puritan principles. Eventually, this sense of moral superiority, together with enlightenment ideas and Lockean liberal assumptions about freedom, individuality, and property, inspired the Founding Fathers to fight for their independence from the British.[52] The US Constitution and the Bill of Rights reflect this philosophy, casting the US political experiment as qualitatively superior to others.

However, some Founding Fathers were sceptical about their country's ability to trigger political change abroad and feared that external actors could corrupt their model.[53] In distrusting imperialistic practices, figures like Alexander Hamilton and George Washington preferred a limited government with diminished foreign ties or commitments abroad, seeing this distancing as a strategic advantage. Colin Dueck calls limited liability the preference for political seclusion: an insular mentality of avoiding engagement in international disputes.[54] Under this principle, the US political experiment should be only projected as a model, an example for others to emulate. In other words, the political experiment's success should influence others by example.

That was first challenged in the 1890s as industrialisation, modernisation, and overall empowerment instigated a progressive reformist movement that believed the US should be an agent of change and actively expand its liberal model into the world.[55] The eagerness to protect the freedom, virtue, and morality of the 'civil man' led to the development of a Manichean tendency in which the country saw itself as the protector of all the good and righteous, whereas any political challenger could be a corrupted and nefarious enemy.[56]

Economic liberalism became an intrinsic part of the US model, and a part of its political elite began to advocate that exporting liberalism and opening overseas markets everywhere was crucial not only for US progress but also beneficial for the entire world.[57] Willian Williams defines this as 'open-door' leadership, in which the continuance of the US creed became intertwined with the expansion of the economic liberal model.[58] That indicates a preference for policies that maintained stability, prevented hostile actors' empowerment, protected the free market, and supported friendly governments. Conversely, enemies are detected when these values are rejected, denied access, or even opposed.

Therefore, the US has a political ethos based on liberal exceptionalism and limited liability, which creates for the state the cognitive function to promote liberal values as a model to be emulated or a project to be imposed globally. Moreover, this identity has an ideational project in that it seeks to promote normative roles that shape others' behaviour. Throughout history, US policymakers have tackled this missionary function by interpreting it as an example or a vindication – in other words, by broadcasting or forcing it.

Dueck identifies four cognitive filters that respond to this duality between limited liability and liberal exceptionalism. First, a leader can use an *internationalist* lens, where the commitment to exporting liberalism is high while the sense of limited liability is low. That means they favour a foreign policy that pushes for opening markets and expanding US international influence. Second, a *nationalist* lens, with weak expansionist commitment and strong limited liability. This lens is dubious about international intervention, reluctant towards globalisation, and sceptical of overseas undertakings. Thirdly, the *progressive* lens is committed to liberal exceptionalism and limited liability, promoting a liberal international order through peaceful means and diplomacy rather than force or direct interference. Finally, the *realist* lens is unconvinced by both exceptionalism and limited liability, being cynical about democracy promotion abroad while recognising that some level of internationalisation can help pursue strategic interests.[59]

This book shows that the US leaders found ways to mix and match these four cognitive lenses to define their policies and strategies. During the 1970s, US Presidents Nixon and Gerald Ford were straightforward realists, sceptical about exporting US values worldwide, and prioritising policies that distanced the country from international issues unrelated to core national interests. Nevertheless, President Carter was linked to progressivism and internationalism, as he campaigned under a narrative of reconciliation with the Soviet Union and protection of human rights worldwide. However, concerning the Persian Gulf, Carter showed pragmatism, giving continuity to Nixon's realist policies.

Iran's state identity: Pahlavi's exceptionalism

Many reigns, successions, coups, and foreign interventions have permeated Iranian collective memory. The first dynasty ruling the territory can be traced back to the sixth century BC during the Persian Empire. The Pahlavis (1925–1979) installed themselves after a military coup in 1925 that overthrew the young Qajar King Ahmad Shan and put in power the general of the Persian Cossack Brigade. Their regime was built under ideals of military order and modernisation while downgrading the Qajar regime's Islamist character as retrograde. Instead, the Pahlavi regime employed a nostalgic discourse of romanticising the Persian Empire and Cyrus the Great, from around 550 BC, one of the largest empires in history and a cradle for culture, religion, art, technology, and science.[60] Allegedly, Cyrus was the first to use the term 'Iran' to describe the Empire's territory; in 1935, Reza Pahlavi altered the country's name from Persia to Iran as a tribute to these times.

The cultural heritage and a deep nostalgia for a period of grandeur gave his regime a sense of qualitative differentiation from the others in the Middle East. The Pahlavi regime deemed Iran exceptional due to its remarkable history, language, ethnicity, and territorial continuity. Under this narrative, Iranians belonged to a unique ethnolinguistic group, the 'Great Civilization' (*tamadon-e bozorg*), with more than 2,500 years of glory that distinguished them from other Arab neighbours that encountered European colonialism. Moreover, the Pahlavi regime romanticised belonging to the Aryan nation (*mellat-e Aryan*) as well as shared roots between Persian and some European languages to stress supposed connections between them. They aimed to detach themselves from other Semitic or Arabic cultures and retain a separate identity that did not blend well across the region and was closer to the West.[61] This exceptionality became known as 'Iranianess' and indicated how the state perceived itself under the Pahlavi regime.

Beyond Iranianess, a deep desire for independence and self-reliance also codified the state identity. Foreign interference was central to the dynasty's political ethos, particularly during the Second World War. While not colonised per se, Iranians faced many powerful intrusions. In this sense, foreign meddling created a yearning for self-reliance and autonomy among the Iranian political elite. This way, despite wanting to be linked with Western modernisation and industrialisation markers, Iran was regularly suspicious of external actors.[62] It yearned to maintain an image of an autonomous political agent. As a result, a sense of independentism was ingrained in this identity, pushing for military empowerment as a way to defend the country. In short, this identity selected policies that would benefit Iran's image as a natural regional leader with a unique history and autonomy, as well as political-military superiority and cultural pre-eminence.

Saudi Arabia's state identity: encirclement syndrome and Islam

The state of Saudi Arabia was not built under the flag of a single nation-alism. Instead, Saudi King Abdulaziz's unification success is fundamentally linked to the Wahhabist clerics from the Najd province, which provided tools to strengthen his armies, overpower other tribes, and exert domination. In other words, the state-building process relied on this religious–political alliance, which legitimised the Al Saud dynasty's rule over an amalgam of different Arab tribes. What made a person Saudi Arabian was territorial belonging, tribal ancestry, and Wahhabi affiliation.

First, let us talk about territory. Located in the Peninsula's heartland and surrounded by vast sand seas that are difficult to access, Najd was probably one of the 'last regions in the old world to open up to the rest of the globe'.[63] It was composed of many small emirates that were mostly left alone to govern themselves and were often threatened by more vigorous rulers from al-Hijaz or al-Hasa. As a result, the region was perceived as a constant source of threats, and order was kept only by negotiating the containment of neighbours' expansionist ambitions and repeated group conflicts. Thus, the Saudi state-building developed with an 'encirclement syndrome', meaning an awareness of being surrounded by enemies, threats, and menaces.[64]

Second, it was in Najd that Muhammad ibn 'Abd al-Wahhab (1703–1792) initiated his new Islamic doctrine, Wahhabism. He was displeased with the evolution of the Islamic societies' relationship with the political elites in the eighteenth century. Thus, he stressed the necessity to return to early beliefs and practices, calling for the rejection of any procedure not based on the Qur'an or the Sunnah.[65] Most importantly, Wahhabism called for the political authorities to protect and promote religious ideas through *jihad.* The Al Saud family tapped on this idea to justify its rule over other groups: to fulfil the duty to protect, promote, and spread the Islamic faith. Via the broad idea of *jihad* – the need to make a personal effort or struggle to be closer to God – Wahhabis drew increasingly into allegiance to the Al Saud, resulting in the eventual incorporation of Hijaz, Hasa, and 'Asir to Najd. Therefore, Wahhabism provided Abdulaziz with a rationale for polit-ical domination, and his rule became intrinsically linked to religion. Islam, not nationalist sentiments, became the primary shared cognitive marker.[66]

Quickly after 1932, the values of Najd spread throughout the country, and Riyadh's *ulama* held influence in much of the citizens' daily lives. They pushed for a return to Islam's puritan version and were critical of practising excessive innovations and foreign ideologies.[67] Moreover, Wahhabism holds that divisions within Islam (like Shiism, syncretism, or polytheism) tend to harm Islam's unitarian vision. Thus, for not approving these divisions, the Saudi identity has significant tendencies towards sectarianism in favour of

Sunnism. Nevertheless, during the 1970s, the monarchy shunned this tendency, relying on pan-Islamism.[68]

Likewise, Saudi Arabia's identity fosters a leadership position among the Muslim community due to its unique Islamic attributes. It sees for itself the mission of protecting Islam, internally and worldwide, being committed to the concerns and beliefs of the *ummah* and safeguarding it from other threatening ideologies. It sees a divine prerogative to preserve the Islamic heritage and cherish the responsibilities of being where millions of people direct their daily prayers.

In conclusion, encirclement syndrome and Islamic exceptionalism require a foreign policy which is aware of the different types of threats that can harm the dynastic rule's survival. For them, regional order is the space for protecting and projecting Islam. Thus, interventionist actors, revisionist ideologies, or secularist political ideas are, at the same time, political adversaries and ontological threats to the regime.

US leadership preferences: the continuity of Nixon, Ford, and Clinton

Richard Nixon and his chief foreign policy advisor, Henry Kissinger, were notorious realists who assumed that strategic interests rather than ideologies should define the international agenda. They aimed to remove the country from conflicts in the 'Third World' like Vietnam and tone down the Cold War's ideological confrontation. They saw excessive involvement in second-tier disputes as an 'unwanted distraction' that overstretched the US' influence and could damage its international position with few gains in return.[69] In Nixon's words, 'as much as we like our own political system, American style democracy is not necessarily the best form of government for people in Asia, Africa, and Latin America with entirely different backgrounds'.[70] Thus, the principles of limited liability were more influential for this administration than the ideas of exporting liberalism.

The Nixon Doctrine aimed to create spaces for 'devolutions of power', in the sense of 'self-reliant regional and sub-regional groupings' that could reduce the 'burden of maintaining a modicum of order and stability in the world'.[71] This meant that Washington would encourage the emergence of regional surrogates to protect Western interests, reducing international commitment while not lessening global influence. In Kissinger's words, 'internal subversion has to be the primary responsibility of the threatened country. The US stands ready to supply material assistance, advice, and technical assistance where that is requested and where our interests so dictate'.[72]

Therefore, this administration had little interest in substituting the British role in the Persian Gulf. They understood it was necessary to develop a strategy for the region, but that did not demand massive US commitment as the environment was not alarmingly vulnerable. In addition, their conclusion was that fostering better relations between Iran and Saudi Arabia and promoting increased cooperation between them should be the ultimate objective. A document from the National Security Council stated that the Persian Gulf was an 'important area in a transitional state. We look to enlightened leadership from Shah, Faisal, and other leaders', and that the 'US can only play a complementary role. Primary reliance will have to be on indigenous leadership'.[73]

> The spread of radicalism in the Gulf would alter the balance within the Arab world and aggravate the Arab–Israeli conflict. Soviet political penetration would affect the East–West geopolitical balance. Our friendly relations with Iran and Saudi Arabia are the mainstay of our influence in the area. The US has communications and intelligence facilities in Iran and overflight and landing privileges in Iran and Saudi Arabia which provide an air corridor to South and Southeast Asia.[74]

Upon reviewing documents from that time, it becomes evident that the administration firmly believed that Iran played a critical role in maintaining regional stability. For example, they concluded that 'unless we remain Iran's principal military supplier, our interests in Iran, including our ability to maintain our own strategic interests there and to influence the Shah in the direction of constructive foreign and domestic policies, will be seriously weakened'.[75] Here it is interesting to stress the importance of Nixon's notorious friendship with the Shah. In his memoirs, the President recalled 'an inner strength in him [the Shah], and I felt that in the years to come, he would become a strong leader'.[76]

Nevertheless, the administration knew that ignoring the general regional suspicion of Iran could have consequences. In a ministerial meeting, it was stressed that 'Arabs could say that the whole thing was an Anglo-Iranian plot to substitute Iranian influence for British influence on the Arabian side of the Gulf'.[77] They had a deep understanding of the complex dynamics of Persian Gulf politics and aimed to develop a policy that reflected this awareness.

> Singly or in tandem, Iran and Saudi Arabia have been touted as candidates to fill the vacuum left by the British. If military power were the sole prerequisite of leadership, Iran could provide a Pax Persica, but the Shah is embroiled in disputes with Kuwait and Iraq at the head of the Gulf and Abu Dhabi down the coast. Cultural and historical differences are added impediments to the exercise of leadership by Iran. Saudi Arabia seems precluded from the role of protector for many of the same reasons, although it does have a good deal of influence with the ruling families in Bahrain and Qatar.[78]

The decision, therefore, was towards a regional policy that included both Saudi Arabia and Iran. For the Nixon administration, it was strategically unwise to strain relations with Saudi Arabia and overlook its role as a leading oil producer and a firm voice against communism. Consequently, they should continue to encourage 'Shah to play a constructive leadership role in regional affairs' and, at the same time, 'seek ways to encourage Saudi Arabia to play [a] more active regional role so Iran's increasing predominance does not overwhelm and frighten other littoral states'.[79]

In short, Nixon wanted to keep the Persian Gulf safe from Soviet influence and maintain close ties with an increasingly powerful Iran while treasuring the Saudi Arabian regional role and stimulating greater cooperation between the two regional actors. This goal did not change when Gerald Ford assumed the presidency after Nixon's resignation in 1974. Neither did it change with Jimmy Carter's election in 1976. While Carter can be defined as a progressive, balancing against the Soviets and containing their influence in strategic regions continued to be a main priority.[80] Zbigniew Brzezinski, Carter's key foreign policy advisor, instructed against pressuring Middle Eastern countries for democratic reforms, as that could be detrimental to the strategic interests of the US. Giving continuation to the Nixon Doctrine, Carter said that he did 'not believe there are any other nations with whom we have had a better friendship and a deeper sense of cooperation than we have found in Saudi Arabia'.[81] He also famously called Iran an 'island of stability in one of the more troubled areas in the world' just two years before the Revolution.[82]

In conclusion, the three presidents agreed on a political strategy that guaranteed the stability of the Persian Gulf without direct involvement. This meant that they were not interested in damaging good ties with Iran by challenging the Shah's growing authoritarianism. While hosting Pahlavi during a visit, Carter said that the US 'national interest [is] to support the Shah so he would continue to play a constructive role in regional affairs', ignoring the Iranians protesting against the regime in front of the White House.[83] However, the 1979 Islamic Revolution abruptly changed Carter's perception of security in the Persian Gulf, driving him to develop a more intrusive strategy by the 1980s.

Iranian leadership preferences: the ambitious Shah

As already mentioned, Shah Pahlavi, with US and UK assistance, stirred a state coup that overthrew the nationalist Prime Minister Mossadegh in 1953. Afterward, he quickly centralised the power in his hands, transforming the regime into something so personalistic that it is hard to distinguish when the status and identity variables end and the leadership variable begins. The Shah saw himself as the state, encouraging sycophancy and servility from the elite and the bureaucracy. While handpicking military leaders and deciding on every matter, he would say: 'I am the army'.[84] According to many historians, his management skills were tricky as he distrusted people around him and refused to delegate duties to subordinates.

Hence, this variable does not provide much filtering here. If status satisfaction revealed promotional behaviour, the Shah sought aggrandisement of his image. Whereas state identity disclosed Iranianess and nostalgia for the Persian Empire, the Shah subscribed to the idea of Iranian superiority and talked fondly about ancient times. In other words, he blended personal goals with national objectives to pursue prestige and hegemonic leadership.

Mohammad Reza Pahlavi became Shah at the age of twenty-two after his father was forced out of power. He was a Western-educated, eloquent man who wanted to be seen as an heir to the Persian Empire's glorious times. Being a strong nationalist, the Shah vehemently believed Iran was entitled to leadership due to its size, military power, and long-lasting imperial history. In an interview, he said he was 'convinced that a return to the Aryan path alone can save humanity from a world escalating towards war, decadence and doom'.[85] But, most importantly, he saw himself as the one who could put Iran on the path of greatness it deserved.[86]

The Shah was determined to modernise and industrialise Iran into the Western moulds. In his view, that would enable the country to belong to a select group of so-called great powers. He said he would transform Iran into 'one of the leading industrial countries which would achieve an enlightened social order', and he often praised the advantages of capitalism and liberalism.[87] When asked about how he saw Iran in the next decade, he answered: 'in the next twenty-five years – that is, within a single generation – we shall rank among the five biggest powers'.[88]

For all these reasons, he interpreted the British withdrawal as an opportunity to improve Iran's leverage in relation to the Western countries and to fulfil his ambitions. It created the perfect context to demand more assistance on modernisation so that Iran could guarantee the order. He aimed to convince that a West-oriented order in the Persian Gulf depended on expanding the Iranian military. For example, the Shah told some US officials that the Persian Gulf countries were 'simply not ready for the added responsibility that would befall them' if there was no new protector of the order.[89]

> the Shah is convinced that Iran must play the dominant role in the Persian Gulf and he is determined that radical Arab or Soviet influence should be prevented, or at least be kept to an innocuous level. He feels that neither Saudi Arabia nor the various principalities can contribute significantly to the control of these

subversive forces and that therefore, the entire burden of ensuring the region's security will fall on Iran as the strongest and most stable riparian power. To meet this burden, Iran, in the Shah's opinion, will require a modern and well-equipped military establishment with most of the equipment to be purchased either from the US or elsewhere.[90]

As an army man himself, the Shah wanted to be seen as the epitome of a militarised, robust, bold, and masculine leadership.[91] He was well aware that the Nixon Doctrine aimed to reduce direct commitments and used it to his advantage, often asking Nixon for arms procurements and assistance in training and capacitation. In a message from Tehran to the US Department of State, it reads:

> rather than trying to treat all countries generally alike, the US and Iran should both try to develop an especially close and cooperative arrangement with countries that shared their basic political and international philosophy, and were in a position to work towards stabilising areas that today were in a precarious position.[92]

Moreover, the Shah quickly understood that more positive relations with Saudi Arabia would improve its prestige among the other Gulf countries and simultaneously satisfy the US leaders. Thus, he often expressed interest in collaborating with local actors, particularly Riyadh. For example, in 1969, he said he was willing to 'enter into an informal or a formal agreement or alliance' with the Saudis as the relationship was 'of great importance' to the region.[93] Additionally, the Shah frequently praised Saudi Arabia's spiritual guidance in the region.[94]

Nevertheless, the Shah did not want his Western preference to be read as submission. In some situations, he tested the alliance with Washington by demanding faster weapon negotiations or taking harder stands towards US oil companies.[95] Indeed, he wanted to be seen as a valuable ally, not as a Western pawn. In his words:

> if in the past we walked along the same path as the west, it was not because we were their camp followers. No, of course not. We believed in the philosophy of human freedom and liberal values, as the west does, and so we worked in cooperation with them. Now let me return to this canard of Iran being 'a western enclave' in the Middle East. The answer is a categorical NO! I would say NEVER![96]

However, by the second half of the 1970s, most of the Shah's opponents accused him of being, indeed, a pawn. Western-style modernisation heightened inequality, destabilised the economy, and increased poverty. Simultaneously, monopolisation of power, corruption, and maladministration reached absurd levels. In addition, oppression and persecution via the SAVAK secret police increased the restlessness among the population.[97]

Meanwhile, the Shah relished his new status as 'one of the world's most important statesmen', the 'Imperator of Oil' – which was bestowed upon him by *Time* magazine.[98] Hence, he grew detached from his population's needs while leaving the administration and distribution of revenues suboptimal. Here were the foundations for the Iranian Revolution.

Saudi Arabian leadership preferences: Faisal, the architect

King Faisal (1964–1975) was one of the most outstanding Saudi monarchs, known for consolidating the country's political institutions and its overall foreign policy orientation. At the age of thirteen, Faisal started his political career as viceroy of Hijaz in 1926. Later, in 1930, he became the country's first Foreign Affairs Minister. By the time he became King, he was the ultimate regime insider, with an extensive tribal, regional, and international network. Joseph Kechichian describes him as a 'cohesive, cogent, and consistent' leader.[99] He capitalised on the unprecedented income of oil revenues to transform the royal family into a corporate ruling group with internal unity by increasing the size of the state and improving the mechanisms of rent distribution. This way, he has been considered the 'architect of modern Saudi Arabia', shaping the governmental structure while securing loyalty from key constituencies.[100]

The King was known to be very pious and a staunch anti-communist, deeply concerned with the ideology's dissemination in the Middle East and its effects on Islamic unity.[101] This way, he believed Saudi Arabia needed to promote Islamic solidarity worldwide, offering economic assistance to other Muslim countries so that they would not turn to the Soviet Union or other communist countries. As a result, Faisal co-founded the Muslim World League in 1962 and the Islamic Development Bank in 1975. He supported the pan-Islamist idea that, against secular or non-Islamic ideologies, Muslim people from all sects should cooperate to strengthen their unity as a community. For example, during a visit to Tehran, he talked about the 'bond that united all Muslims' and called for cooperation to defeat radicalism since 'brotherhood and love are derived from the spiritual teachings of Islam' and 'Islam will remain a clear and straight path that needs no alteration or amendment'.[102] For him, 'those who disavow Islam and distort its call under the guise of nationalism are actually the most bitter enemies of Arabs, whose glories are entwined with the glories of Islam'.[103]

It is possible to frame King Faisal as a pragmatic, realist leader who was aware that the Persian Gulf could become susceptible to Soviet influence without Western protection. Having his country's vulnerabilities in the back of his mind, his disposition was towards appeasing rather than resisting a powerful opponent, waiting for events to unfold before reacting immediately and avoiding irreparable confrontation.[104] He was also worried about Iran's hawkish attitude towards regional hegemony and Iraq's closeness to the Soviets. Nevertheless, when it became clear that Washington would prioritise Iran to fill the power vacuum, Faisal concluded that Iraq was the most significant regional threat and sought to improve ties with the new US surrogate. As a result, he reached an understanding with the Shah 'based on a tacit division of spheres of influence that left the Gulf emirates in the Saudi sphere but allowed Iran to seize the Abu Musa and Tunb islands'.[105]

In short, Faisal understood he could not translate Saudi Arabia's political and financial capacities into military clout in time to compete with Iran or Iraq for regional leadership. Therefore, by engaging with the stronger status quo actor in combination with the US, the King hoped to 'essentially count on Iran to check Iraq, and on the United States to check Iran'.[106] In other words, his assessment established a strategy in which the Saudi Arabian regional behaviour tilted in the direction of the less ideologically threatening actor.

He also sought to improve relations with the US throughout the 1970s. Previously, his staunch criticism towards Israel had created certain tension within Washington's political elite. In his first years of rule, Faisal often pushed Washington to find a more balanced approach to deal with the Arab–Israeli conflict.[107] However, as the 1970s advanced, he became more pragmatic and gradually began to separate the US–Saudi ties from his critiques of Israel.[108] After all, the US were Saudi Arabia's primary weapon and security provider, and the King was concerned with modernising his army for better domestic security.

A revengeful cousin assassinated Faisal in 1975, and his brother Khalid bin Abdulaziz Al Saud assumed the throne. In both foreign and domestic politics, Khalid kept Faisal's agenda until 1979, a year that saw the increase in Saudi Arabia's insecurity to unforeseen levels. While the new King had political experience and prestige in the family, he suffered a history of heart problems, gradually driving his brother, Crown Prince Fahd bin Abdulaziz, to assume more predominance in decision-making. They gave continuance to Faisal's preference for wait-and-see politics, avoiding any proactivity while simultaneously assessing who was the more significant threat to regional stability and forecasting that the US would provide security.

The Twin Pillar Diplomacy triangle

After the British departure, President Nixon elaborated the Twin Pillar Diplomacy, in which the US assisted Iran and Saudi Arabia in their needs, who, in turn, guaranteed a West-friendly order in the Persian Gulf. Washington wanted to promote collaboration between the two status quo countries to ensure stability without having to put its feet on the ground. The Shah aimed to substitute the United Kingdom and improve its power position while keeping the regional order as it was. Riyadh, aware of its vulnerabilities, sought protection from the extra-regional power in vogue. There was a win-win-win situation. Therefore, the first Persian Gulf triangle was a *ménage à trois*, where the US, Saudi Arabia, and Iran shared positive relations. The status satisfaction variable showed us a congruence among the countries' ambitions during the decade, as they all expected the order to continue being West-oriented. It also displayed that the three perceived Iraq as a threat due to its close ties to the Soviet Union. In short, there was no status competition between the three actors: they aspired for different positions that were not mutually exclusive.

The leadership variable revealed that the Shah understood well the Nixon Doctrine's priorities and used them to his advantage, requiring more and more military procurements and diplomatic support. In their turn, the US leaders sensed that Iran lacked cultural and identitarian elements, local appeal or natural partnerships to lead alone – something that the Saudis had due to their religious and ethnic credentials. Hence, knowing Iran provoked suspicions among the Arab Gulf countries, US leaders included Saudi Arabia in their regional strategy despite Iran being a much stronger actor. Just like the Shah, King Faisal was wise to use the political scenario to his advantage and pushed for more engagement with Iran under the US auspices and security assistance.

In this sense, threat assessment and shared interests led to a moment in which, despite diverging identities and political arrangements, no ontological insecurity emanated from the three dyads, allowing for more pragmatism and cooperative ties. Of course, one cannot say that the Iranian identity was complementary to the Saudi one, nor that the latter harmonised with the US one. Nevertheless, a scenario of mutual goals allowed these identities to coexist, not superposing each other and, hence, not producing cognitive anxieties. In a meeting with Prince Fahd, Nixon said he looked to the Middle East as a battleground between 'forces of stability' against extremism and those headed for destruction.[109] Both Faisal and the Shah seemed to see themselves as these forces.

Therefore, the triangle's tendency was collaboration. Iran was the US' leading partner for security, while Saudi Arabia gave the partnership more legitimacy among other Persian Gulf actors. During the period, Iran received military assistance from Washington and provided, in return, intelligence access and a secure air corridor between Europe and Southeast Asia for the

West. This way, Iran became the model example of a local ally the Nixon Doctrine sought. For example, Foreign Minister Ardeshir Zahedi promised that 'they could move quickly and deal with the situation before outside powers such as the Soviet Union became involved' and that they would 'gladly act in this manner if it possessed the requisite military strength'.[110] Moreover, the US leaders saw Iran as a critical advisor for orienting their regional role. On one occasion, Kissinger asked the Shah for advice in a meeting, saying, 'we are selling them [the Saudis] some arms. Does Your Majesty have any objection to this?', and Pahlavi answered, 'not at all. Sell them as much as you like', complementing that 'in the meantime, we should think about getting some Saudi like Fahd or Sultan to start an official co-operation with Iran'.[111]

Nevertheless, the concretisation of the Twin Pillar Diplomacy needed Iran and Saudi Arabia to improve their ties. By this logic, the Bahraini independence in 1971 became a valuable window of opportunity. According to historical records, Iran has long claimed the island, and most of its population believed it should be seized after the United Kingdom's departure.[112] However, the people of Bahrain wanted emancipation without Iranian influence. King Faisal strongly supported the island's independence, releasing together with the emir of Bahrain a joint communiqué to clarify that 'any attack on Bahrain would be treated as one on Saudi Arabia'.[113] Thus, the King met the Shah and insisted that controlling the island could seriously harm Iran's regional leadership ambitions because a leader needs legitimacy and a certain level of local approval to thrive. In meetings, the King advised Pahlavi on the Gulf Arab rulers' positions, guiding him to drop territorial claims and agree to a United Nations solution.[114] So, the Shah started a long process of negotiating his renouncement of Bahrain.

Therefore, the Shah prioritised Saudi–Iranian relations instead of immediate territorial gains, which was probably within reach considering the disproportionality between the Iranian army and the Bahraini one. Furthermore, the Shah calculated that improving the Arab–Iranian relationship could prevent radical ideologies' infiltration and provide his country with the conditions to legitimise its leadership role. Sure enough, after embracing Faisal's assistance on the matter, relations between Iran and the regional monarchies improved. Eventually, when the Shah deployed troops in 1971 to Abu Musa and Tumbs islands, a territory which the UAE also claims, Saudi Arabia's reaction was considerably passive and unwilling to intervene. Faisal said he did not want to participate in that dispute as 'it was now on friendly terms with Iran'.[115]

As mentioned already, Iran and the US lacked identification with the regional actors and risked having their actions rejected without Saudi Arabia's support. Therefore, Tehran and Washington encouraged

Saudi Arabian Islamic leadership, seeing it as a positive element for the order's continuity against Arabism or communism. This way, Saudi Arabia provided ideological and cultural legitimacy to the Twin Pillar Diplomacy, reducing Arab countries' anxiety and legitimising the Iranian superintendency.

Moreover, Saudi Arabia increasingly became an economic pillar within the strategy. While the Twin Pillar configuration did not prevent Tehran or Riyadh from joining the oil embargo in 1973, the King was very cautious about it, focusing on appeasing the US rather than confronting it. Faisal took weeks to raise the initial cut in oil exports, which only happened after direct discussions with the Nixon administration.[116] After that, Riyadh repeatedly coordinated its production to keep the oil prices stable. For example, in 1976, when the Shah attempted to increase the oil prices, Riyadh halted and kept the rates constant, pleasing the West.

In conclusion, while Iran continued to be the security leg of the triangle, Saudi Arabia was becoming the economic one. Riyadh adopted a moderation role among the oil producers, voting against sudden increases in oil prices even if that meant disagreeing with Tehran. Therefore, the triangle consisted of the US assuming a distant partner's role in the order's continuity, whereas Iran promoted itself as the regional leader with Saudi Arabia's collaboration and support. As a consequence, the system experienced one of its most stable decades. However, the 1979 Iranian Revolution completely shattered this scenario.

*

Throughout the 1970s, Tehran, Riyadh, and Washington had positive working relations characterised by one foreign power and two collaborative regional actors. Therefore, despite their differences in power, status ambitions, and state identities, each country played roles that coexisted while sharing interests and threat perceptions. While the Saudis were suspicious about Iran's intentions, the Twin Pillar strategy kept Riyadh's anxiety under control. It created what Arshin Adib-Moghaddam calls 'psychological ease' for the decision-makers.[117] In other words, the three countries had similar concerns with stability and established a collaborative security architecture. The triangulation ended not for lack of continuity but due to the structural changes in 1979 that altered the balance of power in the Persian Gulf. In retrospect, it is ironic that Kissinger warned Nixon that 'if a radical regime were to take over in Saudi Arabia, the US would have little choice but to move closer to Iran'.[118] He was right that if one of the two countries went rogue, the US would have no option but to strengthen the other. He *just* mistook which country would turn against them.

Notes

1 The six emirates were: Abu Dhabi, Dubai, Sharjah, Ajman, Umm al-Quwain, and Fujairah. The emirate Ras al-Khaimah joined the UAE in February 1972.
2 World Bank, GDP growth (annual %) – United States: 1961–2019.
3 Colin Gray and Jeffrey Barlow, Inexcusable restraint: The decline of American military power in the 1970s, *International Security* 10, 1985, pp. 27–69.
4 World Bank, Military expenditure (% of GDP) – United States: 1960–2019, 21 May 2021.
5 After the Bahraini independence, the Jufayr naval facility was acquired by the US Navy and became part of the US Navy operations. It represented a series of task group operations that supervised oilers, provided logistics, and protected companies against invasion.
6 Cooper, *The oil kings*.
7 Iran shares land borders with Afghanistan, Azerbaijan, Armenia, Iraq, Pakistan, Turkey, and Turkmenistan. Moreover, it shares maritime borders with Kuwait, Saudi Arabia, Qatar, the UAE, Bahrain, and Oman.
8 World Bank, GDP per capita (current US$) – Iran, Islamic Rep.: 1960–2019.
9 Abrahamian, A history of modern Iran; Hadi S. Esfahani and M. H. Pesaran, Iranian economy in the twentieth century: A global perspective, *Iranian Studies* 42: 2, 2009, pp. 177–211.
10 Esfahani and Pesaran, Iranian economy in the twentieth century.
11 M. H. Pesaran, The Iranian economy during the Pahlavi era, in Ehsah Yarshater (ed.), *Encyclopaedia Iranica* (Costa Mesa: Mazda Publishers, 1997), pp. 143–156.
12 World Bank, Military expenditure (current USD) – Iran, Islamic Rep.: 1960–2019.
13 World Bank, Military expenditure (% of GDP) – Iran, Islamic Rep.: 1960–2019.
14 Stephen McGlinchey, Arming the Shah: U.S. arms policies towards Iran, 1950–1979 (Doctor of Philosophy in International Relations thesis, Cardiff: Cardiff University, 2012).
15 Abrahamian, *A history of modern Iran*; Ward, *Immortal*.
16 Ward, *Immortal*.
17 Cooper, *The oil kings*.
18 Amin Saikal, *Iran rising: The survival and future of the Islamic Republic* (Princeton: Princeton University Press, 2019).
19 Alvandi, Nixon, Kissinger, and the Shah, p. 367.
20 Ruhi K. Ramazani, ARAB v. Arab–Iranian relations in modern times, in Ehsah Yarshater (ed.), *Encyclopaedia Iranica* (Costa Mesa: Mazda Publishers, 1997), pp. 220–224.
21 David J. Singer, Stuart Bremer, and John Stuckeym, Capability distribution, uncertainty, and major power war, 1820–1965, in Bruce Russet and Betty Crump Hanson (eds), *Peace, War, and Numbers* (Beverly Hills, CA: SAGE, 1972), pp. 19–48.

22 Saudi has land borders with Jordan, Iraq, Kuwait, the UAE, Oman, Qatar, and Yemen. It also shares maritime borders with Iran, Bahrain, Eritrea, Egypt, and Sudan.

23 World Bank, Population, total – Saudi Arabia: 1960–2019; World Bank, Population growth (annual %) – Saudi Arabia: 1961–2019.

24 The first and second Saudi realms (1744–1818 and 1824–1891, respectively) failed to permanently unify the Peninsula's vast territories and multiple tribes.

25 Toby Jones, *Desert kingdom: How oil and water forged modern Saudi Arabia* (Cambridge, MA, London: Harvard University Press, 2010); Tim Niblock, *Saudi Arabia: Power, legitimacy and survival* (London, New York: Routledge, 2006); Madawi Al-Rasheed, *A history of Saudi Arabia* (New York: Cambridge University Press, 2010).

26 World Bank, GDP growth (annual %) – Saudi Arabia: 1969–2019.

27 Jones, *Desert kingdom*, p. 83.

28 Singer, Bremer, and Stuckeym, Capability distribution, uncertainty, and major power war, 1820–1965.

29 Gregory Gause, *Oil monarchies: Domestic and security challenges in the Arab Gulf States* (New York: Council on Foreign Relations Press, 1994); Stephanie Cronin, Tribes, coups and princes: Building a modern army in Saudi Arabia, *Middle Eastern Studies* 49: 1, 2013, pp. 2–28.

30 Cronin, Tribes, coups and princes, p. 2.

31 World Bank, Military expenditure (current USD) – Saudi Arabia: 1960–2019.

32 Josoph Kechichian, *Faysal: Saudi Arabia's king for all seasons* (Gainesville, FL: University Press of Florida, 2008), p. 121.

33 Bradley Bowman, Realism and idealism: US policy towards Saudi Arabia from the Cold War to today, *Parameters* 35: 4, 2005, pp. 91–106; Al-Rasheed, *A history of Saudi Arabia*.

34 Layne, *The peace of illusions*, pp. 35–36.

35 Richard Nixon, Address by President Richard Nixon to the UN General Assembly, United States Department of State, 1969.

36 Foreign Relations of the United States (FRUS), Memorandum from the Executive Secretary of the Department of State (Read) to the President's Assistant for National Security Affairs (Kissinger) (Documents on Iran and Iraq, Washington, DC, 30 January 1969).

37 Foreign Relations of the United States (FRUS), Letter from the Under Secretary of State for Political Affairs (Johnson) to the Deputy Secretary of Defense (Packard) (No. 13, Jordan, 4 November 1970).

38 Foreign Relations of the United States (FRUS), Paper Prepared by the Interdepartmental Group for Near East and South Asia (Middle East Region and Arabian Peninsula No. 2, Washington DC, 1969).

39 Foreign Relations of the United States (FRUS), Memorandum from William Quandt and Gary Sick of the National Security Council Staff to the President's Assistant for National Security Affairs (Brzezinski) (Middle East Region and Arabian Peninsula No. 1, 2 February 1977).

40 Ali Ansari, Shah Mohammad Reza Pahlavi & the myth of imperial authority (PhD thesis, London: SOAS, 1998).

41 Abrahamian, *A history of modern Iran*; Kinch, *The US–Iran relationship*.

42 Petersen, *Richard Nixon, Great Britain and the Anglo-American alignment*, p. 89.

43 Cooper, *The oil kings*, p. 138.

44 Ansari, Shah Mohammad Reza Pahlavi & the myth of imperial authority, p. 341.

45 Fain, American ascendance and British retreat in the Persian Gulf region, p. 175.

46 Cooper, *The oil kings*, p. 21.

47 Alvandi, Nixon, Kissinger, and the Shah, p. 348; Petersen, *Richard Nixon, Great Britain and the Anglo-American alignment*, p. 89.

48 Al-Rasheed, *A history of Saudi Arabia*, p. 128.

49 Kumar, The right kind of 'Islam', p. 1087.

50 Foreign Relations of the United States (FRUS), Memorandum from the Chairman of the Interdepartmental Group for Near East and South Asia (Sisco) to the Chairman of the Review Group (Kissinger) (Middle East Region and Arabian Peninsula No. 133, Washington, DC, 21 November 1969).

51 Colin Dueck, *Reluctant crusaders: Power, culture, and change in American grand strategy* (Princeton, NJ, Oxford: Princeton University Press, 2006), p. 22.

52 Layne, *The peace of illusions*; Michael B. Oren, Power, *faith and fantasy: America in the Middle East, 1779 to the present* (New York, London: W. W. Norton & Company, 2007).

53 Jonathan Monten, The roots of the Bush Doctrine: Power, nationalism, and democracy promotion in US strategy, *International Security* 29: 4, 2005, pp. 112–156, p. 115.

54 Dueck, *Reluctant crusaders*.

55 Monten, The roots of the Bush Doctrine, p. 137.

56 Kinch, *The US–Iran relationship*, pp. 79–80.

57 Arguing that it was 'the white men's burden', the US had its own imperialism experience via Roosevelt's Big Stick doctrine, intervening in Latin America, Hawaii, and the Philippines.

58 Willian Williams, *The tragedy of American diplomacy* (New York: Dell, 1972).

59 Dueck, *Reluctant crusaders*.

60 Ali Ansari, The myth of the white revolution: Mohammad Reza Shah, 'modernization' and the consolidation of power, *Middle Eastern Studies* 37: 3, 2001, pp. 1–24; Abrahamian, *A history of modern Iran*.

61 Kinch, *The US–Iran relationship*, p. 33; Adib-Moghaddam, Discourse and violence.

62 Ray Takeyh, *Guardians of the revolution: Iran and the world in the age of the Ayatollahs* (Oxford, New York: Oxford University Press, 2009).

63 Sharifah M. Al Oboudi, Najd, the heart of Arabia, *Arab Studies Quarterly* 37: 3, 2015, pp. 282–299.

64 Long, *The United States and Saudi Arabia*, pp. 4–8.

65 Christopher Blanchard, *The Islamic traditions of Wahhabism and Salafiyya* (Washington, DC: The Library of Congress: Congressional Research Service, 2008).

66 Al-Rasheed, *A history of Saudi Arabia*, p. 6.

67 Natana DeLong-Bas, *Wahhabi Islam: From revival and reform to Global Jihad* (New York: Oxford University Press, 2004); Niblock, *Saudi Arabia*.

68 May Darwich, The ontological (in)security of similarity: Wahhabism versus Islamism in Saudi foreign policy (No. 263, Hamburg: German Institute of Global and Area Studies, 2014); Jones, *Desert kingdom*.

69 Dan Caldwell, The legitimation of the Nixon–Kissinger grand design and grand strategy, *Diplomatic History* 33: 4, 2009, pp. 633–652, pp. 646–647.

70 Foreign Relations of the United States (FRUS), Address by Richard M. Nixon to the Bohemian Club (Foundations of Foreign Policy No. 2, San Francisco, 29 July 1967).

71 Richard Nixon, Address by President Richard Nixon to the UN General Assembly (United States Department of State, 1969).

72 Foreign Relations of the United States (FRUS), Memorandum from the President's Assistant for National Security Affairs (Kissinger) to President Nixon (Foundations of Foreign Policy No. 41, 20 October 1969).

73 Foreign Relations of the United States (FRUS), Telegram from the Department of State to the Consulate General in Dhahran (Middle East Region and Arabian Peninsula No. 79, 20 February 1970).

74 Foreign Relations of the United States (FRUS), Paper prepared by the National Security Council Staff. 1969–1976 (Middle East Region and Arabian Peninsula No. 82, 4 June 1970).

75 Foreign Relations of the United States (FRUS), Paper prepared by the Interdepartmental Group for Near East and South Asia (Middle East Region and Arabian Peninsula No. 2, Washington DC, 30 January 1969).

76 Richard Nixon, *RN: The memoirs of Richard Nixon* (New York: Simon & Schuster Paperbacks, 1978).

77 Foreign Relations of the United States (FRUS), Memorandum of conversation (Middle East Region and Arabian Peninsula No. 72, 11 March 1969).

78 Foreign Relations of the United States (FRUS), Intelligence memorandum prepared in the Central Intelligence Agency (Middle East Region and Arabian Peninsula No. 122, 21 September 1972).

79 Foreign Relations of the United States (FRUS), Telegram from the Embassy in Iran to the Department of State (Iran; Iraq, 1973–1976 No. 62, Tehran, 26 June 1974).

80 Dueck, *Reluctant crusaders*; Steven A. Yetiv, *The absence of grand strategy: The United States in the Persian Gulf, 1972–2005* (Baltimore, MD: Johns Hopkins University Press, 2008).

81 Bowman, Realism and idealism.

82 Seliktar, *Navigating Iran*, p. 9.

83 Bill, *The eagle and the lion*, p. 226.

84 Bill, *The eagle and the lion*, p. 196.

85 Ruston K. Karanjia, *The mind of a monarch* (London: Allen & Unwin, 1997), p. 261.
86 D. Heisey and David Trebing, A comparison of the rhetorical visions and strategies of the Shah's white revolution and the *Ayatollah*'s Islamic revolution, *Communication Monographs* 50: 2, 1983, pp. 158–174.
87 Heisey and Trebing, A comparison of the rhetorical visions and strategies of the Shah's white revolution and the *Ayatollah*'s Islamic revolution, p. 166
88 Karanjia, *The mind of a monarch*, p. 243.
89 Foreign Relations of the United States (FRUS), Memorandum of conversation (Documents on Iran and Iraq, 1 April 1969).
90 Foreign Relations of the United States (FRUS), Intelligence Note No. 743 from Deputy Director George C. Denney, Jr. of the Bureau of Intelligence and Research to Secretary of State Rogers. 1969–1976. Washington, DC (Documents on Iran and Iraq no. 25, 17 October 1969).
91 Abrahamian, *A history of modern Iran*, p. 68.
92 Foreign Relations of the United States (FRUS), Telegram 4185 from the Embassy in Iran to the Department of State. Tehran (Documents on Iran and Iraq no. 24, 13 October 1969).
93 Foreign Relations of the United States (FRUS), Memorandum of conversation (Documents on Iran and Iraq, 1 April 1969).
94 Kechichian, *Faysal*, pp. 176–186; Gregory Gause, *Saudi–Yemeni relations: Domestic structures and foreign influence* (New York: Columbia University Press, 1990), p. 69.
95 Petersen, *Richard Nixon, Great Britain and the Anglo-American alignment*, p. 53.
96 Karanjia, *The mind of a monarch*, p. 254.
97 Abreviation in Persian for *Sazman-e Etelaat Va Amniat Keshvar*, or, in English, the Organisation of Intelligence and Security of the Country.
98 *Time* magazine cover. *Time* magazine, 4 November 1974. Available at https://content.time.com/time/covers/0,16641,19741104,00.html.
99 Kechichian, *Faysal*, p. 162.
100 Riedel, *Kings and presidents*.
101 Bowman, Realism and idealism, p. 97; Kechichian, *Faysal*, p. 162.
102 Kechichian, *Faysal*, p. 176.
103 Abdullah M. Sindi, King Faisal and Pan-Islamism, in Willard A. Beling (ed.), *King Faisal and the modernisation of Saudi Arabia* (New York: Routledge, 1980), pp. 171–189, p. 186.
104 Nadav Safran, *Saudi Arabia: The ceaseless quest for security* (Ithaca, New York, London: Cornell University Press, 1998), p. 213.
105 Safran, *Saudi Arabia*, p. 126.
106 Safran, *Saudi Arabia*, p. 178.
107 Al-Rasheed, *A history of Saudi Arabia*, pp. 128–129; Bronson, *Thicker than oil*, p. 99.
108 Riedel, *Kings and presidents*, p. 53.

109 Foreign Relations of the United States (FRUS), Memorandum of conversation (Middle East Region and Arabian Peninsula No. 132, 14 October 1969).

110 Foreign Relations of the United States (FRUS), Memorandum of conversation (Middle East Region and Arabian Peninsula No. 21, Washington, DC, 15 May 1970).

111 Foreign Relations of the United States (FRUS), Memorandum of conversation (Iran; Iraq, 1973–1976 No. 27, Washington, DC, 24 July 1973).

112 Roham Alvandi, Muhammad Reza Pahlavi and the Bahrain Question, 1968–1970, *British Journal of Middle Eastern Studies* 37: 2, 2010, pp. 159–177, p. 162.

113 Saud al Faisal bin Abdulaziz Al-Saud, *Saudi Arabia and the international oil market: An executive summary of the special presentation* (Houston, TX: James Baker III Institute for Public Policy, Rice University, 2005), p. 47.

114 Al-Saud, *Saudi Arabia and the international oil market*, p. 141; Alvandi, Muhammad Reza Pahlavi and the Bahrain Question, 1968–1970, p. 168.

115 Al-Saud, *Saudi Arabia and the international oil market*, p. 123.

116 Al-Rasheed, *A history of Saudi Arabia*, p. 140; Petersen, *Richard Nixon, Great Britain and the Anglo-American alignment*, p. 144.

117 Adib-Moghaddam, *The international politics of the Persian Gulf*, p. 14.

118 Foreign Relations of the United States (FRUS), Memorandum from the President's Assistant for National Security Affairs (Kissinger) to President Nixon (Middle East Region and Arabian Peninsula No. 89, 22 October 1970).

4

The stable marriage triangle (1979–1989):
Consolidation of the Carter Doctrine

The events of 1979 altered the relations between Iran, Saudi Arabia, and the US radically. The Revolution that topped down the Shah traversed different classes and reflected dissatisfaction in many spheres. Clerics accused Pahlavi of corruption and deviance, a great part of the bureaucracy and the urban classes feared his growing authoritarian rule, and the *bazaaris* and the lower classes struggled with rampant inflation and recession. The Shah had alienated almost every sector of society and lost essential support while failing to transform Iran into the economically developed powerhouse he had hoped for. In 1977, a series of protests, demonstrations, and strikes against his rule began in many cities.

However, apart from some palliative economic liberalisations, the Shah mostly responded to the protests with repression and violence. The army frequently intervened in public gatherings, arresting and fining people. The secret police, SAVAK, ruled through terror, increasingly resorting to abuse of power and human rights violations. In its peak of repression, the government opened fire against protesters in Jaleh Square in Tehran on 8 September 1978, killing over a hundred people and injuring many more in what became known as 'Black Friday'. This event mobilised a more energetic wave of crippling strikes that paralysed the country. The protests would only stop when the last member of the Pahlavi dynasty left the country.

The Iranian Revolution was broad-based, built on the backdrop of grassroots mass participation, and included a broad spectrum of political, social, and economic groups. While many affluent people left the country and moved their money abroad, others from the army, *Majlis* politicians, and civil servants joined the movement. Nevertheless, the most influential revolutionary leader became *Ayatollah* Ruhollah Khomeini, who returned from exile in February 1979, two weeks after the Shah fled the country. According to Ervand Abrahamian, more than 3 million people waited for Khomeini at Tehran's airport to celebrate the regime's end.[1] During the tumultuous months that followed Pahlavi's fall, the Revolution's ideological outlines became more clearly defined as anti-imperialist, nationalist, and Islamist. The political system that emerged was radically opposed to the previous one. However, its consolidation process was abruptly cut short by Iraq's decision to invade Iran on 22 September 1980.

Iraqi President Saddam Hussein sought to reverse his territorial losses from the 1975 Algiers Accords and gaining control over the Shatt al-Arab waterway. Initially, Iraq scored quick advances in the war, as Iran seemed unprepared for the attacks. However, Iranian resistance surprised all, and by mid-1982, Iran had reconquered its territory and continued to retaliate, entering Iraqi territory. Despite its shattered economy, dysfunctional army, and lack of allies, Iran faced the war as a holy mission and a resilience test. Domestically, the war was seen as a righteous battle against evil, helping the clerics to mobilise society around their rule, close their political circle, repress opposition, and, eventually, consolidate their leadership and power.

For almost six years, Iran overlooked any international pressure to end the conflict or the Iraqi attempts to negotiate a settlement. As the war dragged on, Iran and Iraq modified their tactics and experimented with new weapons, turning the war into a stalemate that neither party could win or quit. Beyond the war of attrition on the ground, they began the Tanker War by 1984, a series of low-grade combats at sea that unsettled the oil shipments' stability in the Persian Gulf. With the fight gaining more and more global contours, Iraq began receiving diplomatic and military support from most Arab countries and the US, earning a substantial advantage against Iran. After attacking Kuwaiti ships carrying the US flag, Iran had to face the US Operation Earnest Will (from July 1987 to September 1988), the largest naval convoy operation since the Second World War. Several Iranian vessels, as well as oil platforms, were bombed.

The war dragged on until August 1988. When the battle reached the cities, there were intense air raids, missile attacks, and the use of chemical weapons against Iranian civilians. With superior firepower and foreign assistance, Iraq was crushing an enemy drained by massive casualties and suffering from a shortage of weapons. While the war consolidated the *Ayatollah*'s narrative of Islamic resistance, Iran's economy was in free fall, cities were destroyed, and the regime revealed clear signs of defeat. The final nail in the coffin was when the US accidentally shot down the Iran Air Flight 655 on 3 July 1988, killing 290 people. On 18 July 1988, less than a month later, Khomeini accepted a ceasefire proposed by UN Resolution 598 (proposed already in 1987), which stipulated that both countries should retreat to their original borders and repatriate war prisoners. The long, bloody, and costly war was over without a clear winner or a peace agreement.

The US power: reassuring order

The 1980s represented a period of readjustment and recalculation for the US. The Cold War détente finished with the Soviet invasion of Afghanistan in December 1979, resulting in a new wave of military build-up and escalating hostile rhetoric between Washington and Moscow. Economically, the decade began with a recession. However, the GDP growth rate returned to be positive in 1981 (2.5 per cent), reaching its climax in 1984 (7.2 per cent), and closing the period at 3.6 per cent in 1989.[2] The inflation rate stayed relatively low, consumption rose, the financial sector bloomed, and investments skyrocketed. The neoliberal agenda of Reaganomics produced initial economic expansion – via, among others, cuts on federal market regulations and taxes – at the cost of massive privatisation, diminished labour protection, and curtailing of union power.

These changes also meant increased social inequalities, spiralling budget deficits, and growing dependency on foreign trade and oil exports. Public debt also increased due to an expansion of the defence budget. Military expenditure went from US$ 126.8 billion in 1979 to US$ 321.8 billion in 1989, which rose from 4.9 per cent of the total GDP in 1979 to 5.8 per cent in 1989.[3] The country was committed to strengthening its capacity for rapid intervention in key strategic locations, restoring naval power, and expanding tactical forces, as well as enhancing defence research centres.[4] It underwent a broad modernisation process of its conventional forces to overcome many communication and control problems and shield the military from obsolescence.

In the Persian Gulf, Washington focused on increasing its military presence, acquiring the capability to respond quickly to instability if needed. In 1980, the idea of a rapid deployment force (RDF) in the Middle East took shape, consisting of two airborne army divisions, two ranger battalions, six air force wings, three carrier task forces, and three amphibious brigades accompanied by airpower.[5] The US naval forces in the Persian Gulf and the Indian Ocean also grew in size, broadness, and scope. Moreover, the Diego Garcia base gained strategic importance. Around US$ 400 million was spent on its reform and expansion so that it could host thousands of sailors and support the largest naval vessel fleets of the US and the United Kingdom.[6]

In 1983, the military reorganised the RDF to create the US Central Command (CENTCOM), a unified regional command with higher bureaucratic stature and autonomy, controlling more than 290,000 personnel across four services.[7] The ability to deploy forces was first tested in Operation Earnest Will, which was a fundamental turning point for the US' power projection in the Persian Gulf.

In short, the 1980s was a period of empowerment for the US as the Cold War rekindled. It also marked the beginning of the US military footprint in the Persian Gulf. Already in 1984, CENTCOM had the following combat forces available: an army with four divisions and one brigade, seven tactical fighter wings, two strategic air bomber squadrons, three carrier battle groups, one surface action group, five marine patrol squadrons, and three marine amphibious forces.[8]

US changeable power

The ties between the US and Iran were severely broken on 4 November 1979, when Iranian students invaded the US embassy and kept several citizens as hostages. The event was one of the first examples of the anti-US resentment that permeated much of the Islamist ideology in Iran and beyond. This sentiment would quickly become a stumbling block on the US image and regional appeal. With the insurgents claiming that they discovered at the embassy a plot to bring the Shah back, many in the Middle East started to see the US as yet another imperialist power acting only for its own benefit.[9] In this context, the Revolution promoted itself as a force to overcome US supremacy. Moreover, the US regional credibility diminished even more with the Iran–Contra scandal, which exposed Washington's duplicity in selling arms to both Iran and Iraq during the war.[10] Therefore, while Washington consolidated its capacity to project power in the region during this period, its regional appeal and popularity changed forever after 1979.

Nevertheless, throughout the decade, the US sought to improve its security ties with the remaining status quo actors in the Persian Gulf. Particularly with the Saudis, Washington signed a defence agreement in 1982 to establish high-level consultation mechanisms and a joint military commission. In a matter of weeks, the US-Saudi military engagement enlarged via assistance to regional actors, providing arms supply, and investing in developing ports, airfields, and air-and-sealift facilities.[11] They also took the needed steps to guarantee that Tehran would not win the war against Iraq. For that, they removed Iraq from its list of terrorist nations in 1982 and restored diplomatic ties in 1984.

By 1989, Washington had diplomatic representation in almost all Persian Gulf countries apart from Iran. It is important to stress that their direct involvement in the Tanker War brought military cooperation with the smaller monarchies to another level. For example, Qatar provided storage facilities for weapons, jet fuel, and medicine, Bahrain offered port and naval facilities, and Kuwait bought significant amounts of US-American military equipment.[12] This way, the US consolidated itself as the guarantor of security in the Persian Gulf – at least in the eyes of the regional monarchies – finally assuming the earlier role of the United Kingdom.

Iranian power: becoming the Islamic Republic

Tumultuous politics marked the first decade of the Islamic Republic. While the Revolution was multifaceted, the clerics, under the auspices of *Ayatollah* Khomeini, assured their political supremacy by establishing a theocratic hybrid republic. The new regime was divided into divine and popular rights, the *Vox Dei* and the *Vox Populi*. The President (chief of the executive) and the *Majlis* (legislative and regulatory power) composed the elected branch. The unelected branch comprised the Guardian Council (religious jurists) and the Supreme Leader, or *Velayat e-faqih*, who oversaw almost all political, military, and judiciary decisions.

Many elements of Iranian power transformed with the Revolution and the war. Geography changed in the first years of the war, as Iraq took around 120 km of Iranian territory, but the frontiers were restored by the war's end. Demographically, it is estimated that 10,000–40,000 lives were lost during the Revolution, and more than half a million, mainly from the middle or higher classes, emigrated.[13] Moreover, between purges and tribunals, it is estimated that around 75 per cent of Shah's senior officers were executed, and up to 30,000 were arrested.[14] Finally, there were 200,000–220,000 deaths on the battlefields, around 16,000 civilian causalities, 350,000–400,000 wounded, and more than 2 million internal refugees.[15]

Inflation, recession, and unemployment followed the many months of civil unrest and strikes against the Shah's regime. After the regime change, Iran faced in November 1979 the first of many US economic sanctions, which froze assets and imposed a trade embargo. Additionally, the war against Iraq was very costly: it consumed around 70 per cent of the Iranian government budget while the public deficit accumulated.[16] Due to the war and growing political isolation, investments sank continuously, and the GDP growth rate decreased from –10.5 per cent in 1979 to –27.5 per cent in 1980, closing at 6 per cent in 1989.[17] Moreover, oil prices sharply declined during the decade, pushing inflation to the ceiling, bankrupting smaller private businesses, and forcing many skilled professionals to emigrate.

Despite the restrictive scenario, the new regime brought benefits to the working and lower classes via subsidies, labour protection measures, and commercial and industrial concessions. Despite the low growth rate, Iranian GDP per capita went from US$ 2.42 thousand in 1979 to US$ 4.27 thousand in 1986 and closed at US$ 2.24 thousand in 1989.[18] Additionally, the Revolution expanded the welfare state, introducing industrial protectionism and price controls that benefited the poorer consumers.[19] In less than a decade, the new regime managed to improve people's daily lives despite the dire conditions of war: infant mortality dropped, the percentage of children in school rose, and illiteracy was almost eradicated.

The military element of power was also severely affected in the period. Military purges in all forces resulted in around 12,000 officers being arrested, dismissed, or forcefully retired.[20] Many generals were reportedly tortured and executed, and hundreds of lower-ranking officers deserted. According to Steven R. Ward, the air forces dropped from 100,000 to 65,000 personnel, while the navy went from 28,000 to 23,000.[21] Nevertheless, Iran kept its advantage over other Persian Gulf countries in terms of quantity and recruiting ability.

As discussed in the previous chapter, the Shah focused on the military build-up and had the highest defence budget in the Middle East. The new regime promised to reduce military-spending, but that was hindered due to the demands of the war. Thus, while the military expenditure as part of the GDP decreased from 5.7 per cent in 1979 to 4.5 per cent in 1989, the military-spending increased from US\$ 4.9 billion in 1979 to US\$ 16.3 billion in 1989.[22] It is important to stress that military modernisation from the previous period depended on US assistance in training, equipment, ammunition, and communication. Therefore, much of the acquired equipment became non-operational with the end of US–Iran diplomatic ties. More precisely, around 30 per cent of the army and 50 to 60 per cent of the air force equipment, as well as 60 per cent of the helicopters, became dysfunctional or inoperative.[23]

A final note should be made on the Islamic Revolutionary Guard Corps (IRGC), a special force to protect the Revolution, monitor people's allegiance, and oversee other institutions. The IRGC was composed mainly of lower-middle classes dedicated to Khomeini's cause, with many willing to become martyrs for the Revolution's sake. Quickly, the IRGC consolidated itself as a crucial (and frequently unaccountable) element of Iranian power, mainly due to its relevance during the war against Iraq. It comprised around 200,000 war volunteers, developed a ministry, and acquired naval and air units.[24] Besides, it started to gain importance as an influential economic actor by the eve of the 1990s. Hence, it became an essential institution for the Iranian power projection.

Iran's changeable power

Iran's new radical and independentist rhetoric drove the country away from its traditional conservative partners and closer to actors that did not conform to a Western-oriented order. The new regime used revolutionary rhetorical artifices that eventually incited fear among some Arab and conservative leaders. Thus, all Middle Eastern countries supported Iraq during the war, except for Syria and Libya. Moreover, many of them also broke diplomatic ties with Iran after the Revolution: while

Iran had fifty-eight diplomatic representations worldwide in 1980, it had only thirty-nine by 1985.[25] In the Persian Gulf, only Kuwait kept diplomatic ties.

By promoting its revolutionary political stand, Khomeini's Islamism appealed to some marginalised minorities and revisionist groups who wanted the region to change. For example, in 1982, Iran sent 1,000 IRGC personnel to Lebanon to support, train, and organise the newborn group Hezbollah. As a result, Hezbollah became one of Iran's most reliable partners in the Middle East, and since then, they have been training other revolutionary groups, like Hamas, Islamist Jihad, and Houthis – increasing the scope of Iranian influence.

Moreover, Iran increased its relations with developing countries and became an active member of the Non-Aligned Movement. It defected from the Central Treaty Organisation (CENTO), the politico-military pact with Western economies, and sought to resume the Regional Development Cooperation Organisation (renamed the Economic Cooperation Organisation in 1985) while focusing on expanding trade ties with Turkey and Pakistan.[26] Additionally, despite rejecting communism, Iran sought to improve relations with the Soviet Union and China, mainly because they became Iran's key trading partners and arms suppliers.

Saudi Arabia's power: a decade of anxiety

While the 1970s represented economic expansion due to the oil boom, the 1980s slowed down Saudi Arabian accumulation of resources precisely because the prices dropped. The oil barrel price went from US$ 39 in June 1980 to US$ 12.7 in June 1986, closing at US$ 13 in 1989. This undermined the kingdom's ability to sustain high levels of welfare politics and modernisation. Thus, the GDP fell from US$ 111.8 billion in 1979 to US$ 95.3 billion in 1989.[27] Moreover, the GDP growth rate was negative for most of the decade, reaching its lowest in 1982 (–20.7 per cent) and closing at –0.5 per cent in 1989.[28] This way, the decade represented a period of deficit budgets, slow socioeconomic improvements, and high indebtedness to international banks.

Demographically, the period exhibited the first historical deceleration, with populational growth going from 5.5 per cent in 1979 to 3.8 per cent in 1989.[29] However, the fertility rate was still one of the fastest worldwide: 7.2 births per woman in 1979 and six in 1989.[30] That meant that the Saudi Arabian population went from 9.13 million to 15.6 million between 1979 and 1989.[31] As these rates indicate a disproportional amount of youth within the social base, there was an upsurge of the migrant labour force to fulfil domestic demand during this period. It is estimated that around 30 per cent of the Saudi population was migrant in the 1980s, with 60 per cent of the labour force being non-national.[32]

Moreover, the economic deceleration echoed in the military budget. In 1979, the Saudi military budget was US$ 17.6 billion, while in 1989, it was US$ 12.7 billion.[33] However, this number only reflected the reduction of income, not an active decision to reorient the budget from defence to other sectors, as the military expenditure share of the GDP continued to be more or less fixed – 15 per cent in 1979, 19 per cent in 1984, and 13.4 per cent in 1989.[34] Despite the decline in oil prices, Saudi Arabia kept this level of defence investment – which was highly dependent on the US for assistance, training, and supply.

Saudi Arabia intensified its acquisition of first-line weaponry systems. For example, in 1981, the US sold them F15 combat and five Airborne Warning and Control System (AWACS) aircraft, making Saudi Arabia the first country in the region to possess both technologies. As a result, the air force improved, having about 165 combat aircraft by 1986, and became superior to the Iranians.[35] The naval force also upgraded, with purchases aiming to qualitatively enhance its capabilities. The country's goal was to reach a level of deterrence capacitation that increased other actors' costs for invasion. However, capacities in the event of a regional war or an attack remained insufficient. Moreover, military personnel continued in small numbers, expanding only from 80,000 in 1980 to 82,000 in 1989.[36]

Finally, Saudi Arabian forces continued to be affected by distortions that blocked professionalisation. A fundamental problem within the military was the disproportion between the small-sized armed forces and the demands created by the country's vast dimensions. Due to this, the kingdom often relied on foreign armies for patrolling and protection, such as from Pakistan.[37] Another problem was the military's division into two commands (conventional armed forces and the National Guard), which affected the general organisation and delayed modernisation projects.[38] These problems led to insufficient operational proficiency to respond to possible ground attacks. Therefore, Saudi Arabia remained vulnerable to regional attacks and depended on foreign assistance.

Saudi Arabia's changeable power

Saudi Arabia enhanced its strategic value to the West as the only remaining pillar in the Twin Pillar Diplomacy. The monarchy became the West's most significant Persian Gulf partner, presenting a staunch discourse against Soviet communism and discouraging other Islamic actors from getting closer to the ideals of the Islamic Revolution. Undeniably, the growing radicalisation of Khomeini's anti-monarchical discourse distressed Iran–Saudi relations until the diplomatic relations formally ended in 1981. For an entire decade, the two largest countries in the region did not share ties at all.

Most importantly, Saudi Arabia improved its regional pre-eminence with the foundation of the GCC on 25 May 1981. Facing mounting regional instability, the Arab Persian Gulf states (Kuwait, Bahrain, Qatar, Saudi Arabia, Oman, and the UAE) developed a regional platform to discuss and coordinate action on multiple issues ranging from security to economy and education. The GCC's objectives included promoting regional security, protecting it from international conflicts, and respecting sovereignty. This way, it enhanced domestic security cooperation and provided a platform to collectively request outside assistance or provide aid to others. As one can imagine, due to its larger size and economy, Saudi Arabia eventually imposed its security perspective on the smaller sheikdoms and assumed the position of the organisation's manager.

Hence, Saudi Arabia became the security 'bigger brother' of the other GCC members, especially from the Western perspective. To respond to the overall regional anxiety that the Iranian Revolution represented, especially to conservative actors, Riyadh intensified its regional partnerships through donations in the name of Islamic solidarity. Finally, Saudi Arabia was also involved in Afghanistan's invasion, taking the lead role among other Muslims in condemning Soviet interference and boycotting Kabul while assisting the US in the conflict.[39] Therefore, the country's power projection in the region increased.

The Persian Gulf's balance of power in the 1980s

Undoubtedly, the Revolution and the following war altered the power balance within the region. Quite quickly, countries that once profited from Iranian protection were supporting Saddam's war. Moreover, with the Twin Pillar order gone, the US had to increase its power projection as its other regional partner, Saudi Arabia, did not have the needed capabilities to assume the surrogate position that Iran had in the 1970s. Finally, although the war devastated both sides, Iraq still got the upper hand. It strengthened its regional power while receiving great international support, whereas Iran became only a shadow of the military power it once was. Thus, although the regional power balance continued to be multipolar, the US power projection in the region increased, and the pendulum of which actor had the most possibility to become a regional power moved towards Iraq.

Under the Soviet Union's political clout, Iraq became one of the most powerful countries in the Middle East, ruled by an ambitious leader who saw himself as the inheritor of the pan-Arabist movement. While Saddam failed to end Khomeini's regime, he blocked a possible diffusion of the revolutionary ideals and showcased Iraq's power capacities. That coincided with the Soviet operation in Afghanistan, a new Cold War arms race, and the resumption of hostile rhetoric between the two superpowers. Therefore, the 1980s were much more restrictive than the 1970s. In a bipolar structure, restrictive environments mean geopolitics is more conditioned by the competition between the superpowers. After the Tanker War, the US assumed a more substantial defensive commitment and military presence in the region, justified by the need to contain multiple sources of threat.

Conversely, Iran's power was reduced due to the Revolution and the long-standing war. First, the military mainly became dysfunctional as it was dependent on US assistance. Second, high-ranking officers fled, were arrested, or prosecuted, wrecking military organisation. Third, the war hampered the processes of consolidating the new regime, forcing the government to devote most of its attention and budget to the conflict. Fourth, financial bottlenecks and growing international isolation inflicted Iran's capability to project power. Thus, the decade threw the most prominent country in the Middle East into economic, military, and infrastructural chaos.

Finally, the decade also decelerated Saudi Arabia's economic development while enhancing its strategic relevance. Although it lacked Iran's or Iraq's military strength, the country had crucial anti-communist credentials, strong ties with the West, a strategic location, and a key religious clout in the Arab world. Moreover, it was the one that brought together the interests of the Persian Gulf monarchies into the formation of the GCC. For these reasons, Saudi Arabia's changeable power improved throughout the period. However, despite continuous military procurement, it continued to be exposed to defence vulnerabilities.

Considering these rearrangements, the balance of power approach becomes insufficient to explain why Saudi Arabia and the US chose to support Iraq against Iran. In Cold War terms, securing a certain level of relations with Tehran would benefit Washington in the bipolar competition and reduce the space for the Soviets to gain leverage in the region. Moreover, Saddam continued with his secular, pan-Arabist, and mostly pro-Soviet rhetoric, which was against Saudi's principles. Thus, Riyadh's decision to support Saddam is not self-evident. Finally, that cannot explain why Iran did not seek an alliance with the Soviets. Ideational, cognitive, and leadership factors intervened in the strategic reassessment within each state explaining why these events transformed the *'ménage à trois'* triangle into a 'stable marriage' kind, with one positive bilateral relationship and two negatives.

US' status satisfaction: reassessing the power configuration

During the first half of the 1980s, the US' anxiety towards the Middle East's order amplified, pushing for a more proactive role. First, the conflicts in Afghanistan, Iran, and Iraq threatened a new oil crisis on the horizon, which was a nightmare scenario for the global capitalist economy. Second, Nixon's security arrangement for the Persian Gulf was dismantled, and Iran became an incognita to be tackled with. The general understanding was that regional interests could be threatened by a possible Iran–Soviet partnership.[40] The following lines exemplify this assessment:

> This is not an estimate that the Soviets will seize the Iranian oil fields. It is rather that the combination of the Soviet need for oil, the power vacuum in Iran, the 'strategic window' of the early 80s, the perceived weakness of US leadership, and the geographic advantages of the USSR make such an action a thinkable course either for an erratic older Soviet leadership or an aggressive younger one. The Politburo might come to see Iran as the *schwerpunkt* of the long Soviet struggle with the US. A successful Soviet operation in Iran, even if it did not lead to a cut-off of other Gulf oil, would affect the power balance almost as decisively.[41]

Therefore, the US became convinced that the security of its own interest in the Persian Gulf was endangered. Being aware that no other actor could replace Tehran's previous role, it decided to increase its direct involvement. A memorandum from the Secretary of Defense concluded that:

> Given great volatility and vulnerability of PG/IO [Persian Gulf/Indian Ocean] region, our most serious short-term and mid-term security problem is assuring Free World access to Persian Gulf oil. While this oil is more needed by Europe and Japan than the US, the resulting economic chaos if it were cut off would undermine US security as well. Moreover, the Gulf is the key area in which our current capabilities are most lacking. Therefore, our top defense priority has been to create a greater ability to deter or defend against Soviet domination of PG oil.[42]

The security advisor Zbigniew Brzezinski informed President Carter that they needed to deal 'with the dangers to the Strait of Hormuz quickly' and develop a 'security framework for Southwest Asia and the Persian Gulf'.[43] For that, they conceived the Carter Doctrine. It idealised for the US a position as order protector so that there were 'no more Irans, no more Afghanistans'.[44] In other words, it broadened the US' ambitions in the Persian Gulf, aiming to check any actors challenging the order. Not only did Washington want the region under Western influence, but it also took the lead in ensuring that.

The Persian Gulf monarchies welcomed this new US ambition. They increased their procurement of weaponry and security ties, indicating an eagerness to see the superpower more involved in the region. Hence, their behaviour ensured Washington that status aspiration and ascription matched. This can be seen in this staff memorandum addressed to Carter:

> The Middle Eastern states, and particularly those of the Gulf, are of course less concerned with the economic well-being of the West than of their own, but their interest in avoiding infection from Iran is as great as ours in protecting them from it. Some are concerned over the general US–USSR power balance (Saudi Arabia) but most (Iraq) would be more concerned over the clear and present danger of a Soviet-oriented Iran.[45]

Here, it is important to stress that the US anxiety towards the regional order was gradually reduced when it became clear that the Iranian Revolution did not open up space for Soviet influence. Moreover, by supporting Iraq in the war and increasing securitarian ties with the monarchies, Washington assured that the Iranian ideology could not spread beyond the country's borders. With Iran being primarily isolated by the second half of the decade and the newly formed GCC aligning its interests with the West, the US' anxiety lessened.

Iranian status satisfaction: revolution and revisionism

The Islamic Revolution turned Iran into a prime example of a revisionist state in the sense that there was dissonance between the status it aspired to and the one it perceived to be ascribed. Under the new regime's logic, the international system was unjust to most people worldwide, and the political and economic order was designed to sustain the hegemony of those at the top at the cost of those at the bottom. This way, Iran positioned itself against the bipolar structure of the world, presenting itself as a non-conformist country. Its slogan 'neither East nor West, but Islamic' promoted the liberation of all Muslims who felt oppressed by imperialist powers worldwide – independently of whether they were on the side of Washington or Moscow.

Khomeini famously said that 'the US is worse than Britain; Britain is worse than the US; the Soviet Union is worse than both'.[46] The intellectuality behind the Revolution's ideas linked Islam with global social justice duty, Third-World struggle, and anti-imperialist resistance, encouraging a battle simultaneously against foreign exploitation and secular materialism. Under this logic, Iranian Islamism was 'an ideology focused on class cleavages and division of the international system between capitalistic powers and the larger developing bloc'.[47] Unsurprisingly, most of this criticism was directed at the US, which was perceived as the foremost upholder – and beneficiary – of the systemic order.

Framing the US proximity to the Pahlavi's regime as its original sin against the Iranian people, the new regime ascribed to itself the moral duty of confronting the Pax Americana, using narratives of global solidarity. For Khomeini, 'so long as the United States and other superpowers continue with their oppression and crimes, our nation too will continue its confrontation and struggle against them, while safeguarding its comprehensive independence with all its might'.[48] Through this, the Revolution's narrative overlapped with other Third-World movements grounded on anticolonialism and non-alignment. It criticised the global political-economic system, asserting that the US-led model damaged countries' development and autonomy. This framing can be seen in this speech at the United Nations by an Iranian diplomat:

> Today, the balance of power rather than the rule of law has been accepted as the basis and only possible method of safeguarding security, not only nationally, but regionally and globally as well. The recourse to the threat or use of force, aggression, the occupation of the lands of others by force and the infringement of sovereignty are all being utilised without being met by any serious opposition on the Part of the United Nations and other international forums. We must acknowledge that in many instances the United Nations has even gone so far as to contribute to the legitimisation of such methods. Is it not true that, in practice, the maintenance of the status quo and even submission to changed situations created by acts of aggression have become the general rule in international relations?[49]

Notably, Iran wanted to be seen as a leader against the Western-inclined order in the Persian Gulf.[50] If the Islamic Republic represented God's wishes, and, as *His* visions were not confined to a single country, it was Tehran's responsibility to assume the position of a broadcaster of Muslim uprisings throughout the Middle East.[51] Therefore, Iran continued to aspire for regional influence, but now with a religious and revisionist overtone. Thus, its status aspiration relied on its capacity to influence Islamist activism, idealising a new pan-Islamic regional unity in which it would have a position of primacy.

This status ambition of exporting the Revolution was neither well received by the other Persian Gulf countries, nor did the new regime gain any new external patrons for that. Iranians saw the Iran–Iraq war as an attempt by Saddam, the West, and other conservative regional actors to 'snuff out the revolution'.[52] For them, it was shocking that the international community was on the side of the invading country that used chemical weapons against civilians. This dissatisfaction with the status quo can be detected in this speech from Minister Ali Velayati at the United Nations:

> Tension in the Persian Gulf has been constantly escalating because of, on the one hand, the Iraqi aggression against the Islamic Republic of Iran and, on the other, the intensification of the United States military presence in the countries of the region; the presence of the United States fleet in the Sea of Oman as part of the destructive and aggressive structure of the 'Rapid Deployment Force' – which, under a new development, is to be called the 'Central Command'; and the creation of new military bases in Persian Gulf littoral States.[53]

Therefore, Iran became quite dissatisfied with its ascribed status, frustrated at being depicted as a regional menace while others armed and funded Iraq. The new regime was convinced that the Western powers systematically worked to prevent it from playing an independent regional role. Moreover, the exclusion of Iran from the GCC provoked resentment. Tehran perceived it as an anti-Iranian military pact, a 'plot to keep Iran out of the Gulf affairs'.[54] Therefore, this variable shows how Iran's interpretation of the international system pushed for revisionist policies that disagreed with mainstream policies, condemned the foreign presence in the Middle East, and supported other revisionist and revolutionary actors.

Saudi Arabian status satisfaction: the remaining pillar

Saudi Arabia viewed the regional system as a constant source of threats. At the same time, it had a very realistic assessment of its own vulnerabilities in terms of offensive or defensive capacities, aware that it could not promote such an order stability alone. Thus, the tensions rising from the Iranian Revolution, the Iran–Iraq war, and the Afghanistan war substantially boosted Saudi's anxiety concerning the regional system. In their view, the Middle East was 'caught in the mounting instability'.[55]

The Saudis interpreted the Iranian Revolution as the fall of a friendly monarchy by a Muslim revolution that established an essentially anti-monarchical new actor in the region. The collapse of the Pahlavi regime eliminated the conservative bloc in the Persian Gulf, reversing Saudi Arabia's previous security gains with the Twin Pillar strategy. Moreover, it meant that the US ultimately failed to shield its most crucial regional ally, raising Riyadh's uncertainty about Washington's commitment to actually protect partners. Finally, the growing Soviet Union's presence in Afghanistan increased the fear of socialist expansion in the Middle East.

However, as time passed, Iran got increasingly isolated, the Soviets lost the war, and the US stepped up its capacity to project power into the Persian Gulf. Moreover, a close security cooperation between Washington and Riyadh was consolidated.[56] In US President Ronald Reagan's words: 'Saudi Arabia has assumed an even more important and active role in the world and regional affairs [and] our mutual interests have developed to include many issues of great importance to the world'.[57] Thus, Riyadh's anxiety towards the order diminished. As the US improved its power projection, Saudi Arabia felt more comfortable with the status quo.

Concerning the war, Saudi Arabia perceived it as a struggle between two revisionist and expansionist actors. Therefore, it feared that whoever the winner was, it would eventually try to dominate others and become a hegemon. Therefore, Saudi Arabia felt the need to step up its capacity to protect itself and the other smaller monarchies from such possible hegemonic expansion from Iran or Iraq. Hence, the foundation of the GCC can be understood in this context. Riyadh's response to its growing strategic importance – as the remaining pillar – was to coordinate the other conservative monarchies' security interests in line with the West's interests. The US enthusiastically approved this 'big brother' role for the Saudis, applauding 'the leading role of Saudi Arabia in the Gulf Coordination Council'.[58]

To conclude, the status satisfaction variable indicates that Saudi Arabia continued to be satisfied with its status, even if it began the period with higher anxiety. The GCC coordination role became a new layer of Saudi Arabia's anti-instability behaviour. This layer was well received by the US, further consolidating Riyadh as the leading partner of the West in the Persian Gulf.

US state identity: facing a new challenger

As one of the most stable political systems globally, the US identity variable does not change throughout this book. As already discussed, the US state identity is based on the sense of uniqueness of the 'American experiment' and the idea that they have the mission of promoting their liberal model founded on principles of freedom, individuality, and private property. This variable shows us how the US decision-making process in foreign policy is oriented by cognitive filters that stress the country's role in promoting its 'exceptional values' as an example to be emulated or imposed on the rest of the world.

Recapitulating, there are four cognitive lenses that US leaders could adopt: internationalist, nationalist, progressive, or realist.[59] Moreover, this identity has a manicheist disposition that explains why Washington tends to assess what is opposing, denying, or rejecting its liberal values as a threat or an enemy. In simpler terms, if the US sees itself as the unavoidable good, all those challenging its dominance of the global order are 'custodians of all that is corrupted'.[60] Therefore, the emergence of the Islamic Republic was perceived as a threat as it accused the US role in the Middle East of being malignant.

As the leadership variable further discusses, Presidents Carter and Reagan sought strategies to promote the US liberal values while checking the expansion of other ideologies threatening their influence. However, they diverged on their chosen cognitive lenses. While Carter was close to the internationalist paradigm, Reagan was a nationalist who redefined much of the Republican Party. For Carter, the US model should have been promoted as an example to be followed, whereas for the Reagan team, force and imposition should not have been taken off the table. Thus, both lenses discouraged any policy that conveyed coexistence with the anti-US 'mad mullahs' ideology.

Iranian state identity: down with *gharbzadegi*!

A profound dissatisfaction with Iran's proximity to the West to the detriment of its own culture, traditions, and beliefs profoundly influenced many anti-Shah intellectuals that guided the Revolution. Among them, Jalah Al-E-Ahmad, who was a member of the communist Tudeh party, popularised the term *gharbzadegi* or 'West-toxification' to warn that non-Western societies were becoming susceptible to a 'disease' not only corrupting their values but also destroying local production and industries. Another key intellectual influencing the Revolution was Ali Shariati, who called for the Iranians to 'return to their self' and rediscover their national roots and Shiism foundations, suppressed by the Shah's inclination to Aryan and pre-Islamic myths.[61]

Khomeini successfully engineered non-traditional Islamic political thinking inspired by these intellectuals that united Iranians from very diverse ideological spectrums. Thus, establishing the new regime meant a victory against *gharbzadegi*. Islam, particularly Shiism, helped Iranians to rediscover themselves and break free from Western dependency and monarchical oppression. Moreover, in Khomeini's interpretation, this toxification was not restricted to the Iranian case but was a worldwide problem. Iran repositioned itself at the centre of a global justice and equality movement, presenting Islam as a tool to emancipate people from oppression and imperialism all over the world. This permitted the country to see itself as a leader articulating global opposition to the superpowers, promoting its Revolution as a moral mission, and justifying its regional and international expansionism.

The Revolution had a pan-Islamic discourse, talking to (and for) all Muslims. For them, Islamism should overcome any separation between state, society, and faith without ethnic, sectarian, or linguistic distinctions. In Khomeini's words, 'there is no difference between Muslims who speak different languages, for instance, the Arabs or Persians. It is very probable that such problems have been created by those who do not wish the Muslim countries to be united'.[62]

As an 'Islamic city on the hill', Iran presented itself as the centre of an up-and-coming Muslim awakening worldwide. This way, it forged ties with Islamic movements abroad while using this regional influence to validate leadership domestically. Still, this identity strongly emphasised Shiism and its ultimate expression of faith: martyrdom. Indeed, oppression, violence, and harassment marked Shiism's history. Traditionally, this sect is a social minority that has been underprivileged and persecuted in many Arab countries. Khomeini remarkably talked about the tragic fate of Imam Hussayn, the 'ultimate *homo Islamicus*', as an example of the Muslim people's resilience.[63] Being the first Shia-ruled government in the Middle East allowed Iran to project itself as a warrior against injustice towards minorities. In this sense, Khomeini refurbished the sect 'from a conservative quietist faith into a militant political ideology'.[64]

Finally, this ideational character created a manicheist understanding of international politics. Because Iran embodied and represented *the* Islamic virtue, any adversary was perceived as a force of disbelief. Similar to the US case, exceptionalism ingrained binary understandings that any actor denying Iran's aspired role was an enemy and a threat. Therefore, this variable pushed for policies that promoted Islamist upheavals, supported actors against the US, and criticised the regional actors' ties with the West.

Saudi Arabian state identity: meeting an ontological threat

Islam gave Saudi Arabia an ideological distinctiveness, determined much of the country's customs, and granted the monarchy the needed sociopolitical legitimacy. The 1980s, however, provoked ontological distress in Saudi's identity because, for the first time, domestic and regional sources were contesting its predominance as the Islamic leader.

Three events caused this ontological threat. First, the Islamic Republic of Iran presented itself as an alternative to Saudi's Islamist model. Khomeini often challenged the dynasty's legitimacy and accused monarchies of not being true to Islamic ideals.[65] Therefore, the Iranian model could promote anti-monarchical sentiments and reduce Saudi Arabia's influence among Muslim communities. Hence, Iran challenged the monarchy with the same instrument that the Saudi political elite used to legitimise its own rule: Islamic values. It set the stage for the competition of Muslims' hearts and minds between the two.

Second, the Revolution kindled dissent among the Shia community in the Saudi Eastern province. During the demonstrations of the *Ashura* in 1979, Saudi Shias organised strikes and riots while flaunting Khomeini's pictures.[66] They were dissatisfied with the country's unequal wealth distribution and Wahhabism's political and cultural predominance. However, the monarchy saw these protests primarily as a product of Tehran's influence. Disruption was also visible during the following *Hajj*, as many Iranians promoted their revolutionary ideas to other pilgrims. These events showed the Saudi monarchy that Iran had the potential to subvert a part of its population.

Third, another threat emerged on 20 November 1979, this time from its own Sunni majority. A group of radical Sunni rebels sieged Mecca's Grand Mosque for fourteen days, declaring that their leader, Muhammad Abdullah al-Qahtani, was the new Mahdi and demanding the overthrow of the Al Saud dynasty. The siege's militants also accused the monarchy of embracing Western-style modernity, becoming corrupt by materialism and incapable of acting as just rulers. The siege shocked Muslims worldwide, and it took the national forces two weeks, plus foreign assistance, to defeat the rioters. More than 118 were killed during the recapture of the mosque, whereas around sixty-eight were later executed. The event tested Al Saud's commitment to Wahhabism and forced the monarchy to reassess its modernisation pace.

Therefore, the regime felt it was being challenged from multiple fronts. Then, to re-establish its political-religious rule's legitimacy, the monarchy reaffirmed its ties with the conservative Wahhabis, adopting a more restrictive and controlling code of social conduct.[67] Moreover, it gave the Nadj's *ulama* more power, hence reducing its own pan-Islamic discourse to favour sectarianism. After 1979, the Saudi state identity could be interpreted through the pan-Islamist and sectarian lenses. Both understood that the country should be involved in the global *ummah*'s decisions to protect Islam worldwide.

However, while the pan-Islamist lens oriented the leaders towards a protector position for *all* Muslims, the sectarian lens distinguished the Sunnis from the Shias, privileging the first. By instrumentalising a sectarian language, the monarchy could exploit a popular anti-Shia sentiment among Sunnis in the Arab world to increase its own popularity – domestically and internationally.[68] As the leadership variable further explains, Saudis kept the sectarian lens throughout the 1980s.

US leadership preferences: establishing the Carter Doctrine

Right after the Revolution, President Carter believed that it was still possible to negotiate some type of working relation with Iran as both were interested in checking communism.[69] His administration was linked with promoting human rights and the internationalist-progressive paradigm, and he was cautious about opposing a massive and broad revolution like the Iranian one. However, the turning point was when the Shah requested the White House shelter. On the one hand, advisors in the Pentagon and the State Department said that this could endanger the US' already weakened position in Iran. On the other hand, close friends of the Shah, like Henry Kissinger and David Rockafeller, and prominent internationalists, including Carter himself, felt 'torn and morally ill at ease' for ignoring the monarch, especially because he needed medical treatment.[70] The President eventually decided to invite him, and on 22 October, the Shah flew from Mexico to New York. On 4 November 1979, Iranians invaded the US embassy, altering the political game entirely.

Every day that passed during the hostage crisis, the more the space for diplomatic solutions became restricted, and many US Americans called for military intervention. However, Carter continuously rejected military intervention, saying that it would endanger the hostages or even trigger a Soviet response. On the contrary, he took steps in stages. First, he attempted to establish back channels with Tehran's moderates on the grounds of 'equality, mutual respect, and friendship'.[71] When these failed, he resorted to shutting down diplomatic ties, freezing Iranian assets, and halting oil imports. In retrospect, Carter's caution yielded positive results, building international consensus against Iran while resisting pressures for direct conflict.[72] Nevertheless, this could not help him with the increasing domestic criticism.

Additionally, losing Iran meant losing the only surrogate actor protecting US interests in the Persian Gulf. In Carter's words, 'in recent years, the Persian Gulf has become vital to the US and to many of our friends and allies. Over the longer term, the world's dependence on Persian Gulf oil is likely to increase'.[73] Thus, as Brzezinski put it, the region was becoming the 'third central strategic zone' of the US policy, and developing a 'Persian Gulf security framework' was imperative.[74] The administration perceived that the remaining partners were hesitant about the US' ability to protect the region as it failed to avoid the Iranian Revolution, the invasion of Afghanistan, and the hostage crisis. A National Security Council (NSC) official observed that Washington was becoming 'a laughing stock in the region'.[75]

To answer these issues, Carter sent a mission to the Middle East in 1979 to 'restore and reinforce confidence in the US among our friends in the region' and 'begin to lay the basis for security collaboration among the US and key states'.[76] The mission should 'forcefully express our recognition of the strategic importance of the region, its strategic location, its vital resources, and its crucial role in establishing healthy patterns of internal development and North–South relations'.[77] They were aware that Saudi Arabia could not replace Iran immediately, but they should stimulate Saudi Arabia's defence capabilities. The Carter administration argued it was necessary to respond positively to Riyadh's requests for armaments, as the 'failure to meet these needs – for the military equipment and the political support it also represents – can have a profoundly adverse impact upon our overall relationship'.[78]

> the time is ripe to open the question of a new US military relationship with Saudi Arabia. This Mission believes that SAG would not only be receptive to but in fact, would welcome a change in the US Saudi military relationship. There is a little doubt that the military relationship occupies a central place in US Saudi relations ... If we accept the premise that the security of Saudi Arabia with its vast petroleum reserves is of vital interest to the US, then it is also true that, as a concomitant of that interest, it is necessary to ensure that the military assistance program in Saudi Arabia is operated with as much efficiency and effectiveness as possible.[79]

By January 1980, the President had announced the Carter Doctrine. The Doctrine asserted the US political involvement in the region by fortifying friendly governments, providing military assistance, and promoting stability. The following dialogue from a special coordination committee exposes its mindset:

Secretary Schlesinger: But we have to develop this capability. A local display of American power is necessary. They [regional partners] feel it in their bones. They can't articulate what they want, but they have to see that we have the capacity to protect them.

Dr Brzezinski: Over the longer term, what we are talking about is an increasing American role in the area which recognises it as vital to our national interests.

Secretary Brown: We've been acting as if we don't need a big presence in the area. First the British were there, and then the Iranians seemed strong. Now both are gone. So we may need to review our assumptions.[80]

In the President's words:

let our position be absolutely clear: an attempt by any outside force to gain control of the Persian Gulf region will be regarded as an assault on the vital interests of the United States of America, and such an assault will be repelled by any means necessary, including military force.[81]

Republican candidate Ronald Reagan continuously used the hostage crisis to attack Carter, running for re-election in 1980. Reagan called the crisis a 'humiliation' and a 'stark symbol of declining US capability in the region', capitalising on the US nationalist sentiments.[82] Reagan portrayed Carter as an indecisive leader while promising to 'make America great again' – something that would be capitalised on by another nationalist politician decades later. Reagan, an actor-turned-politician, had a 'great fondness of Hollywood-spun myths' and one clear goal: restore the US' predominance based on a nostalgic recollection of the 'greatest nation in the world'.[83] He won by a landslide.

Reagan believed that the US carelessly allowed the empowerment of many enemies. He clearly was not keen on continuing the détente with the Soviet Union, as he believed that the US should not have its powers limited. The new president employed a rhetoric of economic superiority, national pride, and exceptionalism to attack the Soviets and justify a growing US involvement in peripheral countries.

Concerning the Middle East, Reagan saw Iran's hostility towards the US as hateful, irrational, and defying behaviour that should not be accommodated. A more realist president may have cautiously remained neutral in the Iran–Iraq war, but the Reagan administration saw Iran's rejectionist behaviour as an attack on the US values and, therefore, a more significant threat. As one security advisor argued, the support to Iraq was 'not out of political affection for Saddam Hussein, but rather because of the instability and chaos his regime's collapse would trigger throughout the Gulf'.[84] On their rationale, the best scenario would be that both Iran and Iraq were weakened, but they could not afford the latter to fall into the radicalisation of the first. Moreover, they believed that if Iran won, the GCC countries would soon fall under the Revolution's influence. In short, the US saw Iraq as a barrier to Iranian expansionism, Saddam's 'violations of international law were reluctantly tolerated'.[85]

In sum, Carter's administration struggled to balance its internationalism and anti-war ideas with a growing restrictive environment for his country in the Persian Gulf. On the contrary, Reagan's foreign policy combined nationalism and revanchism in defining the country's priorities, leading to a more muscular policy in the region. Both administrations agreed that the US needed to increase its proactivity to protect the oil market and regional partners – and so they did. Carter developed the Doctrine, and Reagan pushed it forward.

Iranian leadership preferences: the centrality of Khomeini

Khomeini's political project was far more developed and cohesive than other groups opposing the Shah, and he was skilful in defusing opposition by appropriating and coopting demands from others. A well-known critic of Shah's moral and spiritual corruption, he amalgamated themes of religious grievance, nationalism, and class struggle in his rethoric, gathering followers across different perspectives. He was arrested in 1963, triggering protests countrywide and converting him into a national resistance hero. After his release, Khomeini was forced into exile in 1964, first in Turkey, then in Iraq, and finally in France. His discourse gained much more international prominence in France, as 'Neauphle-le-Château was becoming the political capital of the Iranian Revolution'.[86] He victoriously returned to Tehran in February 1979.

Khomeini exuded a 'mystical charisma, power, and authority, projecting a messianic, invincible, and decisive image', making him a leader not only for the Islamists but also for the urban middle class, *bazaaris*, and leftist students.[87] On the one hand, his Islamic credentials depicted him as the guardian of morality, appeasing the religious crowds. On the other hand, his anti-imperialist discourse appealed to the secular opposition. By linking faith to other socioeconomic grievances, he moved the Revolution beyond the Muslim cause and englobed issues like foreign resentment and inequality. Consequently, after the Shah had left, Khomeini managed to approve in March 1979 a referendum that established the new theocratic regime with almost unanimity.

Khomeini was a staunch believer that Iran needed to export its Revolution against the enemies of Islam. The following extracts exemplify how he combined religion with nationalism and resistance, reducing the space for more conciliatory political views:

> Dear sisters and brothers, in whatever country you may live, defend your Islamic and national honor! Defend fearlessly and unhesitatingly the peoples and countries of Islam against their enemies – America, international Zionism, and all the superpowers of East and West. Loudly proclaim the crimes of the enemies of Islam. My Muslim brothers and sisters! You are aware that

the superpowers of East and West are plundering all our material and other resources and have placed us in a situation of political, economic, cultural, and military dependence.[88]

all the powers are intent on destroying us, and if we remain surrounded in a closed circle, we shall certainly be defeated. We must make plain our stance toward the powers and the superpowers and demonstrate to them that despite the arduous problems that burden us, our attitude to the world is dictated by our beliefs.[89]

For him, Muslim liberation against Western or Eastern interference and exploitation could only be guaranteed through constant struggle and contestation. He was willing to take this leadership role and, in doing so, put Iran at the centre of the global fight for injustice. Therefore, by declaring that 'all Muslim countries are a part of us' and 'the revolution [is] without borders', Khomeini employed the idea he was on a religious mission to strengthen Iran's international position.[90]

Moreover, he used the same framing to condemn other Islamic countries that accepted or even aligned with the superpowers, particularly the US. Here, he openly confronted Saudi Arabia:

If we wanted to prove to the world that the Saudi Government, these vile and ungodly Saudis, are like daggers that have always pierced the heart of the Moslems from the back, we would not have been able to do it as well as has been demonstrated by these inept and spineless leaders of the Saudi Government.[91]

Undeniably, other Iranian revolutionaries diverged from Khomeini's point of view, particularly in terms of foreign policy. Among them was the first Prime Minister of the provisional post-revolutionary government, Mehdi Bazargan, a moderate who followed the nationalist tradition of Mosaddegh. He promoted a vision of non-alignment that enabled working relations with the US, the Soviets, and neighbouring countries. Until the hostage crisis broke out, Bazargan sought not to break ties with Washington but to reform them based on respect and equality. However, after the invasion of the US embassy, he felt compelled to resign.

His successor, Abolhassan Banisadr, was also frustrated with how centralisation on Khomeini difficulted to maintain working relations with the West. He was a Sorbonne-educated economist close to Khomeini – they even returned from France on the same flight. However, he showed discontent with the hostage situation, political oppression, and reduction of religious freedom and gradually entered into conflict with more conservative parliamentarians. In June 1981, he was impeached with the Supreme Leader's support and, facing threats, he returned to France. Eventually, the war against Iraq consolidated political rule of the *Ayatollah* and eliminated secular forces and dissidents from the political elite. A new constitution was approved in October 1981, and the cleric Sayyid Ali Hosseini Khamenei became the new President.

It is important to stress that Khomeini had no open intention of being associated with the Shah's concentration of power, so he encouraged the creation of political factions. While he promoted this as a way of decentralising power, one can interpret this as a way to preserve Khomeinism long after the leader's death. That is so because all these political groups needed to declare allegiance to the Islamic Republic. Thus, two major political camps arose in the 1980s: the *jihadi* (traditionalists or conservatives) and the *ijtihadi* (reformists or internationalists). Among other issues, they varied in how they saw Iran's foreign relations. While conservatives argued that the country should be completely autonomous, reformists defended a certain level of integration with the regional system. By the end of the decade, figures like Hashemi Rafsanjani and Ali Akbar Velayati started to gain political influence and developed another faction, known as *amlagaran* (pragmatic or moderates), which favoured integration into the global economy and limited cooperation with the West.

However, Iranian factionalism became truly relevant to international politics only after Khomeini's death in June 1989. Throughout the 1980s, the decision-making was a task for the Supreme Leader, who had the final say on all political domains. That meant political spaces for challenging him were limited. As a result, his international stand concentrated on promoting and exporting the Islamist revolutionary narrative, confronting Western imperialism, and intensifying the discourse of resistance and martyrdom.

Saudi Arabia's leadership preferences: the rise of the Sudayris

There were two Saudi monarchs in the 1980s: King Khalid bin Abdulaziz Al Saud (1975–1982) and King Fahd bin Abdulaziz Al Saud (1982–2005). King Khalid had extensive diplomatic, political, and military training, having served as the viceroy of Hejaz, an army officer during the Yemeni war, and the interior minister during King Faisal's rule. However, after his second heart surgery in 1978, he delegated most of the decision-making to then Crown Prince Fahd, who became the de facto ruler for at least seven years before he assumed the throne. Fahd was a prominent public figure at international meetings and events, gaining extensive political and diplomatic renown. Interestingly, his rising importance inside the kingdom refined his persona, integrating him more into the monarchy's costumes and expectations. Once a prince associated with yachts, expansive palaces in Europe, and a *bon vivant* attitude, the political environment's restrictiveness after 1979 drove Fahd to a more pious and conservative behaviour.[92]

Fahd's political empowerment represented the emergence of the Sudayri Seven, an influential group of Abdulaziz's sons from the same mother, Hussa al Sudayri: Fahd, Sultan, Abdul Rahman, Nayef, Turki, Salman, and Ahmed. Swiftly, the group took hold of key government posts and guaranteed a relatively cohesive decision-making process during the 1980s and 1990s.[93] The Sudayris are linked to a preference for an ever-stronger relationship with the US and a harsher stance against Iran. Moreover, they tend to lay off calls for affronting Washington, even on issues such as the Palestinean cause, if that could damage their special partnership with Washington.

Khalid and Fahd had to face domestic and international threats that increased the country's sense of vulnerability. When it comes to the Iranian Revolution, Khalid did not immediately condemn or reject it. Initially, he sought a new diplomatic arrangement that did not harm regional stability. In this sense, the Revolution prompted a wait-and-see process in which the monarchy started to evaluate whether Iraq was still the most direct threat or whether the scenario had changed.

They sought coexistence with Khomeini's regime based on their shared Islamist credentials. Reportedly, King Khalid congratulated the *Ayatollah*, calling 'the revolution a beginning to further closeness and understanding', while Fahd added he had 'great respect for Iran's new leadership'.[94] It was visible that the monarchy initially tried to establish a dialogue with the Iranian leadership. Nevertheless, Iranian rhetoric, increasingly more hostile to monarchies and the West, amplified Saudi leaders' judgment that Tehran was not interested in working relations. Gradually, Fahd assumed the sectarian approach to respond to the Iranian rhetoric as well as to discredit Khomeini's image towards the international *ummah*.

Particularly after the Mecca siege, Fahd became more interested in reaffirming Saudi Arabia's unique Islamic role to international audiences. Therefore, he enhanced his own credentials as a religious leader, particularly among the Sunni community. For example, in 1986, he changed his title from 'Your Majesty the King' to 'Custodian of the Two Holy Mosques of Mecca and Medina', denoting the fundamental bond between his rule and the protection of Islam. Fahd also incentivised the expansion of Sunni networks worldwide and pushed for the sociopolitical empowerment of the Saudi clerics overseeing the construction of *madrasas* and Wahhabi educational centres outside the country. Fahd also introduced a weekly meeting with the *ulama*, where he boosted the propaganda against Iran's Islamic credentials.[95]

The Shia protests in the East, the tensions during the *Hajj*, and Khomeini's rhetoric led Fahd to conclude that Iran's ideological threat was more substantial than Iraq's. Thus, after 'waiting and seeing',

Fahd publicly stated that the situation in Iran was 'contrary to the interests of Islam, the entire Muslim world, and the stability of the Middle East'.[96] Under this context, the hostility over the *Hajj* kept growing, as Saudi Arabia accused Iran of inciting the Shias during the peregrinations. In an exchange of correspondence, Khalid asked Khomeini to urge his followers to show more restraint, hinting that Iranian pilgrims were corrupting people in Mecca.[97] Therefore, when the Iranians started gaining some ground in the war against all odds, the Saudis felt compelled to support Iraq directly.[98]

Finally, Fahd sought a robust relationship with the US. In a conversation with Reagan, Fahd said he wanted to 'express my satisfaction with the steady growth of relations between our two countries'.[99] As King, Fahd promoted Bandar bin Sultan as the ambassador to Washington precisely to lobby for better military partnership with the superpower.[100]

It is possible to affirm that the monarchy identified the Iranian Revolution and the Siege of Mecca as examples of the inevitable contra-reaction in Islamic societies if subjected to rapid modernisation. Fahd used this realisation to justify more religious control over society and boost the country's international Islamic networks. Here, the leadership variable sheds light on the link between strategy and domestic threats. The King sought to increase the regime's stability domestically via Islamisation and internationally via Islamic solidarity and more muscular strategic coordination with the US.

The stable marriage triangle

Iran became a revisionist country with an Islamist, anti-imperialist, and anti-US self-image. That provoked anxiety in the US and Saudi Arabia, mainly because they relied on Iran to maintain the regional order. Therefore, the Carter administration designed the role of protector of the Persian Gulf for the US. That led to the intensification of securitarian ties with all the remaining monarchies, but especially with Saudi Arabia – coining, therefore, a marriage of convenience between the two. Washington would guarantee security, and in return, Saudi Arabia would coordinate the GCC interests in accordance with the West's interests. The Carter Doctrine and the GCC's foundation reduced the US and Saudi's fears while checking Iranian influence.

While Washington and Riyadh did try to not isolate Iran immediately after the Revolution, Tehran's behaviour became increasingly a menace to both actors. For the US, the new Iranian ethos was irrational and hostile. For Iran, the US were interventionist and exploitative. Moreover, there is a sense of exceptionalism pervading both the US' and Iran's state identities, driving both sides towards similar manicheist conclusions. Whereas the 'city upon a hill' perceives as an enemy any actor hampering the promotion of its open-door policy, the 'Islamic city upon a hill' frames any rejection of its regional role as an act of imperialism and oppression. Thus, both identities blurred the lines for decision-making and obstructed the space for pragmatism, leading to a series of miscalculations that have marked US–Iranian relations.

This new Iranian identity also clashed with Saudi Arabia's identity, and both started to compete as two different projects of Islamist leadership. Clashes began as Iranians attempted to politicise the *Hajj*. Indeed, for Khomeini, the *Hajj* was an 'ideal stage for demonstrating its [Iran's] continued political vitality' and a 'potent instrument for undermining Saudi Arabia'.[101] In 1987, Iranian supporters in Mecca triggered a violent reaction from Saudi police, resulting in around 400 deaths, more than 270 Iranians. The Supreme Leader accused the Saudi monarchy of being incapable of securing the holy cities, raging that they were 'like daggers which have always pierced the heart of the Muslims from the back'.[102] In the sequence, demonstrators in Tehran sacked the Saudi Arabia embassy, killing one diplomat. In response, the Saudis broke diplomatic relations with Iran, banning Iranians from getting a visa to perform the pilgrimage.

Simultaneously, it was clear to Washington and Riyadh that they needed to intensify their relations as Iran became a liability. King Fahd presented his country as the West's remaining partner against radicalism and communism in the region. Carter initiated a massive arms transfer scheme and training programme for the monarchy. For Reagan, selling advanced equipment and a range of high-tech missiles was to 'help our friends defend themselves against the forces of radicalism and terror'.[103] Interestingly, Fahd agreed to finance Reagan's global campaign against the Soviets (which included a monthly allowance to the Contras in Nicaragua), and both countries gradually increased their commitment to the Afghani *mujahedins*.[104] In return, Saudi Arabia used its dominating role in OPEC to keep the oil prices stable despite the ongoing wars.

Hence, the term 'oil-for-security partnership' emerged. Fahd praised Reagan for 'more than anyone else, realise the extent of the importance of this equipment for strengthening my country's security and protecting it', and Reagan assured that he valued 'the strong and solid cooperative relationship', and he would 'meet our responsibilities towards the pursuit of peace, security, and prosperity'.[105] Saudi and US leaders perceived the Soviet presence in Afghanistan and the Iran–Iraq war as proof of an 'arc of crisis' jeopardising regional security. This partnership was openly conservative, and leaders used a religious overtone to justify it.

Brzezinski told Prince Saud that their main common interest was the 'belief in God and religious values, which affect the way in which we approach things'.[106] Similarly, Fahd stated, 'Saudi Arabia, with its Islamic beliefs and principles, and the United States, with its ideals and values, can together find a common ground against aggression, injustice, and oppression'.[107]

The further deterioration of the Iran–Saudi ties is directly linked to strengthening the US–Saudi friendship. For revolutionary Iran, Saudi Arabia was complicit with West imperialism in the region. Khomeini's rhetoric defined the Saudis as 'vessels' or 'lackeys' of Washington. On his last will, he wrote: 'Saudis, may God's curse go to them, these conspirators against the House of God: they should be condemned firmly'.[108] This language was also visible at OPEC during the period. Iran accused Saudi Arabia of boosting its production whenever there were regional shortfalls as a way to harm the Iranian economy.[109]

In this context, sectarianism became a tool for the Saudi monarchy to check the spreading of Iran's influence. Saudi leadership understood that domestic instabilities – like the protests in the Eastern province and the demonstrations during the *Hajj* – could be tackled with a harsher stand against Shiism and an intensification of the more conservative religious discourse. Therefore, it shows how Saudi Arabia was omnibalancing threats from domestic, regional, and international levels simultaneously.[110]

Regarding the US–Iranian relation, a change in tone from Carter to Reagan is noticeable. Carter's tendency towards progressive internationalism restrained him from military action during the hostage crisis. In contrast, Reagan was not keen on reaching a diplomatic settlement with the country. That did not impede him from allowing a secret deal that sold arms to Iran via Israel, in which the sale money was used to support anti-communist forces (the Contras) in Nicaragua. When the deal came to light in 1986, many in the Middle East were stunned, pointing to the US hypocrisy of selling armaments to both sides in the war. For Iranians, it was further evidence that the US was 'willing and able to circumvent even its own laws' to undermine them.[111] If the hostage crisis was a cornerstone for the US Americans to see Iranians as irrational actors, the Contras affair further strengthened the Iranian view that the US were always up to no good in the region.

It is interesting to stress that the Saudi monarchy attempted to mediate the Iran–Iraq war with the implicit authorisation of the US. To Fahd, Reagan guaranteed: 'we share your concern that an Iranian victory is likely to put further pressure on our friends in the area' and the US 'has limited influence with either belligerent. I would appreciate your majesty views on the prospects for Islamic mediation'.[112]

In 1985, Fahd visited Iran to offer help to end the war. However, Khomeini demanded Saddam's deposal and an observer's position in Mecca and Medina, which the King was unwilling or unable to give.[113] More than once, Saudi Arabia publicly regretted Tehran's intransigence and accused it of being a regional destabiliser.

> The Kingdom of Saudi Arabia has tried during the past eight years to maintain normal relations with Iran in the hope of preserving links and maintaining good- neighborliness; it has tolerated many acts and provocations against itself and its people. But Iran has missed no opportunity during those years to demonstrate a hostile attitude towards the Kingdom and the Arab Gulf countries.[114]

While Iran never directly threatened the Saudis during the war, it attacked Saudi ships in May 1984, triggering significant US deployment to the region. In retaliation, Saudi AWACS ambushed Iranian fighters and shot down two aircraft in June. The US interpreted Iranian activity as evidence of hegemonic intention and intervened more directly in the conflict. Showing signals of severe health problems, Khomeini finally relinquished in July 1988, and Iran accepted the ceasefire. With no substantial interest in conflict resolution but also no significant gains, Iran and Iraq continued their hostile relationship.

Along with the 1953 coup and the Contras affair, the US shootdown of Iran Air Flight 655 became another substantial grievance in the Iranian collective memory. By the decade's end, the anti-US sentiments proclaimed by the Revolution were ingrained into Iranian identity. Therefore, the Revolution affected the US power projection not only by losing an ally but also because Iran's political Islam strengthened anti-US feelings all over the Middle East. Conversely, the fear of Iran exporting its Revolution drove the US–Saudi securitarian partnership.

By the time the war ended, Iran was politically and diplomatically isolated, sharing diplomatic ties neither with Washington nor Riyadh, while the US–Saudi relations were at their most decisive moment. When Khomeini was on his deathbed in June 1989, many expected that his death would also mean the regime's end. However, the ascension of new political voices in Iran coincided with yet another balance of power change in the Persian Gulf: Saddam's 1990 invasion of Kuwait. As the next chapter discusses, these events created space for Iran to rearrange its position within the international community and, hence, transforming the triangle.

*

The events of 1979 pushed the triangle towards a 'stable marriage' type, in which the US–Saudi Arabia relationship grew strong due to a restrictive securitarian environment. In contrast, the other two relations became increasingly hostile. This chapter showed how the Islamic Revolution and the Iran–Iraq War undermined the harmony between Iran, Saudi Arabia, and the US. While these events provoked a massive disturbance in the distribution of power within the system, the balance of power analysis alone does not explain how Saudi Arabia and the US shifted their position in favour of the stronger regional actor, which was traditionally close to the URSS. It also does not explain why Iran avoided maintaining its previously close ties with the West while not pursuing a realignment towards the Soviets. The NCR analysis, however, explained the process of decision-making that drove the consolidation of the US–Saudi special relationship and Iran's isolation.

Like the Twin Pillar Diplomacy period, each of these three countries organised their strategy according to their interpretation of the other two's actions. The US presidents and the Saudi kings justified growing military co-operation as a response to Iran's expansionism. Conversely, Iran promoted revolutionary Islamism as a liberation project from arrangements like the Saudi–US partnership. When it became clear that Iran would not fall under Soviet influence, the anxiety in Riyadh and Washington was reduced. Leaders in Tehran and Washington were guided by manicheist views of their country's role that conveyed an enmity between the two that prevails today. In their turn, Saudis had few chances to escape the spillover effect of this enmity. As the remaining pillar of the previous strategy, it would be naïve to imagine something other than Riyadh boosting its ties with the superpower. Doing that allowed Iran to further condemn the monarchy's behaviour and question its Islamic role. Consequently, sectarianism became a tool for the Saudis to respond to Iranian accusations as well as halt its influence, which quickly became the main threat to a regional order – in both Washington's and Riyadh's perception. A triangulation indeed.

Notes

1 Abrahamian, *A history of modern Iran*, p. 161.
2 World Bank, GDP growth (annual %) – United States: 1961–2019.
3 World Bank, Military expenditure (% of GDP) – United States: 1960–2019; World Bank, Military expenditure (current USD) – United States: 1960–2019.
4 Phil Williams, The limits of American power: from Nixon to Reagan, *International Affairs* 63: 4, 1987, pp. 575–587, p. 581.
5 David Isemberg, *The rapid deployment force: The few, the futile, the expendable, Policy analysis No. 44* (Washington, DC: Cato Institute, 1984).

6 Ward, *Immortal*, p. 273; Hal Brands, *Making the unipolar moment: U.S. foreign policy and the rise of the post-Cold War order* (New York: Cornell University Press, 2016), p. 329.

7 Brands, *Making the unipolar moment*, p. 239; Janice G. Stein, The wrong strategy in the right place: The United States in the Gulf, *International Security* 13: 3, 1989, pp. 142–167, p. 147.

8 Isemberg, *The rapid deployment force*.

9 Oren, *Power, faith and fantasy*, p. 548.

10 From August 1985 to March 1987, the US agreed to sell arms to Tehran in exchange for their help on releasing American hostages held by Hezbollah in Lebanon, despite being openly supporting Iraq on the Iran–Iraq war. To make the plot even more complex, the money of the sell was sent to the anti-socialist militia Contras in Nicaragua with the help of the Israelis.

11 Brands, *Making the unipolar moment*, p. 239.

12 Stein, The wrong strategy in the right place, p. 158.

13 Hiro, Cold War in the Islamic world, p. 62; Ward, *Immortal*, p. 241.

14 Seliktar, *Navigating Iran*, p. 15.

15 Ward, *Immortal*, p. 296.

16 Saikal, *Iran rising*, p. 131.

17 World Bank, GDP growth (annual %) – Iran, Islamic Rep.: 1961–2019.

18 World Bank, GDP per capita (current US$) – Iran, Islamic Rep.: 1960–2019.

19 Abrahamian, *A history of modern Iran*, p. 176; Hadi S. Esfahani and Lyn Squire, Explaining trade policy in the Middle East and North Africa, *Quarterly Review of Economics and Finance* 46: 5, 2007, pp. 660–684.

20 Seliktar, *Navigating Iran*, p. 29.

21 Ward, *Immortal*.

22 World Bank, Military expenditure (% of GDP) – Iran, Islamic Rep.: 1960–2019; World Bank, Military expenditure (current USD) – Iran, Islamic Rep.: 1960–2019.

23 Ward, *Immortal*, p. 246.

24 Abrahamian, *A history of modern Iran*, p. 176.

25 Singer, Bremer, and Stuckeym, Capability distribution, uncertainty, and major power war, 1820–1965.

26 Ehteshami, Iran and its immediate neighbourhood, p. 130.

27 World Bank, GDP (current US$) – Saudi Arabia: 1968–2019.

28 World Bank, GDP growth (annual %) – Saudi Arabia: 1969–2019.

29 World Bank, Population growth (annual %) – Saudi Arabia: 1961–2019.

30 World Bank, Fertility rate, total (births per woman) – Saudi Arabia: from 1960 to 2019.

31 World Bank, Population, total – Saudi Arabia: 1960–2019.

32 Niblock, *Saudi Arabia*, p. 56.

33 World Bank, Military expenditure (current USD) – Saudi Arabia: 1960–2019.

34 World Bank, Military expenditure (% of GDP) – Saudi Arabia: 1963–2019.

35 Aharon Levran, Major Middle East armed forces, in Aharon Levran (ed.), *The Middle East military balance 1986* (New York: Routledge, 2019), pp. 123–205.

36 Singer, Bremer and Stuckeym, Capability distribution, uncertainty, and major power war, 1820–1965.

37 Anthony H. Cordesman, *Saudi Arabia: Guarding the desert kingdom* (Boulder, CO: Westview Press, 1997); Safran, *Saudi Arabia*.

38 Cordesman, *Saudi Arabia*; Levran, Major Middle East armed forces.

39 Safran, *Saudi Arabia*, p. 359.

40 Brands, *Making the unipolar moment*, p. 226.

41 Office of the Chief of Staff Files, Hamilton Jordan's confidential files, Iran, n/d 11/79, Container 34b declassified on 20 August 1997.

42 Office of the Chief of Staff Files, Hamilton Jordan's confidential files, Iran, n/d 11/79, Container 34b declassified on 20 August 1997.

43 Office of Staff Secretary, Folder 10/13/80 Container 180 (Presidential Files, n.d.).

44 Brands, *Making the unipolar moment*, p. 121.

45 Office of the Chief of Staff Files, Hamilton Jordan's confidential files, Iran, n/d 11/79, Container 34b declassified on 20 August 1997.

46 Manouchehr Mohammadi, The Islamic republic of Iran and the international system: Clash with the domination paradigm, in Anoushiravan Ehteshami and Reza Molavi (eds): *Iran and the international system* (London, New York: Routledge, 2012), pp. 71–90, p. 78.

47 Takeyh, *Guardians of the revolution*, p. 16.

48 National Security Advisor, Text of Khomeyni's message on hostage situation (Records of the Office of the National Security Advisor, Carter Administration, 3 October 1980).

49 General A. United Nations, Forty-first session: Provisional verbatim record of the 19th meeting (New York, 1986).

50 Fürtig, *Iran's rivalry with Saudi Arabia between the Gulf wars*, p. 144.

51 Homa Katouzian, The Iranian Revolution at 30: The dialectic of state and society, *Middle East Critique* 1, 2010, pp. 35–53.

52 Chubin and Tripp, Iran–Saudi Arabia relations and regional order, p. 10.

53 General A. United Nations, Forty-first session: Provisional verbatim record of the 19th meeting (New York, 1986).

54 Fürtig, *Iran's rivalry with Saudi Arabia between the Gulf wars*, p. 74.

55 Al-Rasheed, *A history of Saudi Arabia*, p. 151.

56 Niblock, *Saudi Arabia*, p. 68.

57 Ronald Reagan Presidential Library, Folder: Saudi Arabia: King Khalid: (8100189–8102956) Box 29 (Digital Library Collections, n.d.).

58 White House, National Security Decision Directive 139 (Washington, 5 April, 1984).

59 Dueck, *Reluctant crusaders*.

60 Kinch, *The US–Iran relationship*.

61 Ervand Abrahamian, Ali Shari'ati: Ideologue of the Iranian Revolution, *MERIP Reports* 102, 1982, pp. 24–28; Adib-Moghaddam, Discourse and violence.

62 David Meneshari, Khomeini's policy toward ethnic and religious minorities, in Milton Esman and Ilamar Rabinovich (eds): *Ethnicity, pluralism, and the state in the Middle East* (New York: Ithaca Press, 1988), pp. 215–230.

63 Adib-Moghaddam, Discourse and violence, p. 158.

64 Ervand Abrahamian, *Khomeinism: Essays on the Islamic Republic* (Berkeley, CA: University of California Press, 1993), p. 3.

65 Fürtig, *Iran's rivalry with Saudi Arabia between the Gulf wars*, p. 232.

66 For Shia Muslims, Ashura, the tenth day of the first Muslim calendar's month, is a sacred day of mourning and martyrdom, representing the death of Iman Husein in Karbala.

67 Madawi Al-Rasheed, *A most masculine state: Gender, politics and religion in Saudi Arabia* (London: Cambridge University Press, 2013).

68 Hiro, *Cold War in the Islamic world*, p. 64.

69 Yetiv, *The absence of grand strategy*, p. 45.

70 Seliktar, *Navigating Iran*.

71 Oren, *Power, faith and fantasy*, p. 546.

72 Takeyh, *Guardians of the revolution*, p. 43.

73 Ronald Reagan Presidential Library, Collection: Roberts, John G/ Box: 7 (n.d.).

74 Brands, *Making the unipolar moment*, p. 234.

75 Seliktar, *Navigating Iran*, p. 39.

76 Foreign Relations of the United States (FRUS), Letter from President Carter to Secretary of Defense Brown (1977–1980, volume XVIII No. 19, Washington, DC, 9 February 1979).

77 Foreign Relations of the United States (FRUS), Letter from President Carter to Secretary of Defense Brown (1977–1980, volume XVIII No. 19, Washington, DC, 9 February 1979).

78 Foreign Relations of the United States (FRUS), Telegram from the Embassy in Saudi Arabia to the Department of State and the Department of Defense (1977–1980, volume XVIII No. 215, Jidda, 13 May 1980).

79 Foreign Relations of the United States (FRUS), Memorandum from Gary Sick and Fritz Ermarth of the National Security Council Staff to the President's Assistant for National Security Affairs (Brzezinski), 19 June 1979, Washington, DC (1977–1980, volume XVIII, 24).

80 Foreign Relations of the United States (FRUS), Minutes of a Special Coordination Committee Meeting (1977–1980, volume XVIII, Washington, DC, 11 May 1979).

81 Jimmy Carter (23 January 1989): State of Union Address 1980. Washington, DC. Available at www.jimmycarterlibrary.gov/assets/documents/speeches/su80jec.phtml. Accessed on 10 October 2018.

82 Ronald Regan Presidential Library, Collection: Roberts, John G/ Box: 7 (n.d.).

83 Williams, The limits of American power; Oren, *Power, faith and fantasy*, p. 550.

84 Brands, *Making the unipolar moment*, p. 237.

85 Takeyh, *Guardians of the revolution*, p. 93.

86 Behrooz Moazami, *State, religion, and revolution in Iran, 1796 to the present* (New York: Palgrave Macmillan US, 2013), p. 134.

87 Saikal, *Iran rising*, p. 45.

88 Ruhollah Khomeini, *Islam and revolution: Writings and declarations of Imam Khomeini*, Contemporary Islamic Thought (Berkeley, CA: Library of Congress Cataloguing in Publication Data, 1981, Persian Series).

89 Khomeini, *Islam and revolution.*
90 Eva P. Rakel, Power, Islam, and political elite in Iran: A study on the Iranian political elite from Khomeini to Ahmadinejad (PhD thesis, Amsterdam: Amsterdam Institute for Social Science Research, 2008), p. 151; Takeyh, *Guardians of the revolution*, p. 18.
91 *New York Times*, Excerpts from Khomeini speeches, 4 August 1987.
92 Hiro, *Cold War in the Islamic world*, p. 84; Riedel, *Kings and presidents*, p. 86.
93 Al-Rasheed, *A history of Saudi Arabia*, p. 143.
94 Keynoush, *Saudi Arabia and Iran*, p. 101.
95 Niblock, *Saudi Arabia*, p. 65.
96 Okruhlik, Saudi Arabian–Iranian relations.
97 Martin Kramer, Behind the riot in Mecca, *Washington Institute for Near East Policy 5*, 1987, pp. 1–10.
98 Safran, *Saudi Arabia*, p. 364.
99 Presidential Library and Museum, Remarks at the welcoming ceremony for King Fahd bin Abdulaziz Al Saud of Saudi Arabia (Washington, DC, 11 February 1985).
100 Keynoush, *Saudi Arabia and Iran*, p. 118.
101 Chubin and Tripp, *Iran–Saudi Arabia relations and regional order*, p. 16.
102 Martin Kramer, *Arab awakening and Islamic revival* (New Brunswick: Transaction, 1996), pp. 161–187.
103 Presidential Library and Museum, Statement by Principal Deputy Press Secretary speakers on the Congressional disapproval of the United States arms sale to Saudi Arabia (7 May 1986).
104 Al-Rasheed, *A history of Saudi Arabia*, p. 154; Riedel, *Kings and presidents*, p. 90.
105 Ronald Regan Presidential Library, Folder: Saudi Arabia: King Khalid: (8100189–8102956) Box 29 (Digital Library Collections, n.d.).
106 Foreign Relations of the United States (FRUS), Memorandum of conversation (Middle East Region and Arabian Peninsula No. 188, Riyadh, 17 March 1979).
107 Presidential Library and Museum, Remarks at the welcoming ceremony for King Fahd bin Abdulaziz Al Saud of Saudi Arabia (Washington, DC, 11 February 1985).
108 Ruhollah-M. Khomeini, Imam Khomeini's last will and testament (unknown, 15 February 1983).
109 Chubin and Tripp, *Iran–Saudi Arabia relations and regional order*, p. 13.
110 Nonemman, *Analyzing Middle East foreign policies.*
111 Cook and Rawshandil, *The United States and Iran*, p. 27.
112 Ronald Regan Presidential Library (n.d.): Folder: Saudi Arabia: King Khalid, Box 29. Executive Secretariat, NSC (Digital Library Collections). Accessed on 5 October 2018.
113 Fürtig, *Iran's rivalry with Saudi Arabia between the Gulf wars*, p. 68.
114 United Nations, General Assembly: Provisional verbatim record of the Fifteenth Meeting (New York, 28 September 1987).

5

The romantic triangle (1989–2003): The Saudi–Iranian rapprochement

The revolutions of 1989 and the fall of the Berlin Wall announced the ending of the Cold War. By December 1991, the Soviet Union was gone, and the bipolarity that defined international relations had vanished. The 1990s were perceived as a decade of unipolarity. Global political preferences shifted towards an overwhelming assimilation of Western capitalist values and norms in a context in which the US presented itself as the winner of the Cold War. Those who did not adopt the Washington Consensus were cast as rouge states challenging the new order or failed states incapable of embracing the capitalist and liberal model.

This new order first tested its grounds in the Persian Gulf. On 2 August 1990, Iraqi troops invaded and occupied Kuwait. The Kuwaiti military was forced to surrender, and the royal family had to flee. Many motives led Saddam Hussein to the attack. First, he accused Kuwait of not following oil-producing quotas and practising price-dumping, consequently harming the Iraqi economy. Second, Iraq was highly indebted to Kuwait, but it was unable to pay it back. After the Iran–Iraq war, Saddam asked for a debt pardon, but Kuwait refused, adding more fuel to the fire. Finally, Iraq also had historical claims over the Kuwaiti territory, which the Emir obviously denied.

If Saddam succeeded in his occupation, Iraq would most probably become an oil superpower, owning around 10 per cent of the world's oil reserves. Thus, it was up to the US to honour its commitments established with the Carter Doctrine. Seeking how to tackle this crisis, President George H. W. Bush quickly built an international consensus against Saddam. Many, particularly the Europeans, were anxious about the possibility of another major oil price shock and endorsed the US call for direct action to expel the Iraqis from Kuwait. Therefore, on 2 August, the UNSC adopted Resolution 660, demanding an immediate withdrawal of the Iraqi troops from Kuwait and threatening military action. Interestingly enough, Moscow sided with Washington, solidifying the idea of a rising unipolar moment.

Thus, the US military began Operation Desert Shield in Saudi Arabia to prepare for fighting against Iraq. On 29 November, the UNSC passed

Resolution 678, demanding Saddam to depart from Kuwait until 15 January 1991. Finally, a day after the deadline, the US coalition began Operation Desert Storm – an extensive aerial bombing that lasted forty-two days. Iraq was forced into a ceasefire by 27 February. By the end of the commonly called Gulf War, Iraq's army was reduced to half its size, and its navy was destroyed. The Iraqi economy was shattered. With almost no country siding with Saddam, the country was politically isolated.

Nevertheless, Saddam remained in power, reeling against rebel Kurds, Shias, and domestic opposition. While it received massive support from the West and most Arab countries during the Iran–Iraq war, Saddam's regime was now framed as one of those rouge states that 'needed to go'. Throughout the 1990s, Washington orchestrated many rapid preventive operations against Iraq, such as the 1998 Desert Fox. The Persian Gulf's balance of power was, once again, changed. It was up to the countries to reassess their threats and preferences.

US power: the unipolarity moment

Without any rival able to match its military or economic capabilities, Washington had greater autonomy to spread its liberal economic model throughout the 1990s. The economy was booming: the GDP growth rate went from 1.8 per cent in 1990 to 4.1 per cent in 2000, closing at 2.8 per cent in 2003.[1] Whereas the GDP was US$ 5.9 trillion in 1990, it reached US$ 11.4 trillion in 2003.[2] The favourable economic moment was related to lower energy prices, reduced inflation, lower unemployment, deregulation, and the birth of e-commerce. However, this economic boom was concentrated in bubbles, forcing wages down and raising income inequality, especially among migrant and black communities. The 2001 recession indicated that the economy was vulnerable to business cycles and incapable of redistributing capital more equally. After the 9/11 terrorist attacks, homeland security investment massively increased, leading to a new era of public deficits.

The end of the bipolarity enabled a reduction in the military budget, which started with President George H. W. Bush and accelerated with President Bill Clinton. The budget was affected by a national spending reorientation: in 1990, the military budget represented 5.6 per cent of the GDP, 3.1 per cent in 2001, and 3.8 per cent in 2003.[3] Therefore, spending was reduced from US$ 325 billion in 1990 to US$ 298 in 1999, only to skyrocket after the 9/11 attacks, reaching US$ 440 billion in 2003.[4] Nevertheless, the US was still the most extraordinary military power in the world. Moreover, it was the only country capable of projecting its power worldwide through its many defence commitments overseas. For example, around 200,000 troops remained deployed in Western Europe and Northeast Asia.[5]

The quick defeat of Iraq was an example of the US success in the so-called Revolution of Military Affairs, which concerned the technological transformations that were changing the nature of war. Modern warfare turned towards non-armed vehicles and precision weapons capable of hitting targets selectively and avoiding higher civilian casualties. By forcing Saddam out like it did, Washington proved its global technological and tactical superiority. Moreover, its participation in the conflict definitely bound the US to the Persian Gulf security. It brought to Saudi Arabia around 250,000 troops, accompanied by heavy airpower and machinery. When the war started, the coalition had nearly 550,000 personnel, 2,000 tanks, 1,900 aircraft, and 100 warships at its disposal.[6] From those, around 20,000 troops remained in the region.[7] In Saudi Arabia, 5,000 military personnel and 30,000 civilians, plus the Combat Air Operations Centre, remained.[8] Washington also invested heavily in patrol, policing, infrastructure, and logistic improvements via security cooperation with the GCC countries.

Therefore, the US reinforced its power projection in the region by promptly allocating forces and setting preventive missions against Iraq. CENTCOM expanded bases in Bahrain, Oman, Qatar, and the UAE. In 1994, Operation Vigilant Warrior positioned more than 50,000 troops, an air carrier, a battle group, and hundreds of aircraft in the region. Surges like those became frequent, showing the US' capability to deploy forces quickly. In 1995, Operation Desert Fox brought more troops and naval forces to Kuwait and increased personnel in Saudi Arabia to enforce no-fly zones over Iraq. Another deployment in 1999 sent more than 1,000 missiles against 300 Iraqi targets. These recurrent deployments reached new heights as George W. Bush prepared to initiate Operation Enduring Freedom against Afghanistan after the 9/11 terrorist attacks.

US' changeable power

The unipolar moment symbolised a period of self-perceived superiority, high prestige, and low competition for the US. As the only remaining superpower, Washington had a new leadership position and profited from good relations with most countries. NATO's post-Cold War enlargement expanded the US alliances, whereas the broad coalition against Iraq emboldened Washington diplomatically and politically. Focusing on the Persian Gulf, the US fortified its economic, diplomatic, and military relations with all the monarchies throughout the period. Under the scope of the Carter Doctrine, it signed defence agreements with Bahrain, Oman, Saudi Arabia, Kuwait, Qatar, and the UAE, ensuring that CENTCOM had a complex combination of bases, logistical sites, and operational infrastructure at its disposal.

Nevertheless, diplomatic ties with the two largest Persian Gulf countries, Iran and Iraq, remained absent. These two countries rejected the US role as an extra-regional actor and promoted resistance and nonconformity all over the Middle East. Moreover, many Arabs and non-state actors criticised the US political authority in the region, refusing, for example, its solutions for the Israel–Palestinian conflict and condemning the presence of military troops within the monarchies. Among them, there was al-Qaeda, which organised many attacks against the US and its allies throughout the period, leading to the devastating 9/11 attacks. Therefore, it is possible to affirm that anti-Americanism narratives and Islamist terrorist groups' empowerment are directly associated with the US' growing power projection in the Middle East.

The Iranian power: still-standing republic

In June 1989, *Ayatollah* Khomeini passed away, and the transfer of power guaranteed the continuation of the theocratical regime in the hands of *Ayatollah* Sayyid Ali Hosseini Khamenei, the new *Velayat-e faqih*. Despite what many suspected, the government transitioned relatively easily with virtually no disturbance. A constitutional referendum was held on 28 July, eliminating the Prime Minister's position, rearranging presidential obligations, and introducing the Supreme National Security Council. These measures increased the power of the regime's electable executive branch. By the eve of the 1990s, after an eight-year-long war and many sanctions, Iran still looked for ways to stabilise its economic system, but the political one seemed finally consolidated.

Iran began the 1990s in economic distress. The GDP dropped from US$ 124.8 billion in 1990 to US$ 63.7 billion in 1993. With the increase in oil prices in 2001, the GDP started to grow slowly, closing the period at US$ 153.5 billion in 2003.[9] Indicating it maintained its rentier economy, the GDP growth rate fluctuated according to the price of oil: 13.8 per cent in 1989, –1.5 per cent in 1994, and 8.7 per cent in 2003.[10] The currency kept losing value, and foreign debts increased. Despite plans for reform aiming to deregulate and privatise parts of the economy, international embargos and lower oil prices led to a decade of rampant inflation, budget payment problems, and uneven economic development.[11] Iran struggled with high unemployment, feeble health and education sectors, and social inequality.

Militarily, the isolation during the war pushed Iran towards a defence build-up focused on self-reliance and deterrence. The country opted for acquiring denial and retaliatory capabilities, such as long-range ballistic missiles and anti-ship and air defence systems.[12] However, the economic hardship and few diplomatic ties made it hard to reconstruct the military power like in the Pahlavi years. This way, the defence expenditure reflected the revenue variation throughout the decade, ranging from US$ 16.4 billion in 1990, to US$ 1.4 billion in 1994, to US$ 3.7 billion in 2003.[13] Most importantly, the government gave centrality to economic recovery, limiting the military budget to under 2.3 per cent of the total GDP yearly.[14]

It is important to stress that Tehran mastered techniques for rebuilding and repairing existing military equipment that bypassed international sanctions. It invested in deterrence capacitation and asymmetric warfare, including guerrilla tactics and proxy forces. The goal was to make it as hard as possible for others to attack them. Also, Russia, North Korea, and China provided technology for ballistic missiles.[15] Crucial here is to empha-sise that, in January 1995, Moscow signed a deal to rebuild the Bushehr nuclear power plant, which was deactivated in 1979. Nuclear power offers strong deterrence capabilities and can reduce oil dependency. Therefore, Iran started to promote clandestine research activities on dual-use nuclear technologies. That began to garner international concern by the end of the decade, becoming a central issue during the fourth triangle.

Iran had the size, population, and geopolitical importance to become a regional power. Nevertheless, it lacked organisational cohesion, organised and well-equipped forces, and other conventional capabilities. It had an advantage in military personnel, with 440,000 in 1990 and 580,000 in 2003.[16] Moreover, the IRGC kept growing in size, resources, and influence, primarily via its additional branches, the elite Quds Force, and the Basij Resistance Forces. During this period, the IRGC became instrumental in Iranian security architecture due to its ties with regional actors and broad fi-nancial networks.[17] However, the dual military structure – army and IRGC – and the opacity of decision-making within the forces have been a stumbling block to overall Iranian military professionalisation and improvement.[18]

Iran's changeable power

The 1990s improved Iran's international position. First, Tehran created the necessary preconditions to normalise relations with the GCC by condemning the Iraqi invasion immediately and maintaining neutrality during the war. Second, in December 1991, the United Nations acknowledged Iraq as the aggressor of the Iran–Iraq war, ultimately endorsing Iran's claims in the past decade. Finally, without Khomeini's harsh rhetoric, countries in the region seemed more accepting of Iran – or they finally recognised that the Islamic Republic was not a temporary thing. Therefore, Iran resumed diplomatic ties with many neighbours, even hosting the 1997 Organisation of the Islamic Conference in Tehran. An example of this new convivial atmosphere of the

Iranian regime was President Mohammad Khatami's proposition of a global dialogue among civilisations (an antithesis of Samuel P. Huntington's *Clash of civilizations*) at the 1998 UN General Assembly meeting, which other countries warmly embraced.

By the eve of the 2000s, Iran was not the internationally isolated actor it was in the 1980s. Its relations with the GCC improved significantly, and it resumed diplomatic ties with Saudi Arabia in 1991. By the end of the period, Tehran had diplomatic representation in almost all the Persian Gulf states except for Iraq. Iran also mended ties with European countries and expanded its economic, energy, and securitarian relations with the Islamic ex-Soviet states. Finally, it signed economic and securitarian cooperation agreements with China in 1990, Turkey in 1992, and Pakistan in 1995.

Simultaneously, Iran continued to have regional appeal due to its anti-imperialist and resistance rhetoric. In 1991, it hosted an international conference on Palestine as a counterreaction to the Madrid Conference, receiving many key actors against Israeli policies. Moreover, it kept pace with many Islamist political groups, supporting the Lebanese Hezbollah, the Algerian Front Islamique du Salut, the Sudanese Turabi regime, the Palestinian Hamas, the Islamic Jihad Jordanian, the Egyptian Muslim Brotherhood, and the Tunisian al-Nahda Party.[19] It is essential to point out the economic and military links the IRGC developed through the end of the 1980s and the 1990s with countries like Syria, Pakistan, and Sudan. The IRGC has built networks with sub-national, ethnic, religious, and political groups, establishing relationships that expand Iran's strategic interests, influence, and international reach. The Quds Force, for example, conducted operations inside and outside the country, collecting strategic intelligence and providing financial support to other Islamists. By assuring alliances with other revisionist groups, Iran increased its strategic clout while enhancing the popularity of its ideology.

Saudi Arabia's power: restrictive times

Riyadh entered the decade with a substantially weaker financial position than in the 1980s, which was already a decade of deceleration. It faced mounting budget deficits, international debt, and reduced capital reserves due to a decade of low oil prices. Moreover, it had to assume most of Operation Desert Storm's costs and pay for arms contracts arranged before the conflict, amounting to around US$ 60 billion.[20] Forced to borrow from the International Monetary Fund (IMF) for the first time in 1991, the kingdom's foreign debt exceeded US$ 25 billion in 2000, or 15.3 per cent of its GDP. As the 1990s indicated no oil price boom, Saudi Arabia faced cash flow drainage, low infrastructure investment, and growing unemployment. The GDP growth rate went from 15.1 per cent in 1990 to 2.8 per cent in 2002, with the total GDP growing from US$ 117.6 billion to US$ 146.7 billion.[21] This would change only as the oil prices started to increase in 2002. The economy began to warm, closing the period with a growth rate of 11.2 per cent and a total GDP of US$ 214.8 billion in 2003.[22]

Moreover, the demographic boom of the 1970s and 1980s began to pressure the economy as around 50 per cent of the population was under fifteen years old. The elevated natality is a persistent socioeconomic issue for Saudi Arabia, as successive younger generations get increasingly marginalised, with few job prospects and more dependent on welfare state benefits. During the 1990s, such stagnation started to pressure the government. Some people complained about economic mismanagement and questioned why the US soldiers remained in their territory.[23] Many young Saudis were disillusioned with West-like modernisation and joined fundamentalist groups to express their frustration – creating new domestic securitarian pressures for the regime.[24]

Pressured, the King published the Basic Law of Government in 1992, which formalised the responsibilities of many governing institutions. While the document appeased the *ulamma* by reinforcing the link between the family and conservative religious values, it did not satisfy fundamentalists (such as Osama bin Laden), who kept accusing the monarchs of political and religious corruption. Between 1995 and the end of the period, Saudi Arabia had to grapple with growing terrorist attacks in its territory, especially against foreigners based there – the 1996 Khobar Towers attacks being the most infamous.[25]

Regarding the military, almost twenty years of high defence-spending were insufficient to protect them during the Gulf War or domestic terrorism. This did not stop the Saudis from applying for even larger arms procurements immediately after the war, even if they had to renegotiate or cancel several contracts for lack of payment capacity. Military expenditure in the period continued to represent a relatively moderate percentage of the GDP: 12.4 per cent in 1990, 14.3 per cent in 1998, and 8.6 per cent in 2003.[26] Interestingly, the Saudis attempted to reduce their dependency on US arms supplies by diversifying suppliers, but the strategy bore very few fruits.[27]

Like the previous period, Saudi Arabia focused on defence capabilities, investing in armour, air defence weapons, and anti-tank artillery.[28] They also acquired a relatively sizeable possession of modern air defence weapons. Nevertheless, their inventory was still the third largest in the region, after Iran and Iraq. While the country managed to develop the necessary facilities, infrastructure, and equipment to support its forces in peacetime, it did not adopt a modern management system adequate to support mobile combat operations. By the end of the period, the country remained highly dependent on US security and military technology and lacked the training to operate most of the acquired equipment.[29] Moreover, the military personnel remained low: 146,000 in 1990 and 215,000 in 2002.[30] This way, despite the high investment, military resources and expertise remained weak in Riyadh's capacity to project power.

Saudi's changeable power

With the end of the Cold War, the new political configuration opened space for Saudi Arabia to resume its relations with Russia, China, and the newly unified Yemen. It signed a border agreement with Yemen in 2000 as well as a free-trade agreement with Syria in 2001, and a customs union with the GCC members in 2003. It also officialised diplomatic ties with Iran and engaged in bilateral diplomatic activities with Egypt and Syria, improving its regional reach and political clout. On the other hand, the Gulf War exposed the GCC's inability to act as a cohesive actor in the conflict, as the monarchies preferred bilateral agreements with the US. That weakened the organisation as a collective security initiative and increased the monarchies' dependency on Western providers.

Unsurprisingly, Saudi Arabia's ties with the US Americans strengthened by receiving the troops. At the end of 2001, 316 US Americans worked in training missions with the Saudis and other Marines, Navy, and Air Force personnel.[31] That gave Saudi Arabia a sense of security in the post-Cold War scenario as it maintained its strategic relevance to the superpower. However, that did not come without domestic and regional controversy. As already mentioned, some regional actors saw the US role as increasingly invasive and not in favour of Muslim interests. Indeed, the 1990s were marked by a growing anti-Americanism in the Islamic world that spread over Saudi Arabia. By hosting the troops and increasing its military dependence, the Saudi monarchy was often accused of subservience, diminishing, thus, its regional appeal.

Finally, the US–Saudi relationship was shaken by the 9/11 events, as a wave of harshly critical commentary from journalists and politicians stressed the limits of the two countries' cooperation. Considering that fifteen out of the nineteen aircraft hijackers were of Saudi Arabian nationality, Riyadh's international image was up for harsh scrutiny. Washington imposed visa restrictions, froze assets of various Islamic charities, and incarcerated hundreds of Muslims in black-site prisons. Nevertheless, Saudi Arabia's political, economic, and securitarian relations with the West continued to be strong, mainly because of oil and collaboration in counterterrorism operations.

The Persian Gulf's balance of power in the 1990s

The Gulf War sedimented the bipolarity's end and demonstrated the US' ability to protect the regional order. Washington strengthened its permanent military presence so it could quickly be deployed and made necessary defence arrangements with all the GCC countries to ensure its interests in the region. Moreover, the conflict shifted alliances once more: previously supported virtually by all Arab countries and most of the West during the war against Iran, Iraq was now bad news in the Middle East – or, in the lexicon of the times, a rogue state. If, in the 1980s, the pendulum for regional hegemony gravitated towards Baghdah, it had ultimately lost that orientation in the 1990s.

Very dependent on their hydrocarbon sector, Saudi Arabia and Iran felt the second decade of low oil prices heavy on their economies. Far from a period of ascension, they were in dire need of reassessment. However, the changes in how the world perceived Iraq played in Iran's favour, improving its image and external relations and expanding ties with the GCC, Europe, and the ex-Soviet countries in Central Asia. In turn, Saudi Arabia improved its position as a US securitarian partner despite economic hardship. Unlike Iran and Iraq, it was not grappling with war damages, political isolation, or economic sanctions. However, it was still behind Iran and Iraq regarding military personnel and could not sustain extended operations if needed. Additionally, the permanence of the US troops harmed their image among the Arab masses. Therefore, no pendulum was going towards either actor's direction.

Finally, while the UN sanctions weakened Iraqi conventional capacities and the war isolated it politically, the country continued to threaten Iran and the GCC countries. Iraq retained around 50 per cent of its pre-war military capacity and managed to reconstitute around twenty-eight of its fifty-seven forces divisions.[32] Throughout the decade, both Tehran and Riyadh supported and maintained working ties with different Iraqi opposition groups in the hopes that they would eventually overthrow Saddam. The US also coordinated several operations to disrupt Saddam's regime during this period. These operations showcased that Washington had entered a new chapter in its warfare history due to the employment of a combination of superior airpower, weapons of more advanced technology, lightning-fast ground mobility, and new tactics. It found itself in a uniquely relaxed position throughout the 1990s, no longer worrying about the Soviet Union, with unmatched military power and cheap access to oil.

This chapter argues that the 1990s was a decade of missed opportunities for improving all the relations within the triangle and developing a more sustainable regional security. The three agreed that Iraq was the most significant threat. Relations between the US and Saudi Arabia were solid and primarily security-oriented. Nevertheless, only Saudi Arabia managed to find a modus vivendi with Iran. In contrast, the hostility between the US and Iran continued despite attempts to reduce it. Therefore, to explain why the triangulation evolved from a 'stable marriage' to a 'romantic triangle' instead of returning to a '*ménage à trois*', it is necessary to explore the intervening variables.

US status satisfaction: the sole superpower

The unipolar moment meant for the US that the liberal, capitalist, and democratic model could be universalised. That drove it to expand its global influence. After the success in Kuwait, President George H. W. Bush's 'new order' seemed to be established, with the US being the most powerful country in the world. In this scenario, the US promoted itself as the 'benevolent leader' with an unequivocal solution to the world's problems: its own political model. President Clinton later coined the term 'indispensable nation', labelling the US as a country that cannot 'allow itself to be challenged with impunity by much less well-endowed political actors'.[33]

However, adapting to unipolarity was tricky, generating a sense of confusion regarding the US' global role and reach. Due to its previously discussed missionary tendencies, the absence of a clear rival made the US aware of any actor contesting or rejecting its superpower position. Hence, through the decade, Washington behaved as a 'worried sheriff', trying to impose its dominance.[34] The narrative of indispensability urged their involvement in successive conflicts in Bosnia, Iraq, Kosovo, and Somalia – with mixed results, to say the least.

Despite the systemic change, Washington did not abandon the Carter Doctrine. The Persian Gulf was crucial because a stable oil market was necessary to expand neoliberal economic values all over the world. Therefore, maintaining the region safe from hegemonic powers was essential. The GCC countries embraced this logic, enhancing their bilateral security ties with the US and reinforcing that the environment was permissive to Washington's interests.

Moreover, it is possible to assume that its role was endorsed by those who supported the intervention against Iraq – especially those that enabled US troops to remain. Therefore, the US was overall satisfied with its ascribed status in the region. Nevertheless, two countries rejected that position: Iraq and Iran. Hence, these 'rogue states' should be contained or converted. Nevertheless, the disproportional power distribution between

Washington, Tehran, and Baghdad meant that the first could draw policies that excluded the last two from its regional security arrangements entirely.

In sum, as a bastion of the capitalist neoliberal model, the US sought to prevent any hegemon from dominating strategic geopolitical regions such as the Persian Gulf. However, as the other variables discuss, the tendency to see international politics as an ideological battle and the absence of a competitor reduced systemic clarity for the country. In some ways, there was 'a misplaced nostalgia for the simplicity of the Cold War and containment' among US politicians.[35] By not altering its ambitions with the end of the Cold War but only expanding them, the US was creating an unmanageable task for itself in which every act of political defiance, no matter where in the globe, could lead to a perception of threat in Washington.

Iranian status satisfaction: recalibrating the tone

The Gulf War did not alter Iran's ambitions, nor its status satisfaction, but affected how permissive it perceived the environment to be. On the one hand, Iraq was isolated, which improved Iran's image. The international community was more willing to accommodate the regime. Hence, Iran amended diplomatic ties with many countries. Moreover, it showcased more moderation in its political standings, and that was well received by its neighbouring countries. This way, the reduced isolation enhanced the country's ascribed status.

On the other hand, the increased US military presence was detrimental to Iran's ambitions, as it was strongly averse to extra-regional actors' interference. As already explained, Iran's ambitions were to be an active player in constructing a regional security architecture. Therefore, its perception of potential risks escalated as thousands of US-American troops arrived. Moreover, the coalition did not overthrow Saddam, who continued to be a lurking threat, disagreeing with Tehran throughout this period over reparations, prisoner exchanges, and border demarcation.

Thus, while the export of the Revolution rhetoric was not abandoned, it gained a facultative feature that could be replaced by promoting Iran's experiment as an example to other actors. In this sense, the missionary spirit was accommodated, and, analogous to the US' ambitions, exporting the Iranian model became the ideal scenario, but that should not be held against national interests. In restrictive environments, the opportunities for revolutionary advances were limited, and pragmatic diplomacy took precedence. However, that does not mean Iran has stopped being a revisionist country. The country continued to be dissatisfied with the fact that most of its neighbours ratified the Carter Diplomacy, which excluded Iran from the Persian Gulf securitarian architecture.

In conclusion, although its position had improved, its peers kept rejecting the leadership Iran believed was naturally hers. Hence, Iran remained dissatisfied with the ascribed status, and the variable continued leaning towards revisionist policies. Nevertheless, an empowered US forced Iranians to calculate their available options with caution, as the system was mostly restricted to its revolutionary rhetoric. Thus, the revisionist behaviour acquired a pragmatic undertone that accepted occasional accommodation.

Saudi Arabian status satisfaction: threats change, again

While Riyadh initially feared its geostrategic relevance would be reduced with the end of the Cold War, the efficiency of the Gulf War reduced the monarchy's anxiety. It showed how ready the US was to ensure its role as a protector of regional order in a post-Cold War scenario. Moreover, by hosting the remaining US troops and training centres, Saudi Arabia gained a new level of strategic relevance. In President George H. W. Bush's words, 'the security of Saudi Arabia is vital – basically fundamental – to US interests and really to the interests of the Western world'.[36]

As already discussed, Saudi Arabia idealised a system in which an extra-regional actor protected the Persian Gulf stability by checking the emergence of a local hegemon. Therefore, the weakening of Iran and Iraq after a decade of fighting, plus the Gulf War, reduced Riyadh's concerns towards the status quo. Nevertheless, it also forced Saudis to reassess who was the most prominent regional threat to order: this time, it was not Iran but Iraq. The Saudis believed that the US decision not to overthrow Saddam Hussein increased the Iraqi threat within the regional environment. Iran, on the other hand, was reducing its own aggressive rhetoric and seeking better regional integration.

Thus, the systemic change altered who Saudi Arabia perceived as the main threat in the Persian Gulf. The need to omnibalance different domestic, regional, and international threats pushed Saudi Arabia to see Iraq as the strongest regional threat. By exploring the possibilities of accommodation with Iran, Saudi Arabia did not become a revisionist actor. It continued to aspire for a security partnership with the extra-regional power, who should, in return, uphold Iran's and Iraq's hegemonic ambitions. The improvement of ties with Iran was possible precisely because Saudi Arabia relied on the US to guarantee order, enabling, therefore, the pursuance of other motivations beyond security. The systemic change only made the environment more permissive and opened a window for improving Saudi–Iran relations.

US state identity: the exceptional model

A fundamental rationale for the US strategy has been to have a clear competitor or rival to compare their values and confirm their superiority. So far, the US creed (individualism, capitalism, and liberal democracy) had opposed the Soviet Doctrine. However, in the 1990s, there was no apparent rival, which provoked inevitable ontological distress. While the policymakers kept having access to the four cognitive lenses (internationalists, nationalists, progressives, and realists), they also had to find ways to interpret the unipolarity moment and the novelty of lacking a clear enemy. How does one define what the US international role is if there is no clear opposing idea of what it is not? Thus, policymakers could see this optimistically, perceiving the unipolarity as favourable for expanding their model via an example, or pessimistically, observing the moment as a global threat, in which case they had to protect their way of living vigorously.

While President George H. W. Bush was a strong realist and sceptical about overly promoting the liberal model, the next two administrations had opposing views concerning unipolarity. President Clinton followed the positive line of thinking, interpreting the unipolar moment as a signal that the world was receptive to the liberal model. Under this version, it was a matter of time for US-American values to become universalised. Therefore, the country's function was no longer to check the influence of the 'red blob' but to expand the 'blue blob' via institutions and policies.

On the other hand, a pessimist interpretation would detect the increasing globalisation as a process that multiplied threats and enemies, endangering the long-term hegemony of the US. President George W. Bush, particularly after the 9/11 attacks, aligned with this interpretation, which helped him build his War on Terror agenda. This view pushed policymakers to inflate threat perception and the definition of enemies, which could be any revisionist state, anti-imperialist ideology, or even the potential emergence of hostile actors, state or non-state.

Iranian state identity: enabling pragmatism

Since the Revolution, Iran's identity has been based on Islamism, Shia values, and anti-imperialist sentiments. It also saw itself as a revolutionary trailblazer and a role model for Muslim emancipation. However, this goal of spreading the Revolution could not sacrifice the state's survival. After almost a decade of war against Iraq, it became clear that Iran could not rely on any external actor to guarantee its survival. A sense of independentism (the need to not depend on anyone) forced Iran's political elite to refocus on regime survival. Thus, with the stabilisation of the political system with Khamenei replacing Khomeini, it became more discernible that this identity permitted pragmatism when necessary.

Therefore, Iranian leaders could grasp that exporting the revolution was not feasible when the environment was too restrictive – thus, pragmatism took precedence over ideological disposition. A more ideology-oriented leader concentrated on the resistance rhetoric, following a more manicheist understanding of international politics. During this triangle period, the Supreme Leader, *Ayatollah* Khamenei, had little predisposition towards pragmatism, and he pushed the revolutionary narrative often – particularly for domestic crowds. Conversely, more pragmatic leaders would reduce this narrative to favour issues that could improve regional alliances, assure economic negotiations, or reduce geopolitical tensions. Both Presidents Akbar Hashemi-Rafsanjani (1989–1997) and the reformist Mohammad Khatami (1997–2003) identified with this more pragmatic interpretation of the state identity.

It is essential to stress that pragmatism does not mean that any principles of the Revolution were lost. Leaders had to follow the cognitive lenses that fostered Iran as a genuine regional leader safeguarding Muslims everywhere, fighting injustice and oppression. Nevertheless, pragmatism oriented them against policies that could erode the regime's autonomy and survival, while ideological interpretations were more risk-prone.

Saudi Arabian state identity: back to pan-Islamism

As already discussed, Islam provided Saudi Arabia with ontological security through an exceptional religious quality that distinguished it from others. Leaders could opt for a more pan-Islamic and/or sectarian approach. While the first focused on all Muslims, the second focused on the Sunni community, particularly distinguishing them from Shias or other revisionist ideologies. When others threatened the Saudi sense of uniqueness, and the environment was perceived as restrictive, leaders were driven towards sectarian interpretations as a way to differentiate the country from others.

However, the Saudi leadership could also reduce the sectarian tone when it saw the environment as less restrictive to national interests and less ontologically threatening. Indeed, during the period, King Abdullah returned to a pan-Islamist lens, promoting Saudi Arabia as a religious leader in the region for all Muslims. Therefore, this lens facilitated the improvement of relations with non-Sunni regional actors and minimised the country's sectarian discourse towards international and domestic audiences.

US leadership preferences: from Bush I to Bush II

This period covers three presidencies that diverged on their enthusiasm towards the unipolarity moment: Republican George H. W. Bush (1989–1993), Democrat William Clinton (1993–2001), and Republican George W. Bush (2001–2009). The first President, George H. W. Bush, was a man of the Cold War. Among his many posts in the government, he served, for example, as Nixon's United Nations ambassador, Ford's China ambassador, and Reagan's Vice President. He was considered a quintessential realist and interpreted liberalism promotion with scepticism, something to be tapped only when serving the country's political advantage.[37] His foreign policy experience was decisive for the Russian transition and the reconfiguration of the European security arrangement. He saw the Cold War's end as a window of opportunity to create a 'new world order' according to Washington's interests. In his words:

> the totalitarian era is passing, its old ideas blew away like leaves from an ancient, lifeless tree. A new breeze is blowing, and a nation refreshed by freedom stands ready to push on. There is new ground to be broken and new action to be taken. There are times when the future seems thick as a fog; you sit and wait, hoping the mists will lift and reveal the right path. But this is a time when the future seems a door you can walk right through into a room called tomorrow.[38]

In the Gulf War, his interest was to restore the status quo ante.[39] Giving continuity to the Carter Doctrine, the goal was to eliminate Iraq's possibility of rising as a regional hegemon while protecting local partners. The President showed no interest in spreading liberal principles and values in Iraq – like his son would later do. In a realist fashion, he aimed to check Iraqi power expansion and showcase US power projection while avoiding long-term political engagement.

George H. W. Bush was also a pragmatist and emphasised the need to work with many influential leaders, regardless if they were in line with US values or not.[40] Under this logic, he reached out to Iran indirectly in 1989 for the first time since the Revolution, arguing that 'goodwill begets goodwill'. Similarly, US officials James Baker and Brent Scowcroft commended Iran's neutrality in the war and were vocal about taking the relationship further.[41] They aimed to obtain Tehran's assistance in freeing US hostages kept in Lebanon. Thus, their justification for improving ties was based on benefiting the US, not for the sake of any internationalist cause.

However, the Democratic majority in Congress hindered most of these attempts as they saw no political advantages in reaching out to Tehran. They rejected Iran's anti-Israel rhetoric and its opposition to the peace process. The US political elite disagreed on whether rapprochement with Iran was worth the sort of 'exasperating and fruitless negotiations that had characterised the hostage crisis and then the arms-for-hostages fiasco'.[42] Many political actors were critical of the rising trade with Iran despite the absence of diplomatic ties. Interestingly, it was during the 1990s that the Israeli lobby's activism in Washington became highly noticeable. Calls for increasing pressure against Iran worked on Clinton's first term.

As a candidate, Bill Clinton capitalised on the idea that Bush was a president stuck in Cold War times. Clinton portrayed his opponent's statecraft as 'plodding, unimaginative and slow to respond to change'.[43] With the motto 'it is the economy, stupid!', he reduced the relevance of great power competition to praise the rise of globalisation and market liberalisation, showing optimism towards unipolarity. Clinton interpreted the US identity via an internationalist lens, believing the permissive environment supported promoting liberal ideas.

First as the attorney general and then as governor of Arkansas, Clinton was linked with the New Democrat movement, which defended cultural liberalism with a more neoliberal stance regarding the welfare state, tax regulation, and fiscal constraints. As President, he oversaw the country's most prolonged economic expansion in peacetimes and signed major international accords such as the North American Free Trade Agreement (NAFTA). His staff included liberals who believed the country should encourage a global upwards spire of prosperity and market integration via free trade and assertive multilateralism. In Secretary of State Madeline Albright's (1993–2001) words: 'we are America; we are the indispensable nation. We stand tall, and we see further than other countries into the future'.[44] According to Clinton,

> we live in times when the spirit of America – our freedom, our vitality, our strength, our respect for others, our commitment to the future – this is a driving force in the lives of millions and millions of peace-loving people all around the world. That is why we're trusted to support the people of the Middle East and the people from South Africa to Haiti to Northern Ireland

to the former Soviet Union in their courageous efforts to escape the shackles of the past and realise their dreams for tomorrow ... like people all over the world who are drawing on our strength and our spirit to make their dreams real, we Americans must renew our own faith in the greatness and unlimited potential of our country.[45]

This world view led Clinton to prioritise the Israel–Palestine peace solution in his Middle East agenda. It is essential to stress that the pro-Israel lobby in Washington gained power and influence during the Clinton administration – both in the Senate and Congress.[46] In the Persian Gulf, he reinforced the Carter Doctrine by formulating the Dual Containment strategy to restrain Iran and Iraq. Clinton aimed to push the two to accept the US' diplomatic, political, and economic predominance, even via force. Interestingly, both Khamenei and Saddam Hussein vehemently criticised how the Israel–Palestine situation was unfolding and blamed Washington for what they felt was unfair towards the Palestinians.

Clinton perceived the US to be so dominant that it could exclude the two 'pariah states' from the Persian Gulf security framework until they changed their behaviours or regimes.[47] In National Security Advisor Anthony Lake's words: 'we no longer have to fear Soviet efforts to gain a foothold in the Persian Gulf by taking advantage of our support for one of these states to build relations with the other'.[48]

Nevertheless, Dual Containment was not equal for both countries. The administration was increasingly assuming a policy of regime change for Baghdad while being more flexible towards Tehran. In his second term, Clinton stated publicly that he did not discard the possibility of dialoguing with Tehran.[49] In fact, after the 1993 and 1995 Oslo Accords, he had more political space to reach out to Iran without domestic critique. Hence, from 1997 to 2000, the administration sent signals to Iran while recognising past mistakes. Clinton publicly recognised Iran's grievances, stating that Iranians had the 'right to be angry at something my country or my culture or other that are generally allied with us today did to you 50 or 60 or 100 or 150 years ago'.[50] Most impressive was Albright's speech at Washington's American Iranian Council, where she praised Iran as a 'blossoming democracy', admitted the US involvement in the 1953 coup, and said Washington and Iran were 'idealistic, proud, family-oriented, spiritually aware and fiercely opposed to foreign domination nations'.[51]

However, the chapter shows this willingness to improve relations was contingent on Iran altering its perceived hostile behaviour first. Clinton's administration employed a tone that often reflected condescendence, demanding Iran to first change towards what the US Americans believed was appropriate for them to then act. Simultaneously, the legislative routinely branded Iran as a 'rogue, terrorist, outlaw or backlash state'.[52] Here, it is important to stress that a world view that implicity or explicitly claims that all countries want to be like the US is never well received by people with a history of anti-imperialist struggle. Therefore, the internationalists showcased their difficulty in dealing with countries that did not agree with the US' role.

Finally, there is George W. Bush. While campaigning, Bush presented himself as a conventional Republican with realist tendencies, more sceptical towards international humanitarian missions and critical of Clinton's multi-lateralism.[53] In his words, 'if we are an arrogant nation, they [other nations] will resent us. If we are a humble nation, but strong, they will welcome us'.[54] He campaigned on more restrainment, promising an external policy driven by national interests rather than a continuation of Clinton's internationalist adventurism.[55] Ironically or not, his administration is mainly remembered for being the opposite of that.

The President had little time to implement his envisioned foreign policy. The World Trade Centre and the Pentagon terrorist attacks on 9 September 2001 forced the administration to adopt a new, assertive strategy. For that, the President embraced neoconservatism – associated with names like Irving Kristol and Robert Kagan. Neoconservatives maintained a neoliberal view of economics while assuming aggressive and proactive international behav-iour. They believed that the end of the Cold War meant a triumph of the US' ideals and the confirmation that they needed to keep upholding their values worldwide in a very proactive way, or else dominance would fade.[56] In this context, the 2001 attacks functioned as a window of opportunity for them to set their political agenda at the forefront of US politics.

One should not think that the process of neoconservatisation of the Republican Party happened in a vacuum – it has been a work-in-progress project since the final years of the Cold War. However, 9/11 gave them a clear enemy: Islamists based in non-liberal countries. Interestingly enough, neoconservatives thrive on narratives that put Christianity as a religion endangered by external actors, and that seems to have resonated with Bush's Evangelical credentials. Assuming that the emergence of terrorist cells within Islamic communities was due to the lack of liberal democracy, the adminis-tration came to terms with endorsing regime-change missions. If diplomacy, deterrence, and containment could not help transform these 'rouge states' into lesser threats, neoconservatives called for the deployment of military power as an instrument of global change. In Bush's words:

> on 11 September, 2001, America felt its vulnerability – even to threats that gather on the other side of the earth. We resolved then, and we are resolved today, to confront every threat, from any source, that could bring sudden terror and suffering to America … America must not ignore the threat gathering against us. Facing clear evidence of peril, we cannot wait for the final proof – the smoking gun – that could come in the form of a mushroom cloud.[57]

The Bush Doctrine was announced in his 2002 State of the Union address and asserted that non-liberal democracies possessing weapons of mass destruction were the biggest enemies of the US – and that pre-emptive action was available. He declared that the country was at war against terror, unleashing the 2001 intervention in Afghanistan. Therefore, for the first time since 1980, the Carter Doctrine was put to the sideline. While the Carter Doctrine estimated that Washington would use forces if its regional partners were under clear threat, the Bush Doctrine aimed at deploying preventive forces to eliminate potential sources of future attacks and change regimes that did not follow the liberal-democratic model.

Therefore, Bush's rhetoric abandoned any sense of realist restraint as he tilted towards an internationalist-vindicative interpretation of the US cognitive function. His rhetoric became extremally moralistic: the country was fighting an 'eternal battle' against evil.[58] In this context, he famously enlisted Iran and Iraq as part of an 'axis of evil' menacing the world's stability. His decision to finally invade Iraq in 2003 under the argument that Saddam was hiding nuclear weapons altered, once again, the Persian Gulf's power balance.

Iranian leadership preferences: the plurality of Rafsanjani and Khatami

So far, this variable has been linked to one man's overwhelming power: first the Shah Pahlavi (1953–1979) and then *Ayatollah* Khomeini (1979–1989). That changed with the Supreme Leader's death and the emergence of greater political factionalism. Throughout the period, two presidents ruled under the aegis of *Ayatollah* Khamenei: pragmatist Akbar Hashemi-Rafsanjani (1989–1997) and the reformist Mohammad Khatami (1997–2003). Despite the *Ayatollah*'s dominant power, these presidents had certain space for political manoeuvre, especially concerning foreign policy, and could tilt decisions in their direction.

Ali Khamenei became the new *Velayat e-faqih* on 4 June 1989, and in the following month, the *Majlis* Speaker Akbar Hashemi-Rafsanjani became President by popular vote. Before being selected as the new Supreme Leader, Khamenei was Iran's President from 1981 to 1989. He was an active figure during the protests against the Shah and well connected to Khomeini. After the Revolution, Khamenei always maintained himself close to power, guaranteeing positions within the Revolutionary Council and the Ministry of Defence. He was also one of the founders of the traditionalist political faction. While clearly a man with political insight and influence, Khamenei lacked Khomeini's popularity or charisma in his first years as a leader.

Moreover, his appointment did not meet all the needed qualifications – for example, he was not a senior cleric – so he had to gradually negotiate with the religious actors and other political factions to construct his authority and assure their loyalty.[59]

For traditionalists, Iran's primary international function was to promote Islamism and reject external interference. Khamenei's biggest foreign concern was cultural infiltration, showing distress by the possibility of Western values subverting the republic's ideals.[60] In his words, 'Iran's enemies, more than artillery, guns, and so forth, need to spread cultural values that led to moral corruption'.[61] For him, there was no bigger enemy than Washington, which he called a 'hegemonic oppressor'.[62] He was against compromising or negotiating with the 'arrogant power', sure that 'the United States has devised a comprehensive plan to subvert the Islamic system'.[63] Therefore, he considered anyone who decided to bargain with Washington to be naïve.

Conversely, President Rafsanjani had a much more practical view of the role Iran could play internationally. Before 1979, he was a well-succeeded businessman from a prominent pistachio-exporter family. A disciple of Khomeini during his Islamic studies in Qom, he was a major fundraiser of the *Ayatollah* when he was exiled. After the Revolution, he assured a position of power within the Revolutionary Council, and when it was dissolved, he was elected for the first *Majlis*, becoming its speaker in 1980. A patriotic, popular, and influential entrepreneur and politician, Rafsanjani was elected in 1989 with an easy majority. For many, he was 'charismatic, capable, articulate, and eloquent'.[64]

Rafsanjani's ideas swung more towards pragmatism and away from the hardliners as he sought to protect Iranian interests and expand its power under what he considered possible.[65] As President (he was re-elected for a second term in 1993), his goal was to reinsert Iran into the international community and reconstruct its economy by attracting investments, improving technological expertise, and reviving domestic markets. For that, Rafsanjani believed reducing the confrontationist ideological rhetoric was essential to improve relations with regional and European countries.

The President belonged to the pragmatic faction, which believed a more tolerant regime was necessary for economic recuperation, and that put them often in opposition with the hardliners. Thus, to avoid resistance from within, Rafsanjani surrounded himself with technocrats, ministries, university professors, and liberal clerics who had more confidence in the regime's resilience in the face of foreign infiltration than Khamenei and the hardliners.[66] His administration was less sceptical towards improving relations with the West as long as that happened on an equal footing and mutual respect. Moreover, upgrading relations with the Arab world and reaching a modus vivendi with the GCC countries was a priority for Rafsanjani, as he said:

> we and they [GCC countries] both have the desire to resolve problems pertaining to bilateral relations. In my opinion, our relations will be normalised in the not too distant future. We did not have expansionist intentions from the beginning, just as our southern neighbours do not have aggressive designs ... We urge our southern neighbours ... to cooperate with us in order to resolve existing issues concerning the oil market, maritime laws and Resolution 598 [i.e. relations with Iraq].[67]

Factionalism gridlock has dominated Iranian politics. The interplay of divergent factions' interests has often led to contradictions, unfulfilled promises, accusations from different sides, and overall difficulty in implementing political change. While Khamenei and Rafsanjani were interested in working together at the beginning of the presidential term, disagreements between their factions over foreign policy and accusations of corruption led to a growing estrangement between both leaders. Traditionalists were against any proximity measure with the US, whereas pragmatics believed some level of understanding was possible. Rafsanjani advised his diplomats to make the US officials 'comprehend that if they are sincere in improving relations with us, the only way is to show goodwill such as releasing our assets ... [this] would enable us to begin a process of détente'.[68] However, with growing factional disagreements, Rafsanjani was forced to renounce these foreign policy goals by the second term.[69]

Nevertheless, this objective of reinserting Iran into the international community was kindled with the presidential election of the reformist Mohammad Khatami in 1997. Khamani was a cleric with two diplomas in philosophy from the universities of Tehran and Esfahan, two secular institutions by the time he graduated. During the 1970s, he studied Western philosophy in Germany and was the head of the Islamic Center in Hamburg. Consistently positioning himself as a moderate, he was elected to the *Majlis* and assumed other ministerial positions in the 1980s. His presidential campaign was under a platform of political reform and advocated for a more open Islamic civil society. Khatami was elected with around 70 per cent of the votes, having the support of intellectuals, the middle class, students, women, and liberals.[70] The *Majlis*, nevertheless, remained highly conservative, and tensions with the new moderate president were there from the start.

Concerning foreign politics, Khamenei sought better integration. He called for a 'dialogue among nations', arguing that all nations, despite cultural and ideological differences, should be able to interact positively with each other.[71] In his view, Islam should be a very useful tool for seeking such cooperation, as the religion emphasises tolerance and coexistence. He believed this dialogue should:

> understand and utilise religion in a way that it is not incompatible with freedom and progress, rather it sets us on a clear path towards the future. Not only in the world of Islam, but in the entire global arena, we must condemn self-centeredness, discrimination, avarice, arrogance and violence anywhere and in any form, so we can have a calm and secure world for all.[72]

Khatami had set three international objectives: normalising relations with the GCC countries, reconciling with the Europeans, and finding an overture to the US. He said that 'our strategy policy is the expansion of friendship with all regional countries. We believe that existing problems in the region can be solved by wisdom, negotiations, and understanding', and that whenever 'regional countries become closer together, they can prevent foreign intervention in the region, which eventually leads to creation of peace'.[73] Therefore, he continued Rafsanjani's policies but with a more internationalist, constructive angle that went beyond the economy. In Khatami's words, Iran was 'in favour of relations with all countries and nations which respect our interests, dignity, and interest', and that 'if we don't have relations with an aggressive and bullying country such as America, it is due to the fact that America does not respect those principles'.[74]

Therefore, both Rafsanjani and Khatami sent signals to the US for rapprochement. Those signals were restrained in the first administration but substantial in the second. For example, in January 1998, Khatami gave an interview with CNN, praising the US-American people, noting both societies' similarities, comparing the US and Iranian revolutions, and even regretting the suffering provoked by the 1980 hostage crisis.[75] He also initiated an exchange programme of scholars, athletes, and businesspeople to the US soon after his election.

Notwithstanding this, factionalism gridlock remained, and many conservatives opposed Khatami's attempts from the get-go. The discussion among the factions was whether the economic benefits of having ties with the US would damage the Revolution's integrity and anti-imperialist resistance. Despite the President's popularity, key actors within the government, especially in the *Majlis* and the IRGC, rejected even the possibility of an agreement with the US. Most importantly, Khamenei openly diverged from the president's intentions towards the West, making it hard for an actual meaningful resolution to come to fruition.

Nevertheless, both Khatami and Khamenei perceived the 9/11 attacks as restricting the environment. Indeed, Iran was one of the first countries to condemn the attacks and send its condolences to US Americans. It became evident to the Iranian leaders that the US would invade Afghanistan with or without regional assistance. Thus, it is possible that Khamenei realised that sending some appeasing signal to Washington was 'a necessary evil' as Bush's new doctrine could come at the cost of Iran's own autonomy.[76] Nevertheless, as these signals were not captured and Iran was added to the 'axis of evil', the people felt it was time to elect Khatami's antithesis in 2005: Mahmoud Ahmadinejad.

Saudi Arabian leadership preferences: the rise of Abdullah

Saddam's decision to invade Kuwait took the monarchy by surprise, pressuring King Fahd to act somewhat quickly. Some princes, including Crown Prince Abdullah, called for an Arab solution via diplomacy and compromise, while others, represented mainly by the Sudayri clan, believed it was mandatory to call foreign troops to increase protection.[77] Fahd's previous experiences with the Siege of Mecca most probably had him realise that, if invaded, the Saudi army was not powerful enough to control different fronts. Moreover, being a Sudayri himself, Fahd tended to perceive the environment, especially after the Gulf War started, as very restrictive for any policy that diverged from the US interests. Therefore, Fahd asked for US military assistance.

As discussed throughout the book, Saudi Arabian strategic preference was to balance Iran against Iraq or vice versa with the support of the US. In this context, Iranian accommodation signals and prompt accusations of Iraq's policies resonated positively with the Saudis. Thus, in 1991, King Fahd restored diplomatic ties with Iran, received the Iranian Foreign Minister in Riyadh, and allowed an Iran delegation to perform the *Hajj* after years of boycott. Nevertheless, it is hard to associate the decision to mend relations with Iran with Fahd only. By the early 1990s, King Fahd's health weakened, and after a stroke in 1995, his brother, Crown Prince Abdullah, became the de facto ruler.

Abdullah has shown greater interest in the development of a more endogenous regional security arrangement. The only son of a Bedouin mother, he had no full brothers and often diverged from the Sudayris on foreign policy concerning, notably, regional matters.[78] Abdullah was closer to King Faysal and became his National Guard commander in 1963. During Khalid's reign, Abdullah assumed the position of Deputy Prime Minister, a role he kept during Fahd's reign as well – something that indicates his continuous closeness to power. During this period, he showed his negotiation skills in mediating regional crises such as the one between Syria and Jordan (1980) and the Lebanese civil war (1990).

Abdullah is described as a nationalist and pragmatic leader, 'more closely attuned to domestic voices than Fahd' and aware of the need to promote gradual socioeconomic reforms.[79] He also emphasised regional collaboration and the independent pursuit of national interests. Among these, the Palestinian cause seemed very close to his heart, and he was less willing than previous leaders to wind down the country's positioning on the Palestinian–Israeli conflict for the sake of Western appeasement. For example, Abdullah pressured for more significant action, even refusing an invitation to the White House until 'something was done'.[80] In his words, 'a time comes when people and nations part. We are at a crossroads. It is time for the US and Saudi Arabia to look to their separate interests'.[81]

For those reasons, he was perceived as 'less friendly' or 'not so intimately tied to the United States'.[82] However, that did not mean he wanted to alter the relations with Washington. Abdullah was a realist and did not allow the relationship to get tainted. The autonomy rhetoric was for regional and domestic audiences, not for Western partners. During the Clinton years, Washington and Riyadh cooperated on a wide range of issues, from peace diplomacy to counterterrorism. Nevertheless, a less nationalist leader or a more US-leaning one may have just subscribed to the Dual Containment strategy without challenging it. However, Abdullah reached out to Iran to manage their tensions under the frame of developing a more endogenous regional arrangement.

Here, it is essential to stress the weight of constructing a more endogenous regional system on the Crown Prince's foreign policy agenda. Abdullah cultivated for himself an image of an efficient leader committed to the Arab cause, domestic socio-economic improvements, and regional causes. Portrayed as a 'natural reconciler', he was very popular among the Saudis and had close ties with many tribes and Arab leaders inside and outside the country.[83] He aimed to improve Saudi Arabia's overall position among neighbouring countries. After Saddam's defeat and Khomeini's death, he saw the regional environment as less restricted for that, which allowed him to seek more constructive regional proactivity. He also realised that showing flexibility in dealing with Iran could strengthen Riyadh's regional appeal. Moreover, it could improve the country's image, tarnished by critics concerning the permanence of foreign troops.

Finally, Abdullah employed a pan-Islamist approach instead of a sectarian one. Closer to his father and King Faisal, he used an inclusive Islamist world view that could guarantee the country a more influential position among spiritual communities.[84] Thus, he called for an 'interfaith dialogue' to reduce the sectarian tone among clerics and members of the monarchy. Abdullah said: 'we have to eliminate the obstacles which block the way [towards amity] and giving counsel on a reciprocal basis between Muslim countries'.[85] Again, improving ties with Iran would be instrumental for this vision. By reaching out to Iran, Abdullah could show his country's willingness to reduce anti-Shia sentiments, push Riyadh away from radical Islamism, and display more autonomy.

However, the 9/11 attacks made the environment restrictive once again, and after the revelation that most attackers were Saudis, the relationship between Saudi Arabia and the US was in danger. Despite the initial refusal to assume responsibility for the events, Abdullah condemned the attack and oriented King Fahd to send condolences. Moreover, in a pioneering move, he proposed during the 2002 Arab Summit Meeting a peace initiative for the Israel–Palestine conflict, promising Arab normalisation if Israel withdrew from occupied territories. He also travelled to Texas in April of the same year to meet President Bush to discuss anti-terrorism measures. Those were clear signals of appeasement and inclination towards Western interests. He eventually understood that intelligence and security cooperation with Washington was a bigger priority to guarantee the national interest than reforming the regional system's cooperation.

The romantic triangle

The systemic change created conditions for the triangle to transform, as the three actors shared a threat perception concerning Iraq. The balance of power could have led to a triangle like the first one (1969–1979), where the three countries had positive relations. However, the intervening variables explain how the triangle evolved instead into a 'romantic triangle', in which one actor, Saudi Arabia, shared positive links with the other two, whereas the US–Iran relations continued to be negative. They also show how Iran and the US were interested in improving ties but failed due to their own constraints. Washington's hyper-sensibility to actors rejecting its 'indispensable nation' role and Iranian factionalism gridlock harmed any attempt to appease tensions during the period. Eventually, the Iran–Saudi cooperation was undermined due to the continuity of the US–Iran enmity.

This romantic triangle had two primary tendencies: the Iran–Saudi rapprochement and the US–Iran failure to reach out to one another. A shared perception of environmental openness allowed Iran and Saudi Arabia to assume pragmatic attitudes regarding regional matters, bringing them closer together. On the one hand, their identities continued to fuel unease between them, and their aspired position for Islamic leadership created competition. On the other hand, a shared perception of improved power position, a less restrictive environment, low oil prices, and the agreeance concerning Iraq created the opportunity for rapprochement. Thus, the rise of pragmatic leaders in Tehran (Rafsanjani and Khatami) and Riyadh (Abdullah) was crucial as they managed to profit from this window of opportunity and mend ties.

President Rafsanjani aimed to reconstruct Iran's economy by rehabilitating the country internationally, primarily via better relations with neighbouring countries. Similarly, Crown Prince Abdullah reduced the country's sectarian tone to constructively engage with other regional actors. Two major oil-producing countries in financial distress were aware of the benefits of improving their economic ties. Thus, they began the first steps to normalisation by lifting trade restrictions. They also decided to work together in OPEC to tackle declining oil prices and cooperating in production quotas. In 1992, Foreign Minister Velayati and King Fahd proposed a joint economic commission.

President Khatami's election coincided with Abdullah's consolidation as the de facto leader, catalysing the normalisation of relations into active cooperation. In this context, Khatami's 'dialogue among civilisations' coincided with Abdullah's 'interfaith dialogue'. A turning point for the Iranian image among Arab countries was when Tehran hosted the Organization of the Islamic Conference (OIC) Summit in December 1997. Abdullah himself attended the meeting, embracing Khatami for photo ops. Many high-level meetings between representatives of the two countries proceeded. Minister Al-Faisal visited Iran several times and, in 1998, he signed a comprehensive cooperation agreement covering finance, culture, trade, science, sports, and technology. In 1999, during a tour to Arab states, Khatami visited Riyadh to discuss a common geopolitical approach concerning oil, Iraq, and other regional issues. Moreover, they signed a Memorandum of Understanding in 2000 to promote trade, investment, and navigation and a security agreement in 2001 focusing on drug-trafficking, terrorism, immigration, and border control. In rare public appearances, King Fahd would urge other Persian Gulf countries to follow Saudi Arabia and improve their own ties with the Iranian nation.

Until the first half of the 2000s, Iran and Saudi Arabia were advancing their cooperation. They openly showed commitment to finding common ground on regional security matters and showed willingness to discuss a defence pact in the future.[86] However, the US–Iranian hostility was a significant constraint on the Saudi–Iranian relationship. Washington was Riyadh's leading security partner, whereas Tehran denounced the US regional role as part of an imperialist agenda. That put Saudi Arabia in a delicate pivot position in the triangular relationship that was hard to maintain in the long term.

Both Iran and the US have exceptionalist identities that oppose one another. That makes any attempt to change relations a complicated and volatile movement. George H. W. Bush appreciated Iran's neutrality during the Gulf War and welcomed the idea of reducing animosity between the two countries. However, his 'goodwill begets goodwill' approach failed to resonate in Iran at the pace the US administration hoped for. After Khomeini's death, Iran's politics became very factionalised, and Khamenei was still consolidating his power. Therefore, any attempt towards normalisation demanded delicate diplomacy on an equal footing approach to not push the conservative faction away. By the time Rafsanjani managed to help with the hostage situation in Lebanon, George H. W. Bush had already snubbed Iran's help due to the delay. Right afterwards, the US Congress signed the 1992 Iran–Iraq Arms Nonproliferation Act, suspending trade with Iran and banning the transfer of technologies.

In his turn, Clinton was inclined towards measures that excluded states that did not conform to the US liberal norm. Under this mentality, he imposed the Dual Containment strategy, which barred Iran and Iraq from the regional security arrangement. Considering that Saddam became the most prominent threat, a realist approach would expect Washington to apply the 'the enemy of my enemy is my friend' tactic and turn towards Iran for appeasement, as it did in the 1980s with Iraq against Iran. However, Clinton was no realist leader, and non-conformist countries like Iran should be contained. Moreover, Clinton was more susceptible to Congress' pressure and passed two executive orders in 1995 to forbid trade with Iran.[87]

These difficulties harmed Rafsanjani's most significant move to reinsert Iran into the international community and improve the country's economy. In March 1995, the Iranian Oil Ministry was about to sign a US$ 1 billion contract with Conoco Inc., a US company, to explore the Sirri oilfield. Initially, the tender was set to be given to French oil company Total. Still, Rafsanjani made the political gamble of offering to Conoco through a Dutch affiliate, in what people interpreted as a way to test the US willingness to advance economic ties.[88] However, the Clinton administration forbade Conoco to sign the deal as it was inconsistent with the Dual Containment strategy. Rafsanjani lamented: 'we chose to show our commitment to rapprochement by allowing a major energy deal to proceed. We had hoped that this would lead to the beginning of wide-ranging cooperation with the US on a political level'.[89] The following year, Clinton signed the 1996 Iran–Libya Sanctions Act (ILSA), which imposed sanctions on foreign companies that invested more than US$ 20 million in Iran.

On 25 June 1996, a terrorist attack bombed the Khobar Towers near US military bases in Dhahran, Saudi Arabia, killing nineteen US personnel.

The US government and the CIA had a case pointing towards Iran but had no evidence to go to court. The Saudis arrested suspects but refrained from handing over the results of their investigations to Washington. Here, it is possible to assume that Abdullah's regional cooperation preferences influenced the kingdom's decision not to fully cooperate with the US. Some analysts argue that the monarchy was divided on whether or not to give the information at the risk of damaging the détente with Iran.[90] Ultimately, and against the US wishes, Riyadh did not release any statement condemning Iran.

A new moment for US–Iranian appeasement began with Khatami's election, which coincided with Clinton's second term. The US seemed optimistic about Iran's reformist movement, sending diplomatic letters and proposing direct talks.[91] Madeleine Albright stated that 'we began to adjust the lens through which we viewed Iran' and that the administration welcomed Khatami's 'call for a dialogue between our people'.[92] Accordingly, they relaxed visas for Iranians in 1997; provided ILSA waivers to foreign companies that wanted to negotiate with Iran and enlisted the Iranian opposition MEK party (*Mojahedin-e Khalq*) as a terrorist organisation in 1998; and repealed some sanctions over food, medicine, and other humanitarian goods in 1999.

However, Iranian factionalism made it impossible for Khatami to respond with concrete policies. Despite his attempts to reciprocate the positive signals, he was engaged in an internal struggle against conservatives and the Supreme Leader concerning foreign policy. Some authors argue that conservatives discarded Albright's approach due to one particular sentence, which was: 'despite the trend towards democracy, control over the military, judiciary courts and police remains in unelected hands'.[93] For some, Clinton was not reaching out to Iranians as peers but as subalterns, still accusing them of being undemocratic. Therefore, Khamenei was not convinced of the advantages of giving a win for the reformist faction, so he shut down any response to Clinton's administration.

Eventually, a third window of opportunity for improving relations came after the 9/11 attacks. In fact, the US decision to invade Afghanistan, as problematic as it was, became an ideal occasion for Iran, Saudi Arabia, and the US to work together. A war against the Taliban appeared to be in the interest of the three countries. Iran promptly engaged in the 6+2 Talks, did not oppose the invasion, and collaborated with Operation Enduring Freedom by offering intelligence and planning assistance and persecuting al-Qaeda and Taliban members.[94] In their turn, the Saudis supported Iran's participation in peace initiatives while granting US Americans access to their command facilities. They also provided humanitarian and financial aid to the operation.

In November 2001, the United Nations held a conference in Bonn to discuss Afghanistan, and Iran and the US collaborated there. Until 2002, officials from both countries also participated in peace talks in Geneva. It is believed that, for the first time, Khatami had the authorisation from Khamenei to improve relations with Washington.[95] Many high-level officials in the US administration, including Colin Powell, seemed to be interested in opening new possibilities for dialogue.[96] For these reasons, Bush's second-term inauguration speech worked as a watershed. By calling Iran a supporter of global terrorism, reformists in Iran felt betrayed, and conservatives felt as though their suspicions were validated. Khatami said to be 'confident that Bush put the final nail in the coffin of Iran–US relations ... any improvements in relations must be ruled out, at least during my presidency'.[97] Khamenei responded with outrage.

Therefore, it is possible to affirm that the US failed to take advantage of the Saudi–Iran rapprochement. Saudi Arabia and Iran demonstrated that pragmatic leaders could soothe ideological and identitarian disputes to improve regional cooperation. Ironically, a willingness to improve ties was also present within the US and Iranian leadership. However, considering how deeply ingrained the US–Iran mistrust is, what was probably missing was an interested third party that could translate their intentions. Saudi Arabia was an excellent choice for mediation. As Abdullah said:

> I do not think it would be difficult for the brotherly Iranian people and its leadership and for a big power like the United States to reach a solution to any disagreement between them ... There is nothing that will make us more happy than to see this sensitive part of the world enjoy stability, security and prosperity ... If the United States asks us we will not hesitate to contribute to efforts to bring stability to the region.[98]

This missed opportunity is related to the US' excessive confidence in its indispensable role. It allowed them to produce a strategy that excluded crucial actors, ignored the growing anti-Americanism, and responded to Iranian overtures condescendingly. This behaviour was combined with bad timing, as the post-Khomeini political scenario was still in its infancy. Moreover, by intensifying its narrative against Iran through sanctions, the US jeopardised the Iran–Saudi rapprochement. As the weakest link within the triangle, Riyadh could not hold for much longer being the pivot actor if tensions increased between the other two. Ultimately, the Saudi–Iran rapprochement also demanded an improvement between Tehran and Washington.

*

The period from 1990 to 2003 was one of the lost opportunities. For the first time since 1979, the three actors shared the perception that Iraq was the leading regional threat. However, that alone does not show how the rapprochement between Iran and Saudi Arabia happened, and the many failed attempts from Iran and the US to do the same. Explanations are located on ideational, identitarian, and leadership variables. On the one hand, Rafsanjani's and Khatami's pragmatism, as well as Abdullah's vision, were vital. On the other hand, Iran's and the US' expectations of their own international role made communication challenging between the two, and they could not find the timing or the equal footing to negotiate.

The 9/11 terrorist attacks restricted the environmental perception for both Tehran and Riyadh. Facing the imminent threat of US intervention in the region, Saudi Arabia began to appease the US to improve its tarnished relations to guarantee security. Also feeling threats increasing, Iran showed even more pragmatism, with Kathami and Khamenei interested in cooperating with Washington. Nevertheless, neoconservatives blinded the Bush administration to these signals, and his 'axis of evil' discourse dissolved this moment of opportunity.

Whereas leadership preferences and status satisfaction explain the motivations for Iranian and Saudi pragmatism, state identity clarifies why advances can only occur via a process of trust-building. That is not to say that the Saudi–Iranian trust-building process was extraordinarily successful. However, they were managing to reduce the suspicions engendered within their identities in favour of mutual goals. However, the continuity of this reconciliation under a restrictive scenario demanded an improvement in the US–Iranian ties, which continued to be permeated by miscommunication and accusations. By 2003, the opportunities visible at the beginning of the period faded. Ultimately, the US decision to invade Iraq, which sidelined both Riyadh and Tehran, entirely altered the triangle's dynamics.

Notes

1 World Bank, GDP growth (annual %) – United States: 1960–2019.
2 World Bank, GDP (current US$) – United States: 1960–2019.
3 World Bank, Military expenditure (% of GDP) – United States: 1960–2019.
4 World Bank, Military expenditure (current USD) – United States: 1960–2019.
5 Yetiv, *The absence of grand strategy*, p. 161.
6 Brands, *Making the unipolar moment*, p. 304.
7 James Wynbrandt, *Brief history of Saudi Arabia* (New York: Facts on File, 2004), p. 266.
8 Niblock, *Saudi Arabia*, p. 117.
9 World Bank, GDP (current US$) – Iran, Islamic Rep.: 1960–2018.
10 World Bank, GDP growth (annual %) – Iran, Islamic Rep.: 1961–2019.
11 Saikal, *Iran rising*, p. 130; Said A. Arjomand, *After Khomeini: Iran under his successors* (Oxford, New York: Oxford University Press, 2009), p. 59.
12 Ward, *Immortal*, p. 309.

13 World Bank, Military expenditure (current USD) – Iran, Islamic Rep.: 1961–2019.

14 World Bank, Military expenditure (% of GDP) – Iran, Islamic Rep.: 1961–2019.

15 Keynoush, *Saudi Arabia and Iran*, p. 35.

16 World Bank, Armed forces personnel, total – Iran: 1984–2018.

17 Arjomand, *After Khomeini*, p. 61.

18 Ward, *Immortal*, p. 304; Saikal, *Iran rising*, p. 149.

19 Anoushiravan Ehteshami, Foreign policy of Iran, in Hinnebusch and Ehteshami (eds), The foreign policies of the Middle East states, pp. 261–289.

20 The costs were from different kinds: direct subvention to the countries that had sent troops, loans to others, especially to the Kuwaitis that took refuge in Saudi Arabia, logistical support for the coalition forces based in Saudi territory, repair of Kuwaiti and Saudi infrastructure damaged in the war, and the costs of the operations of its own forces.

21 World Bank, GDP growth (annual %) – Saudi Arabia: 1968–2019.

22 World Bank, GDP (current US$) – Saudi Arabia: 1968–2019.

23 Al-Rasheed, *A history of Saudi Arabia*, p. 159.

24 Mordechai Abir, *Saudi Arabia: Government, society, and the Gulf crisis* (London, New York: Routledge, 1993).

25 In June 1996, a truck bomb at the Khobar Towers in Dhahran killed nineteen US military. Moreover, in November 1998, a car bomb killed Americans and Indians citizens by National Guards' offices in Riyadh. Also, in 2001, al-Qaeda fired a missile at an American fighter at the Prince Sultan Air Base, and, in 2002, car bomb attacks killed German and British nationals.

26 World Bank, Military expenditure (% of GDP) – Saudi Arabia: 1963–2019.

27 Cronin, Tribes, coups and princes, p. 24.

28 Anthony H. Cordesman, *Saudi Arabia enters the 21st century: The military and internal security dimension: IV. The Saudi Army* (Washington, DC: Center for Strategic and International Studies, 2002), pp. 42–44.

29 Pollack, Saudi Arabia and the United States, 1931–2002, p. 84.

30 World Bank, Armed forces personnel, total – Saudi Arabia: 1985–2018.

31 Cordesman, *Saudi Arbaia enters the 21st century*.

32 Steven A. Yetiv, The evolving Persian Gulf (1979–97): A comparative analysis, *Defense Analysis* 15: 2, 1999, pp. 147–166, p. 147.

33 Tudor Onea, Putting the 'classical' in Neoclassical Realism: Neoclassical Realist theories and US expansion in the post-Cold War, *International Relations* 26: 2, 2012, pp. 139–164.

34 Derek Chollet and James Goldgeier, *America between the wars: From 11/9 to 9/11* (New York: Public Affairs, 2008), p. 131.

35 Chollet and Goldgeier, *America between the wars*, p. 71.

36 Brands, *Making the unipolar moment*, p. 122.

37 Hal Brands, George Bush and the Gulf War of 1991, *Presidential Studies Quarterly* 34: 1, 2004, pp. 113–131; Lawrence Freedman, *A choice of enemies: America confronts the Middle East* (New York: Public Affairs, 2009); Seliktar, *Navigating Iran*.

38 United States, Presidency public papers of the presidents of the United States, George H. W. Bush: Washington, DC (Volume 1A, Part 1, 1989).

39 Brands, *Making the unipolar moment*, p. 227.
40 Chollet and Goldgeier, *America between the wars*, p. 31.
41 Seliktar, *Navigating Iran*, p. 82.
42 Freedman, *A choice of enemies*, p. 298.
43 Brands, *Making the unipolar moment*, p. 279.
44 Interview, Secretary of State Madeleine K. Albright, Columbus, Ohio, 19 February 1998.
45 United States, Presidency, Public papers of the presidents. William J. Clinton. Book II – August 1 to December 31, Washington, DC, 1994.
46 Stephen M. Walt and John Mearsheimer, *The Israel lobby and U.S. foreign policy* (New York: Farrar, Straus, and Giroux, 2007); Trita Parsi, *Treacherous alliance: The secret dealings of Israel, Iran, and the United States* (New Haven, London: Yale University Press, 2007).
47 Alex Edwards, A neoclassical realist analysis of American 'dual containment' policy in the Persian Gulf: 1991–2001 (PhD thesis, 2013), p. 114; Yetiv, *The absence of grand strategy*, p. 103.
48 Anthony Lake, Confronting backlash states, *Foreign Affairs*, March/April 1994.
49 Seliktar, *Navigating Iran*, p. 100.
50 Presidency United States, Public papers of the presidents of the United States: William J Clinton (Book I, Washington, DC, 1999).
51 Madeleine Albright, Remarks before the American-Iranian Council: As released by the Office of the Spokesman, news release, 17 March 2000.
52 Gary Sick, The United States in the Persian Gulf: From twin pillars to dual containment, in Lesch and Haas (eds), *The Middle East and the United States*, pp. 237–253, p. 304.
53 Dueck, *Reluctant crusaders*, p. 148.
54 Dimitri K. Simes, Learning to lead: President George W. Bush, *The National Interest*, 9 October 2002.
55 Riedel, *Kings and presidents*, p. 131.
56 Chollet and Goldgeier, *America between the wars*.
57 White House, The national security strategy of the United States of America, Washington, DC, 2002.
58 Kinch, *The US–Iran relationship*, p. 100.
59 Saikal, *Iran rising*, p. 98.
60 Arjomand, *After Khomeini*, p. 177.
61 Sadjadpour, *Reading Khamenei*, p. 18.
62 Musavian, *Iran and the United States*, pp. 102–112.
63 Sadjadpour, *Reading Khamenei*, p. 18.
64 Saikal, *Iran rising*, pp. 99–100.
65 Anoushiravan Ehteshami, *After Khomeini: The Iranian Second Republic* (London, New York: Routledge, 1995), p. 25.
66 Takeyh, *Guardians of the revolution*, p. 164.
67 Ehteshami, *After Khomeini*, p. 138.
68 Musavian, *Iran and the United States*, p. 110.
69 Saikal, *Iran rising*, p. 102.
70 Musavian, *Iran and the United States*, p. 142.

71 Saikal, *Iran rising*, p. 185.
72 Hossein Salimi, Foreign policy as a social construction, in Anoushiravan Ehteshami and Reza Molavi (eds): *Iran and the international system* (London, New York: Routledge, 2012) pp. 130–150, p. 146.
73 Reza E. Amiri, Ku Samsu, Hasnita Binti Ku, and Hassan G. Fereidouni, The Hajj and Iran's foreign policy towards Saudi Arabia, *Journal of Asian and African Studies* 46: 6, 2011, pp. 678–690, p. 684.
74 Pollack, The Persian puzzle, p. 310.
75 Interview, Mohammad Khatami, 7 January 1998.
76 Takeyh, *Guardians of the revolution*, p. 207.
77 Riedel, *Kings and presidents*, p. 104.
78 Fahad Alsultan and Pedram Saeid, *The development of Saudi–Iranian relations since the 1990s: Between conflict and accommodation* (New York: Routledge, 2016), p. 55.
79 Okruhlik, Saudi Arabian–Iranian relations.
80 Riedel, *Kings and presidents*, p. 132.
81 Stanley Weiss, It's time to talk about Saudi Arabia, *The Huffpost*, 23 October 2015.
82 Wynbrandt, *Brief History of Saudi Arabia*, p. 270; Okruhlik, Saudi Arabian–Iranian relations, p. 114.
83 Hiro, Cold War in the Islamic world, p. 148; Alsultan and Saeid, *The development of Saudi–Iranian relations since the 1990s*, p. 55.
84 Josoph Kechichian, Saudi Arabia will to power, *Middle East Policy* VII: 2, 2000, pp. 47–59, p. 48.
85 Hiro, *Cold War in the Islamic world*.
86 Okruhlik, Saudi Arabian–Iranian relations, p. 122.
87 Executive Orders numbers 12957 (March 1995) and 12959 (April 1995).
88 *New York Times*, Burned by loss of Conoco deal, Iran says U.S. betrays free trade', 20 March 1995.
89 Musavian, *Iran and the United States*, p. 122.
90 Adel Al Toraifi, *Understanding the role of state identity in foreign policy decision-making: The rise of Saudi–Iranian rapprochement (1997–2009)* (PhD thesis, 2012), p. 202; Keynoush, *Saudi Arabia and Iran*, p. 140; Pollack, *The Persian puzzle*, p. 282.
91 Edwards, *A neoclassical realist analysis of American 'dual containment' policy in the Persian Gulf*, p. 139.
92 Madeleine Albright, Remarks before the American-Iranian Council.
93 Freedman, *A choice of enemies*, p. 307; Hiro, *Cold War in the Islamic world*, p. 161; Musavian, *Iran and the United States*, p. 159.
94 Musavian, *Iran and the United States*, p. 168.
95 Takeyh, *Guardians of the revolution*, p. 129.
96 Seliktar, *Navigating Iran*, p. 128.
97 Musavian, *Iran and the United States*, p. 169.
98 Alaa Fouad, The OIC summit in Tehran: Herald of a new beginning?, *Insight Turkey* 12, 1998, pp. 121–128.

6

The stable marriage revised (2003–2014): Establishing a new rivalry

After declaring military victory in Afghanistan, the US administration turned to Iraq as the next step to implement its Forward Strategy of Freedom, which would bring, in their opinion, 'the hope of democracy, development, free markets, and free trade to non-liberal democracies'.[1] The US invasion was justified by the idea that Iraq held dangerous weapons of mass destruction (WMD) that could be offered to groups plotting new terrorist strikes against US Americans and allies. Despite lacking substantial evidence that Iraq had chemical or biological weapons, Bush's war had bipartisan congressional approval and significant domestic support.

This way, Operation Iraqi Freedom, a 'shock and awe' mission, was launched on 19 March 2003. Washington counted on the assistance of the United Kingdom, Australia, and Poland in its invasion phase. They believed it was possible to construct a liberal democracy in Iraq, consolidate free-market capitalism, and secure oil markets. While receiving little support from allies, the operation mounted 37,000 air raids, launched 23,000 precision-guided missiles, fired 750 cruise missiles, and dropped around 1,500 cluster bombs.[2] On 1 May, Bush declared the mission accomplished, dissolving the Iraqi army and proceeding to the political transition phase. On 13 December, Saddam Hussein was captured and, three years later, executed for crimes against humanity, war crimes, and genocide.

Turmoil in Iraq deepened with a widespread insurgency against foreign occupation and growing sectarian tension. That did not stop the US from handing political control to a feeble Iraqi interim government in June 2004. However, the political field was already dominated by sectarian disputes, and the political vacuum left by Saddam resulted in widespread civil conflict. During the first attempts at political reconfiguration, the Shias' preeminence triggered Sunnis to boycott the electoral process and intensify acts of insurgency and terrorism.

After a general election in December 2005, the Iraqi National Assembly began to draw the conditions for the succession of the interim government, which did not reduce hostilities. With Iranian backing, Shia groups such as the Mahdi Army and Badr Brigade started a violent offensive against the Sunnis after a Shia shrine was bombed in Samarra in 2006, escalating the sectarian conflict further. The election of Shia Nouri al-Maliki as Prime Minister in the same year resulted in further alienation of Sunnis from politics. The chaos empowered Sunni rebel Abu Musab al-Zarqawi, who broke off from al-Qaeda to form his Iraqi branch (*Jamaat al Tawhid wal Jihad*). After his assassination in 2006, Abu Omar al-Baghdadi renamed the unit the Islamic State of Iraq. The level of sectarian violence kept increasing, and in January 2007, the US dispatched over 21,500 soldiers in a new military surge.[3] In 2009, President Barack Obama started to remove troops from Iraq, returning the Green Zone to the Iraqi government. The withdrawal was completed in December 2011.

The poorly planned invasion, the hectic post-conflict mission, and increasingly violent sectarianism frustrated the Iraqi political transition. The number of Iraqi deaths during and after the invasion was exorbitant, and the conflict generated a migration crisis in the region that was without precedence. Moreover, the political vacuum enabled interference from many different actors, particularly from Iran. The conflict became even more daunting after ISIS was founded in 2013. By June 2014, ISIS declared a new caliphate by seizing the second-biggest Iraqi city, Mosul. That drove Iran and the US to deploy direct military action against the group.

The US power: still almighty?

If the 1990s represented a reassuring decade for the US primacy as a global power, the 9/11 attacks were a brutal wake-up call, exposing gaps in the country's defence capabilities. Its first response was to create the Department of Homeland Security, unify agencies of the intelligence community, and relocate specific responsibilities between foreign and security institutions. Moreover, it increased its military budget from 3.1 per cent of the GDP in 2001 to 4.9 per cent in 2010, going from US$ 440.5 billion in 2003 to US$ 752.2 billion in 2011.[4] While this number was reduced after the 2008 economic crisis, it continued, by far, to be the highest military budget in the world.

The invasion and subsequent occupation of Iraq resulted in a massive deployment of US forces to the Persian Gulf. Strategically, one of their first moves was to transfer CENTCOM operations from the Saudi Arabian Prince Sultan airbase to the Qatari Al' Udeid airbase and expand it. Military engineers upgraded the Qatari base as well as ports and runway facilities to support warships and transport aircraft.[5] The US also cooperated with the UAE in improving the Al Dhafra airbase, one of the region's most critical facilities and strategic bases.[6]

While the US started pulling out forces from Iraq in 2011, they kept around 800 intelligence staff, 16,000 diplomats, and security officers.[7] Moreover, they signed multiple military cooperation agreements with Iraq. By 2013, it had military personnel based in Qatar (627), Bahrain (1,100), Saudi Arabia (500), Kuwait (1,164), the UAE (5,856), Oman (22), and Turkey (1,867).[8] This presence allowed Washington to influence political, social, and security outcomes, facilitate weapons sales, security cooperation, and training operations, showcase force deployment, organise stabilisation missions, start offshore missile attacks, and orchestrate full-scale combat operations.[9] In other words, the US had the capacity to project military power like no other regional or non-regional actor in the Middle East.

Therefore, the US remained the most powerful military actor globally. It had a considerable edge regarding weapons systems (with a substantial capability to project power via sea, land, and air), technology, training, and military alliances. However, it was undeniable that the troops' presence and the chaotic aftermath created war fatigue among US Americans. It is estimated that the war cost around US$ 1.7 trillion, plus US$ 490 billion in benefits and US$ 212 billion in reconstruction efforts.[10] Moreover, there was a visible domestic dissatisfaction with the perceived interminable operations and the high military-spending, especially if contrasted with the poor economic numbers.

During the 2000s, international competition increased, and inequality and poverty rose. The GDP growth rate, which was 4.1 per cent in 2000, dropped to 2.8 per cent in 2003, –2.5 per cent in 2009, and 2.5 per cent in 2014.[11] The massive 2008 financial crash resulted from a housing-price bubble and uncontrolled consumer-borrowing.[12] After the banking sector's collapse, the state had to intervene to reduce damages, unemployment increased, investment declined, several businesses went bankrupt, and consumption plunged. As a result, the GDP dropped for the first time ever in 2009 (from US$ 14.7 trillion in 2008 to US$ 14.4 trillion in 2009), causing a recession.[13] Moreover, the national debt skyrocketed. The chain of effect of this economic collapse was global, with more than 104 countries experiencing some adverse impact.

Finally, the international community was beginning to pass through several changes that enabled the emergence of new actors that challenged the economic and political dominance of the US. Most notably, the rise of China started creating waves. It is interesting to note, in terms of numbers, how the economic gap reduced between the US and China throughout the period: the US GDP was US$ 11.4 trillion in 2003, while the Chinese was US$ 1.6 trillion; in 2014, the US GDP was US$ 17.5 trillion, while the

Chinese was US$ 10.4 trillion.[14] China's demand boom also enabled the rise of other emerging actors, like Brazil, South Africa, and India, and the return of older ones, like Russia. The emergence of the BRICS (Brazil, Russia, India, China, and South Africa intergovernmental organisation) and South–South cooperation narratives began to steadily contest the US' almightiness.

US changeable power

Contrary to its first Iraq invasion in 1990, the US' decision to invade Iraq in 2003 was seen as a unilateral move criticised by many close allies. Therefore, while the operation showcased colossal military power, it did not have much international support. No Arab country supported the mission or contributed with troops, although Saudi Arabia allowed the use of its airbases and Kuwait provided free fuel. Nevertheless, after the fall of Saddam's regime, the GCC countries – notably Qatar, Kuwait, and the UAE – boosted their security ties and arms deals with Washington. Moreover, Washington re-established diplomatic and security links with Iraq. Therefore, it is possible to say that the US managed to impose, even if begrudgingly, its dominance in the region. Iran was the only Persian Gulf country that did not have a US embassy.

However, the war tainted the country's image in the region even further, aggravating the anti-US Americanism discussed in the previous chapter. For many, the narrative of spreading democracy was just a cloak for neo-imperialist ambitions and a desire to control the oil reserves in Iraq.[15] Moreover, supporting democracy while endorsing undemocratic leaders in other places made Washington appear as a hypocrite to many people in the Middle East. The fact that no WMD was found in Iraq only boosted the feelings against the superpower. A 2006–2007 public pooling in the Middle East found that 79 per cent agreed that Washington aimed to weaken and divide the Islamic world.[16] Another survey from 2008 showed that 83 per cent had negative views about the US' role in the region.[17] As expected, terrorist and radical groups tapped into these sentiments to recruit new members.

Finally, how the US reacted to the protests that overtook the Middle East on the eve of 2011 harmed their approval among traditional regional partners. The Arab Uprisings were a series of popular movements that started in Tunisia and spread across the Arab world, representing a general dissatisfaction with socioeconomic conditions, inflation, unemployment, and corruption. To the Saudis and Emiratis, Washington did nothing to protect traditional partners like Hosni Mubarak in Egypt or Ben Ali in Tunisia. They also disliked the US non-interference in Syria and its difficulty in handling the Iraqi civil war. While ties continued to be strong, especially in intelligence-sharing, training, and security cooperation, there was a crisis of confidence among the GCC towards the US by the end of the period.[18]

Iranian power: a squandered rising power

The first half of the 2000s empowered Iran. First, threats were reduced as the fall of Saddam meant Iran no longer shared 1,599 km of borders with a long-standing enemy. Second, the 2000s commodities boom raised the price of an oil barrel to three digits, and Iran's economy grew accordingly. For example, the GDP increased from US$ 153.5 billion in 2003 to US$ 598.9 billion in 2012.[19] That meant a growth rate of 8.7 per cent in 2003, closing the period at 4.6 per cent in 2014. This allowed the government to redistribute oil rents through subsidies, social benefits, and loans that improved the overall quality of life compared to previous periods. However, it is essential to note that this growth could have been much higher without international sanctions.

This period is also marked by Iran's plans to develop a complete nuclear fuel cycle. The government was aware of the importance of reducing oil dependency to improve economic stability. The oil sector's productivity was below its potential and with serious difficulty in capturing investments due to long-standing sanctions. However, the International Atomic Energy Agency (IAEA) began to suspect that Iran had non-energy-related intentions in nuclear power. In 2006, the agency accused Tehran of not complying with the Non-Proliferation Treaty, provoking the first round of UNSC sanctions. Iran responded by announcing it could enrich uranium to 20 per cent purity. In February 2010, another round of sanctions followed. This cycle continued throughout the period, with the imposition of sanctions with tighter financial curbs, restricting investment possibilities for companies and banks and complicating the economic situation for Iranians. When oil prices began to drop in 2013, the country entered a stagnation phase. Some estimate that sanctions cost Iran around US$ 133 million daily in revenues.[20]

The oil boom also instigated a spike in military procurements, particularly from China, Russia, and North Korea. The defence budget rose from US$ 3.71 billion in 2003 to US$ 16.4 billion in 2012.[21] With a military doctrine which was mainly defensive, these expenditures were primarily focused on hybrid warfare capacitation that provided resistance to external incursions, anti-ship technology, and long-range ballistic missile capacities.[22] It aimed to increase deterrence by stocking unconventional retaliation capabilities that raised the costs of an attack. Moreover, Iran continued to improve its ability to work via proxies that enabled it to expand its influencing capacity in regional operations while having plausible deniability.

Since 2003, the IRGC has increased its intelligence and military hold in Iraq, primarily via its Quds Force, providing training and armaments to Shia groups.[23] However, when it came to conventional forces, Iran still depended in significant part on old equipment acquired by the Shah, which was outdated and lacked replacement and technical support. Nevertheless, the country's main improvement was acquiring anti-ship missile systems during the period. In January 2005, the CIA confirmed that Iran had the maritime capability to close the Strait of Hormuz, which could compromise the normal flow of the oil market.[24] Likewise, it has been reported that Iran started producing Shahab medium-range ballistic missiles, 'a hybrid progeny of the Soviet Scud, the Chinese CSS, and the North Korean Taep'o Dong series', which can reach up to 2,000 km distance.[25] In fact, the nation has developed a rather decent reverse engineering technology that enabled military build-up despite growing sanctions. As a result, by the end of the period, Iran had one of the region's largest mid-range ballistic missile inventories.[26]

However, Iran's defence system's dual structure (army and IRGC) and problems within its chain of command are often pointed out as hard-to-overcome weaknesses.[27] They can compete for limited resources, and have poorly integrated forces, inadequate cooperation and communication, and high politicisation. Moreover, crippling sanctions made it almost impossible for Iran to acquire high-tech weapons and modernise its conventional capabilities.[28] By 2014, as the economic advances reversed, military expenditure also reduced. In Thomas Juneau's words, Iran squandered its window of opportunity.[29]

Iran's changeable power

Once a foe, Iraq became an Iranian ally after the fall of Saddam, and in 2008, Ahmadinejad became the first President to visit Baghdad, declaring a new chapter in their ties. Moreover, Iran has increased its influence in Afghanistan since the US invasion. At the same time, it strengthened its relations with Syria via security pacts between 2004 and 2007. Finally, the 2006 Lebanese conflict gave Iran more manoeuvre space for it to increase its commitment to Hezbollah, which expanded during the 2000s. With the oil price boom, Iran had more income to redistribute strategically to its partners. Therefore, it established a more robust position within the Middle East.

Yet, Iran's perceived nuclear empowerment drove some GCC members to readjust their posture towards the country. There was more vigorous criticism from Saudi Arabia, the UAE, and Bahrain after the IAEA's reports, as they feared a regional nuclear escalation. Moreover, with amounting sanctions, Europeans and, on a smaller scale, Russians and Chinese found it hard to continue enhancing ties with Iran without suffering the consequences of secondary sanctions.

Here, it is important to stress that Iran profited from this general state of dissatisfaction towards US meddling in the region and enhanced its revolutionary rhetoric.[30] As Hamas, Hezbollah, and Islamic Jihad improved their regional influence and power, Iran also got more powerful. In other words, Tehran acquired political leverage by intertwining its assistance to proxy groups with a shared ideology of resistance while avoiding the direct costs of war. Interestingly, the anti-imperialist rhetoric resonated beyond the region, with many Global South countries getting out of their way to defend Iran's nuclear ambitions. Particularly in Latin America, Iran deepened ties with Venezuela, Cuba, Brazil, Nicaragua, and Bolivia. Moreover, it also enhanced ties with India, China, and Russia under the cloth of anti-hegemonic partnerships.

Nevertheless, Iran's revolutionary appeal had limitations. For example, while it tried to promote the 2011 Arab Uprisings as a delayed 'Islamic awakening' like the 1979 Revolution, this had little resonance. Virtually no protester or movement wanted to be seen associated with Iran.[31] It is possible to assume that its regional appeal had decreased already in 2009 when tens of thousands took to the streets to protest Ahmadinejad's re-election in what became known as the Iranian Green Movement. Instead of answering the people's concerns about the procedure, the IRGC and the army, with Khamenei's authorisation, crushed the protesters with violence, imprisonment, and persecution. Moreover, many universities were closed, and selected domestic and foreign media were banned, resulting in widespread international condemnation.[32] Therefore, Iran's popularity in the Middle East was put into question by the second half of the 2000s.

Saudi Arabian power: on a rising path

After almost two decades of low economic growth, the 2000 oil price boom beginning in 2003 heated the economy to unforeseen numbers. The GDP rose from US$ 215.8 billion in 2003 to US$ 519 billion in 2008, closing at an impressive US$ 756.3 billion in 2014.[33] The pouring of petrodollars was massive, and the monarchy could invest big time in both its own economy and abroad while reducing its balance deficit. Much of this money was reinvested in ARAMCO, guaranteeing that the company had access to the most advanced and secure technology in oil exploration, extraction, storage, and transportation.

Moreover, governmental debt, which reached almost 60 per cent of the GDP in 2004, decreased progressively throughout the period, reaching 1.5 per cent in 2014.[34] There was also important trade diversification due to the steadily increasing crude oil sales to Asian markets, particularly China.

Nevertheless, the decade of high oil prices did not manage to push Saudi Arabia away from the dangers of being a rentier economy. The country remained highly dependent on international oil price fluctuation, and there was no effective measure of reinvesting the rents into other economic sectors to promote diversification, encourage the private sector, and expand domestic markets. By the end of the period, the oil industry remained responsible for 45 per cent of the GDP and 90 per cent of the export earnings. The other sectors of the economy continued to be small in comparison. Like many other countries with abundant extractive natural resources, Saudi Arabians traditionally relied on public jobs while benefiting from almost inexistent taxation, and highly subsidised services like electricity, water, and gasoline.[35] While the distribution of petrodollars has guaranteed this type of social contract, Saudi Arabia felt demographic pressures by the end of the 2000s. From 1982 to 2003, the population rose from 7 million to 22 million.[36] This meant an increasingly unemployed youth that could provoke socioeconomic tension. Moreover, the levels of inequality increased, whereas the dependence on cheap foreign labour did not reduce, signalling a need for fiscal and labour reforms that were mainly overlooked during this period.

Concerning the military sector, Saudi Arabia's expenditures grew exponentially, from US$ 18.7 billion in 2003 to US$ 80.76 billion in 2014.[37] In total, the defence budget, which already consumed 8.6 per cent of the GDP in 2003, rose up to 10.6 per cent in 2014.[38] It is interesting to note that the progression of spending accelerated after 2011 when it became visible that the kingdom's air and land warfare capabilities had enlarged considerably.[39] In 2014, Saudi Arabia became the fourth-largest military spender, behind only the US, China, and Russia.

Saudi Arabia sought to have a fully effective air force as the first line of deterrence while guaranteeing over-the-horizon US assistance to deal with enduring regional conflicts.[40] By the eve of the 2010s, the Saudi air force became the most sophisticated in the region, with AWACS radars for surveillance, modern intelligence apparatus, and capable of limited offensive and defensive operations. Moreover, they invested significantly in armoured fighting vehicles, surpassing Iran in numbers. Saudi Arabia has also enhanced much of its naval defence ability. However, it still rested behind Iran in artillery, rocket inventory, and personnel.[41] As discussed in the last three chapters, Riyadh suffers from difficulty in recruiting and mobilising.

Despite all this high investment, the gap between Saudi Arabian military capacities and the sophistication of its acquired equipment continued to be very high, requiring continued foreign technical expertise and assistance.[42] Moreover, it lacked a consistent command structure and chain of communication among its many military branches, often leading to the inability to handle complicated operations. Nevertheless, in 2011, the military showcased its ability to mobilise a battalion-sized force of around 1,000 troops in Bahrain, successfully controlling Shia protesters. In short, the period represented a great moment of expansion for Saudi Arabia, which also exposed some societal and military limitations.

Saudi Arabia's changeable power

While Saddam was perceived as a threat, Saudi Arabia positioned itself against the US military action, fearing regional instability. Nevertheless, this disagreement did not affect their ties. Washington and Riyadh continued collaborating in a wide range of economic, military, and counterterrorism activities. Moreover, expanding its trade partnerships meant that the monarchy could boost its economic and military cooperation with China and make overtures to Russia. Most importantly, the relations with other Middle Eastern countries during the 2000s continued positively, even showing some improvement with Syria before 2011. There was also an unprecedented degree of interaction between Saudi Arabia and Pakistan, including a secret agreement on nuclear cooperation.[43] Relations with Iran, however, have stalled since 2007, as we further analyse.

It is crucial to look into Saudi Arabia's role in the region's turmoil during the 2011 Arab Uprisings. Overall, its changeable power emanated from its leadership position within the GCC, its authoritative place among the Islamic community, and its status as an oil powerhouse. As the protests shook the regional political scenario and weakened traditional Arab leaders, the Persian Gulf monarchies, mostly only scratched by the wave of demonstrations, gained influence and prestige among other Arab countries. Since 2011, the GCC has become more militarily powerful, more diplomatically ambitious, and less responsive to outside pressures – in what some called the Gulf Moment.[44]

As a result, Saudi Arabia broadened its regional reach and assisted many Arab countries struggling with political and economic crises, increasing its influence over them. Between 2011 and 2014, Riyadh pledged roughly US$ 22.7 billion in regional aid, particularly to Bahrain, Egypt, Lebanon, and Oman.[45] In addition, it has become a prominent supporter of Sunni rebels in Iraq and Syria, a key ally to the Egyptian government since the 2013 military coup, and a direct enforcer of order in Yemen and Bahrain, intervening militarily in both countries. Therefore, it is possible to say that, since 2011, Riyadh has secured for itself a high level of influence among its neighbours.

The Persian Gulf's balance of power after 2003

Regarding power balance, Iraq could no longer be a candidate for regional leadership after its invasion, which meant relative empowerment for the US, Saudi Arabia, and Iran – all foes of Baghgad. While the regional system remained multipolar, the two most powerful countries in the aftermath of Saddam's regime were Iran and the US. Saddam's hasty defeat ensured the US could move forces quickly, with or without international support. Conversely, the new power configuration also left Iran stronger by enabling it to build a system of complex political and proxy campaigns that broadened its security and influence.

Nevertheless, Saudi Arabia also steadily improved its power despite not being so directly benefited by the geopolitical shift. By the end of the 2000s, Riyadh managed to use the oil money to invest more in its infrastructure and military forces, becoming less dependent on the US both to ship its oil and train its officers. Besides, it established a remarkable set of regional alliances and partnerships, ensuring a less threatening environment. While Iran remained stronger militarily, with a more significant mobilisation force and a superior missile capability, the Saudis were catching up, improving in relative terms in virtually every category and showcasing more up-to-date equipment and aircraft.

Therefore, Iran and Saudi Arabia emerged as the Persian Gulf's most substantial regional power brokers. Some authors started talking about a 'cold war' between the two actors immediately after Saddam's fall.[46] However, this term is not necessarily the most appropriate one, as Iran–Saudi ties remained on working terms until 2006. In fact, the 2000s began at the most cordial moment between Iranians and Saudis. However, by the eve of the 2010s, a scenario of rivalry between the two was set – one that involved a growing sectarian war on words and proxy conflicts in several arenas. This chapter shows how the period represented a moment of transition from constructive rapprochement to a Saudi–Iran rivalry, with no direct alteration in their ties with the US, despite certain US–Saudi distancing and partial US–Iran appeasement.

At first glance, the balance of power explains the changes that drove the triangular relations towards a rebooted stable marriage triangle. With Iranian power growing, Saudi Arabia balanced externally with its traditional ally and internally by increasing military expenditure. Nevertheless, such an assessment disregards the complex, nuanced process of shifting reliance and growing frustration among the three actors that led to this scenario – something the intervening variables reveal. Moreover, the intervening variables help us understand how an

Iranian nuclear deal was achieved and which factors influenced simultaneously this negotiation and Saudi Arabia's newfound foreign policy proactivity.

US status satisfaction: recentring on counterterrorism

As discussed in the previous chapter, Washington acted as a 'worried sheriff' with the unmanageable task of monitoring the global community. The previous chapter detected a lack of clarity regarding identifying an enemy or rival. However, the 9/11 attacks posed 'global terrorism' as the new foe whom Washington could fight against. In the words of President George W. Bush, 'the gravest danger facing America and the world is outlaw regimes', and the US needed to 'be prepared to stop rogue states and their terrorist clients before they are able to threaten or use weapons of mass destruction'.[47] Therefore, the War on Terror respecified the US ambitions and inserted counterterrorism into the list of top priorities in the Middle East.

This variable is relational, meaning that it requires a glance at how others within the regional system perceived the US ambitions. While Iran continued to reject Washington's regional role, the systemic change contributed to the US status satisfaction because it transformed Iraq from a foe to a partner, reducing security threats. Moreover, the GCC countries maintained their reliance on Washington's defence assistance. These two factors gave the US a more open environment for its ambitions. However, its military permanence and the lack of multilateral commitment in conflicts have also catalysed anti-US sentiments as well as criticism from local partners. The war in Iraq, the empowerment of revisionist regional actors, and the continuation of terrorism on a much larger scale with ISIS demonstrated that the US policies since 2003 had failed. This way, local resistance to these policies became increasingly pervasive.

There were signs of status discrepancy by the mid-2010s, not because the US ambitioned more than it was ascribed but because it was ascribed more than it was willing or able to be. The decision to not intervene to protect traditional partners during the 2011 Arab Uprisings raised questions about how much Washington was still interested in keeping its 'indispensable nation' function. Nevertheless, that did not mean that the US was less of a status quo actor, nor that its ambitions had changed. For the 2003–2014 period, the status satisfaction variable still pushed the country towards protecting regional order, securing partners and the oil market, and promoting counterterrorism activities. In other words, it still idealised the regional order protector position. Still, it began showing symptoms of exhaustion.

Iran's status satisfaction: new threats, new opportunities

The events of 2003 had a dual effect on Iran's environment perception. On the one hand, Iraq's transformation from a foe to a friend reduced direct threats and amplified Iran's influence. On the other hand, there was a massive increase in US troops in the region. Moreover, being listed as an 'axis of evil' increased Tehran's suspicion that it could be the next target of the War on Terror. Thus, far from concluding that a systemic shift only reduces or increases a country's threat perception, the Iraq invasion simultaneously brought opportunities and risks for the Iranian leadership to handle.

Iran sought to capitalise on the growing anti-US feeling to increase its own relevance among many regional social movements and non-state actors. Iranian leaders' rhetoric against imperialism and its defence of Palestine captivated a significant part of the Middle Eastern audiences.[48] Moreover, the international pressure against its nuclear programme provided new grounds for Iranians to argue against the West's unfair rule of world politics. On their understanding, Washington and its allies denied Tehran its leadership position by blocking its economic development, constraining its regional behaviour, and refusing its inclusion on any negotiation table. The US was acting like, in the words of Ahmadinejad, a 'nuclear colonialist', deliberately isolating Iran.[49]

Thus, defining the period as entirely restrictive or permissive for Iran is unfeasible. While Saddam's exit and Shia groups' empowerment were positive, growing isolation due to the nuclear conundrum and more substantial US military presence were negative. Presidents Khatami, Ahmadinejad, and Rouhani assessed this duality differently. While Khatami worried more about the damages of isolation and the threat of a US attack, Ahmadinejad focused on Iran's upsurge of influence in the region, charging his rhetoric with ideas of revolution, resistance, and anti-imperialism. Nonetheless, Ahmadinejad significantly impacted the country's political image, negatively affecting Iran's diplomatic ties. By 2007, relations with the GCC countries were very strained. Moreover, international sanctions reversed many of Khatami's gains within the international community. By the time Rouhani became President, tensions and scepticism made Iran highly isolated among other regional actors, ensuring it continued a revisionist state.

Saudi Arabia's status satisfaction: seeking a higher position

The Saudis grew steadily dissatisfied with the regional status quo throughout the period, as they became suspicious of Iran and did not see the US as reliable as before. This section shows how a sense of threat perception and uncertainty, together with a growing power position, enabled the monarchy to expand its ambitions and project a new status-seeking behaviour.

In Riyadh's perception, Saddam's replacement by Shia politicians opened the doors for Iranian regional hegemony. The monarchy believed the US had offered Iraq to Tehran on 'a golden platter', encouraging, instead of inhibiting, Iranian expansionist aspirations.[50] Moreover, the revelations about Iran's nuclear programme rang several alarms in Riyadh. To them, such capacities, together with missile superiority, provided Tehran with the means to impose its will in the Persian Gulf and the broader Middle East.[51] Whether this perception reflected reality or not, it is essential to detect mounting anxiety in Riyadh towards the regional order due to Iranian empowerment.

Moreover, Saudi Arabia interpreted Iran's empowerment through a 'Shia Crescent' prism, an idea that Iran was organising and providing financial and military support to a transnational network of Shias. The idea was first coined by King Abdullah II of Jordan and referred to Iran's ability to influence and coopt Shias in Lebanon, Iraq, Yemen, Bahrain, and other countries as agents of insecurity, tension, and conflict in the Middle East. While that was closer to a conspiracy theory than reality, many Arab leaders and media insisted on this narrative, warning about a Shia plot against the order.[52] Saudi Arabia was particularly apprehensive about protests in its oil-rich Eastern province, where most of its Shia population resided. Therefore, Saudis gradually sensed the need to engage in an entangled (ideological and geopolitical) competition for leadership against Iran, with each supporting opposite sides in many regional conflicts.

Saudi Arabia's anxiety was also related to a seeming US disengagement. Some US decisions triggered Riyadh to suspect that the extra-regional power was not as keen as before to guarantee order. First, Saudi Arabia disapproved of Bush's ambitions to intervene and promote democratic reforms. They believed a forced democratisation process in the Arab world could initiate social unrest, potential threats, and revisionism.[53] Second, the Iraqi conflict after 2003 revealed the US' limitations in imposing its will or warranting any type of stability. Third, Obama's reticence during the Arab Uprisings, coupled with his promise to shift priorities away from the Middle East, implanted a fear of abandonment in the monarchy. These events led Riyadh to question whether the US would act to secure the GCC's security in the future.

The 2011 protests brought light to an emerging set of challenges to long-standing governments in the Middle East. At the same time, it reduced the regional influence of other Arab countries, like Egypt, Libya, and Syria. In this context, Riyadh could promote itself as the new Arab leader, with economic and military resources to endorse regional order. Being only loosely affected by protests, the monarchy assisted countries like Morocco and Lebanon in their economic recovery and Yemen, Bahrain, and Egypt in halting demonstrators. Likewise, Riyadh started to support non-state actors resisting Iran-backed governments more openly in Syria and Iraq. In this sense, framing its regional role under the Arabic clout simultaneously served to improve its position and check Iranian influence.

Henceforth, increased power combined with a new sense of uncertainty about the US and the Iranian positions gave Saudi Arabia a new ambition: proactively protecting the regional order. Thus, this variable pushed for a status-seeking behaviour, instigating the Saudi leadership to be more proactive in the maintenance of a preferable order, with or without the US leadership. The US and the other GCC countries did not send any clear signals against Saudi Arabia stepping up to this goal, indicating that they positively received its new ambition. Therefore, there was no status dissonance; Riyadh did not seek to be a revisionist actor or change the order. Instead, it aimed at increasing and improving its own role in safeguarding the order as it was.

US state identity: enmity clarity

As discussed in the last three chapters, this is the only variable that does not change throughout our analysis. In a 'new era of danger' after the 9/11 attacks, many in Washington believed it should spread its liberal ideas to tackle the root causes of global extremism. In an efficient twist of logic, neoconservatives framed terrorism in the Middle East as a non-democratic product and claimed that the US should preventively act to guarantee the global predominance of democratic ruling as a way to protect themselves from future threats. Thus, the neoconservative thinking was not an aberration in the US thought but something consistent with the spectrum of its state identity, which called for the promotion of the US model via force or example.[54]

In this context, President George W. Bush began to mix and match nationalist and internationalist lenses to frame a new national enemy. This cognitive frame oriented the country towards rebuffing multilateralism and rejecting negotiation with non-liberal parties if that revealed a possible reduction of the influence of the liberal model worldwide. In contrast, the Obama administration returned to a combination of progressive and realist lenses, seeking a projection of self-image that worked as a model to be followed without much hands-on action. Thus, President Obama was guided by power-sharing ideas while aiming at reducing the country's direct engagement in non-crucial conflicts.

Iran's state identity: pragmatism and ideology

As discussed in the second triangle, the principles of independentism, pan-Islamism, anti-imperialism, and Shia's resilience defined Iran's state identity. These elements built a mission to assist other Muslim populations in emancipating themselves while constructing an order under the Iranian leadership. In other words, they saw themselves as an Islamist role model for others to follow – one that neither collaborated with the global division of power nor was complacent with the US influence in other regions of the world.

This missionary characteristic meant Iran tended to expand its revolutionary experiment to the Middle East when the conditions permited. Therefore, this ideational identity provided two ways for interpreting the country's regional role: pragmatic or ideological. While the pragmatic lens oriented leaders to seek independentism and to guarantee the stability of the regime, the ideational lens argued for exporting the Revolution, promoting anti-imperialist rhetoric, and instigating religious rivalry. During the period, Presidents Khatami and Rouhani were much more pragmatic, focusing on sovereignty, independentism, and regional inclusion when assessing their options. Conversely, President Ahmadinejad returned to ideological lenses, stressing the revolutionary and anti-imperialist values that formed the regime.

Saudi Arabia's state identity: orbiting sectarianism

The events in 2003 also did not affect Saudi Arabia's cognitive variable. The country sought to protect and promote Islam worldwide, while it was permeated by a sense of vulnerability towards regional order. For analytical purposes, this variable filtered out strategies that ran the risk of reducing Saudi Arabian authority among the *ummah*, increasing the influence of other Islamic authorities, or engendering regional stability. For that, leaders could lean towards pan-Islamism or sectarianism accordingly. Distinct understandings of opportunities, preferences, and threats were related to the different lenses being employed.

During the period, this variable filtered out options such as promoting the Arab Uprisings when that meant threatening Saudi Arabia's regional position. Moreover, this identity boosted fears about the rise of rival Islamist projects in the region, particularly the Iranian one, due to its revisionism and Shia tendency. Therefore, King Abdullah's positioning tilted towards sectarianism to interpret the country's identity when realising the environment was progressively restrictive.

US leadership preferences: the contrast between Bush and Obama

George W. Bush subscribed to neoconservatism, a wing of the Republican Party that encouraged pre-emptive action against possible threats to the US dominance. He sympathised with regime change operations and showed a very binary world view of right vs wrong. In his words, 'either you are with us, or you are with the terrorists'.[55] The idea that the US had the mission to spread its ideals worldwide hit a cord with Bush's religious beliefs.[56] He believed that a crusade against terrorism was part of the US mission against 'forces of darkness'.[57] Neoconservatism also pushed for nationalist readings about the country's global role, detected in Vice President Richard Cheney and Secretary of Defense Donald Rumsfeld. They assumed that only a retaliatory campaign against al-Qaeda was insufficient; it was necessary to display to the world the severe consequences of attacking the US.[58]

The Bush Doctrine's assumption that ousting autocrats like Saddam would result in the instalment of a liberal democracy exposed this administration's shallow understanding of the Middle East dynamics. For Secretary of State Condoleezza Rice, 'the United States pursued stability at the expense of democracy in this region, and we achieved neither. Now we are taking a different course. We are supporting the democratic aspiration of all people'.[59] Hence, under the argument that spreading liberal democracy was advantageous for the whole world, Bush took the US outside the track of the Carter Doctrine for the first time since 1980 by using preventive force to provoke regime change in the region.

The Bush administration defined its enemies not only in terms of national threat but also by those who could live up to its value system. In their view, Iran did not make the cut; thus, it should be listed as an 'axis of evil'. Throughout this administration, any attempt from Iran to provide strategic assistance would not be taken seriously, as it was perceived as an enemy and, hence, up to no good. The idea that Iran was untrustworthy also guided their position regarding Iran's nuclear programme. During the Bush years, Iran was considered ineligible for having a complete nuclear programme. The President and his staff took a much more aggressive and non-negotiable tone than what was seen before.

In the Persian Gulf, Bush pushed for regional economic liberalisation and further integration of the GCC into a growingly globalised economy. Many economic cooperation projects and free trade agreements were signed between the US and the member countries. In other words, the plan of forcefully expanding democracy remained reserved only for those who contested the US role. This hypocritical stand did not go unnoticed by many in the Middle East who criticised the US selective agenda. Also, US Americans increasingly questioned the reason for maintaining such expensive foreign operations – mainly when the country experienced a major financial crisis. Thus, during the 2008 US presidential elections, there was a genuine national discussion regarding the future of the US role in the Middle East.

Democratic candidate Barack Obama capitalised on domestic war fatigue. He famously opposed the Iraqi war and promised that, if elected, he would bring all combatant troops back and restart a diplomacy-first foreign policy. The first black US President and the son of a Kenyan immigrant born in Hawaii, Obama was unmistakably cosmopolitan and with a pretty different set of values from his predecessor. In terms of international politics, he campaigned on the promise of reducing the neoconservatives' vindicative tone and returning to a more multilateral, consensual, and restrained attitude towards global issues.

With Obama's election, the leadership turned to a realist-progressive lens. In his words, 'call me a realist in believing we can't, at any given moment, relieve all the world's misery' and 'we have to choose where we can make a real impact'.[60] He expected to reduce commitments in the Middle East without endangering local partners. Thus, his priority was to return to the Carter Doctrine that was abandoned by Bush. Obama was sceptical about the advantages of promoting regime change in the Middle East and other world regions. In his view, the US should guarantee its interest through a more conventional approach without pre-emptive use of force. He employed terms such as 'bridging divides' instead of 'good vs evil', stressing the importance of acting in concert with allies and sharing responsibilities. Therefore, multilateralism and encouraging traditional partners to contribute more to their own security were central to Obama's strategy.

> Part of his mission as President, Obama explained, is to spur other countries to take action for themselves, rather than wait for the U.S. to lead. The defense of the liberal international order against jihadist terror, Russian adventurism, and Chinese bullying depends in part, he believes, on the willingness of other nations to share the burden with the U.S. This is why the controversy surrounding the assertion – made by an anonymous administration official to

The New Yorker during the Libya crisis of 2011 – that his policy consisted of 'leading from behind' perturbed him. 'We don't have to always be the ones who are upfront,' he told me. 'Sometimes we're going to get what we want precisely because we are sharing in the agenda.'[61]

Concerning the Middle East, Obama hoped to reduce anti-Americanism by committing to treat Muslim countries as equal partners. During a visit to Egypt in June 2009, he spoke about 'new beginnings', citing references from the Koran and the Bible to state that 'Islam is part of America'.[62] He also said, 'America does not presume to know what is best for everyone' but stressed that one of the US' primary concerns was the Iranian nuclear project. Probably aware of the growing power of Iran in the region, Obama made it clear during the electoral campaign that he wanted to change the way of approaching Tehran. In his view, the strategy to coerce with sanctions without preconditions was not working. As he argued, 'American interests are advanced by direct negotiations with our enemies, not engaging in self-imposed ostracism'.[63]

Obama argued that a solution to the nuclear problem was required to ensure the US geopolitical priorities. Therefore, he imposed a dual-track strategy based on offering incentives while clarifying the penalties that could follow. His first move was to remove the preconditions for beginning negotiations. His administration made some attempts in reaching out, such as sending a celebratory message during Nowruz (the Iranian New Year celebration) in March 2009, stressing the Persian culture's richness, the Iranians' peace-loving nature, and the constructive regional role that Iran can play.[64] In his words:

> I've made it clear to Iran's leaders and people that my country is prepared to move forward. The question now is not what Iran is against, but rather what future it wants to build. I recognise it will be hard to overcome decades of mistrust, but we will proceed with courage, rectitude, and resolve. There will be many issues to discuss between our two countries, and we are willing to move forward without preconditions on the basis of mutual respect. But it is clear to all concerned that when it comes to nuclear weapons, we have reached a decisive point. This is not simply about America's interests. It's about preventing a nuclear arms race in the Middle East that could lead this region and the world down a hugely dangerous path.[65]

As Iran did not initially respond, Obama started the second track of his policy, increasing pressure. New bilateral and multilateral sanctions, which were more severe and punitive than the ones before, were imposed in 2010. Secretary of State Hilary Clinton explained that 'by following the diplomatic path we are on, we gain credibility and influence with a number of nations who would have to participate in order to make the sanctions regime as tight and as crippling as we would want it to be'.[66]

The strategy of first offering carrots and only then imposing sticks worked for Obama, who managed to sign the first deal between the US and Iran in 2013, the Geneva Interim Agreement, which is further discussed in this chapter.

Obama had a clear perception of policy limitations. Aware of shifting global politics, he had signalled the intention to recalibrate global priorities to prepare for an Asian-Pacific era since his first year in office. He seemed aware that a more comprehensive strategy towards Asia required a simultaneous retrenchment in the Middle East, which meant 'pulling back, spending less, cutting risk, and shifting burdens to allies'.[67] In his view, regional partners should increase their involvement in protecting the order, reducing the US responsibilities. In the Persian Gulf, Obama was insistent that the GCC countries should find ways of accommodating Iran. In his words, 'it requires us to say to our friends as well as to the Iranians that they need to find an effective way to share the neighbourhood and institute some sort of cold peace'.[68] However, many countries saw this process as a regional disengagement, arguing that it displayed a tacit admission that the US power, influence, and willingness had limitations.[69]

Therefore, Obama's realist-progressive inclinations tilted the decision-making towards multilateralism, retrenchment, and a preference for immediate gains. The progressive inclination promoted the US as a model to be emulated, mostly rejecting the previous administration's vindicative character. When the Arab Uprisings started, Obama chose caution, avoiding supporting or condemning protesters. He paid lip service to the US missionary spirit by focusing on diplomacy and statecraft and rebuffing the use of military force when national interests were not threatened. That explains Obama's decision to redeploy thousands of troops only against ISIS and not to the Syrian war, as the first represented a direct threat to the US interests, whereas the second did not.

Iran's leadership preferences: disagreeing on how to engage

The period comprises three presidencies: the reformist Khatami (1997–2005), the hardliner Ahmadinejad (2005–2013), and the pragmatic Rouhani (2013–2021). Each disagreed on how to achieve Iran's best interests internationally, tilting the country's behaviour to cooperation, non-compliance, and cooperation again. Whereas Ahmadinejad sought to promote Iran as a non-conformist regional power, Khatami and Rouhani intended to integrate it diplomatically and economically into the international system. The main difference between the last two rested in the level of Khamenei's support and the factional gridlock each faced.

First, President Khatami was a reformist who aimed to normalise Iran's international relations and improve ties with regional and Western countries. Immediately after the invasion of Iraq, he tried reaching out to Washington, perceiving the increasingly restrictive environment, and fearing becoming the next target. Using the Swiss Embassy as an intermediator, Khatami sent a letter to Bush that became known as the 'grand bargain'. It expressed Iran's willingness to discuss its support to Hamas and Hezbollah, the Iraq situation, and the nuclear programme. According to Gary Sick, the grand bargain was:

> an agenda for a diplomatic process to resolve all of the outstanding bilateral differences between the United States and Iran. On the Iranian side, they acknowledged that they would need to be prepared to deal with our concerns about their WMD activities, their links to terrorist groups like Hezbollah and Hamas, and they said in there that they would be prepared to eliminate military support for these organisations and to work to turn Hezbollah, for example, into a purely political and social organisation in Lebanon. They recognised that this would be something they would need to do as part of a rapprochement.[70]

It is not entirely clear how much Khamenei was involved. Still, it is possible to assume some endorsement because it was highly broadcast in the Iranian media – which he had much control over. However, the US decision to ignore this effort was a nail in the coffin for Khatami's policy. It also directly boosted the popularity of a new conservative faction, the so-called hardliners (or neoconservatives), who accused him of being lenient and submissive to the West. Targeting Khatami's alleged willingness to surrender Iran's rights, hardliners called for a return to the Revolution's tenets, using a class struggle lexicon and a robust nationalist rhetoric.[71] Eventually, a growingly conservative *Majlis* ensured that Khatami completed his term without a resolution on the topic.

With the support of the IRGC, the hardliners won most of the *Majlis* seats in 2004 and, in 2005, elected Tehran's mayor, Mahmoud Ahmadinejad, as the new President. The son of a low-income family, Ahmadinejad joined the Revolution as an activist student, becoming an IRGC member during the war against Iraq. He spoke for the urban working and lower classes, calling for economic justice, state patronage, and weeding out corruption. He also gained the sympathy of those disillusioned with Khatami's liberalising policies. In Ahmadinejad's view, it was necessary to return to Khomeini's ideals, and he employed words like social justice, Islamic struggle, and martyrdom to mobilise support for his policies. This way, he portrayed himself as the ultimate representative of the 'children of the Islamic revolution'.[72]

Since the beginning of his government, Ahmadinejad had a confrontative attitude towards the West and sustained an uncompromising revisionist stand. He understood the growing anti-Americanism in the Middle East as a permissive signal to boost an antagonist discourse. Hence, he substituted Presidents Rafsanjani's and Khatami's pragmatic approach for an ideological one, underscoring the Iranian cognitive function as revolutionary and anti-status quo. In short, his administration had three main foreign policy goals: assume prominence in the Palestinian cause, bolster regional non-state allies, and achieve nuclear enrichment capacity. He became known for his belligerent, unrestrained language, especially when attacking Israel. Interestingly, his attitude also brought Iran closer to non-regional countries such as Venezuela, Bolivia, and Belarus, which shared dissatisfaction with the global power distribution.

Hardliners framed the nuclear project as a major national pride issue. To them, the West attempted to halt Iran's ambitions by denying it the right to develop nuclear technology. In this sense, hardliners simultaneously framed the country's isolation as proof that the system was unjust and Iran was resilient. Ahmadinejad tilted the Iranian international stance in this matter towards non-commitment. Needless to say, Iran's isolation escalated after Ahmadinejad's re-election, as controversial results provoked waves of protests in Tehran and other major cities.

His second term revealed a growing schism between traditional conservatives and the hardliners, which eventually reflected on foreign policy. Khamenei gradually showed frustration with Ahmadinejad's confrontation and general disobedience, and to counter the President's power, he set up a new Strategic Council on Foreign Relations in 2006.[73] As Khamenei's function was to balance factions, it is possible to conclude that he lessened his ideological tone in relation to Ahmadinejad because the latter's views were becoming detrimental to regime stability. In clear disaccord with Ahmadinejad's revanchism, Khamenei said in public that 'the day the relations with America prove beneficial for the Iranian nation, I will be the first one to approve that'.[74] It is believed that by 2012, the communication between the President and the *Ayatollah* completely broke down.[75]

The 2013 elections presented a winning coalition between pragmatics and many conservatives under the candidature of the cleric Hassan Rouhani. He resumed the pragmatic approach, deeming that no anti-imperialist stand should harm Iran's national interests. He was a respected academic, diplomat, political activist, and British-educated lawyer. He was also the ultimate insider, having served in the *Majlis*, the Assembly of Experts, the Expediency Council, and the Supreme National Security Council. These credentials gave him access to different factions and extensive knowledge about the regime's strengths and weaknesses. Most importantly, Rouhani had good relations with Khamenei, who saw the new President as a loyalist who could reconnect Iran to its original popular base while improving foreign relations.

Rouhani campaigned as a moderate centrist and promised to limit factional gridlock to 'save the economy, revive morality, and interact with the world'.[76] He argued that a better economy demanded ending sanctions, which would be only available through better relations with the West. That did not mean he disagreed that Iran should oppose the current status quo. Like Rafsanjani, Rouhani believed Iran was better prepared to be a regional power and promote its vision of a more endogenous Persian Gulf security arrangement if it managed to reduce its international isolation. In his words, 'Iran's economy has the potential to be among the world's top ten in the next three decades', and '[economic opening] does not mean letting go of the nation's ideals and principles'.[77]

Therefore, Rouhani asserted that working relations with the US could be possible if the two countries treated each other equally. In his words:

> the relationship between Iran and the United States is a complicated and difficult question. There is a chronic wound, which is difficult to heal. However, it is not impossible provided there is goodwill and mutual respect between the two countries. ... It seems that extremists on both sides are determined to maintain the state of hostility and hatred between the two states, but logic says that there should be a change of direction in order to turn a new page in this unstable relationship and minimise the state of hostility and mistrust between the two countries.[78]

At least during his first years as President, Rouhani had Khamenei's backing to push forward a nuclear settlement with the US. Khamenei stated that a deal was possible if it did not forgo Iran's right to develop its national programme.[79] For the first time since the Revolution, the *Ayatollah* and the President voiced a common favourable position on the issue. During Rafsanjani's administration, Khamenei's authority was under construction, making it risky to reach out to Washington. During Khatami's term, conservatives clashed with reformists. However, during Rouhani's term, Khamenei had the upper hand with a conservative–pragmatic coalition and enough authority to dismiss the President if the initiatives backfired. That allowed Rouhani and his Foreign Minister Mohammad Javad Zarif to move quickly, reaching the interim agreement with the P5+1 in Geneva in November 2013. Khamenei praised the negotiators, calling them 'children of the revolution' with a 'heroic flexibility'.[80]

Despite the change in the negotiation tone, the administration continued to push for Iran's rights to nuclear enrichment. In Rouhani's words, the 'atomic fuel cycle and generating nuclear power is as much about diversifying our energy resources as it is about who Iranians are as a nation, our demand for dignity and respect and our consequent place in the world'.[81] Finally, it is necessary to call attention to Zarif's and Rouhani's diplomatic skills. They employed an innovative – and effective – communication strategy to explain their ambitions and reduce international hostility. In Rouhani's words,

> our success in these negotiations showed that by observing all principles and all the red lines of the Islamic Republic and by expressing the reasonable and logical positions of the Iranian nation, we can call on global powers to respect the rights of the people of Iran. These negotiations showed that we can take future steps towards resolving all disagreements in a determined way.[82]

In conclusion, a shift between presidencies significantly altered Iran's strategic predilections. One can see that the changes are associated with different perceptions about environmental restrictiveness and different identitarian preferences. Moreover, it stresses the significance of factionalism for Iran's international behaviour. Explaining the nuclear negotiations is impossible without discussing Ahmadinejad's and Rouhani's different priorities and the quality of their relations with Khamenei.

Saudi Arabia's foreign policy executives: Abdullah's adjustment

During this period, the monarchical rule was in Abdullah's hands, first as Crown Prince (1982–2005) and later as King (2005–2015). As discussed in the previous chapter, King Fahd suffered from severe health problems, and Abdullah became the de facto ruler by the 1990s. The previous chapter has already presented Abdullah as a leader with pan-Islamic and regionalist preferences. He favoured an endogenous regional security system in which Saudi Arabia could thrive as a central and pivoting decision-maker. This chapter shows a variation of Abdullah's threat perception from one period to another. While he perceived a more permissive environment enabling improvement with Iran in the 1990s, the invasion of Iraq reverted this scenario, leading to a policy change corresponding to a sense of restrictiveness.

Like the first invasion of Iraq, Abdullah was against a foreign intervention, stating that the Iraqis and other people in the region would not welcome US soldiers.[83] Nevertheless, after the declaration of war, there was little left to do besides give quiet assistance and distance Saudi Arabia from the aftermath. After the involvement of so many Saudi nationals in the 9/11 attacks, it could be costly for Saudi Arabia to defy Washington's decision. Moreover, the fight against terrorism was a serious challenge to the monarchy, as a hidden Osama bin Laden and allies called for overthrowing all the monarchies of the Arab Peninsula. Therefore, the King believed that guaranteeing – and improving – a security partnership with the US was seen as crucial. One should not overanalyse Abdullah's remarks on the 'illegitimate foreign occupation' in Iran, as these were oriented to domestic audiences; externally, he restrained his criticism to avoid spoiling the US–Saudi relationship.[84]

Nevertheless, the most significant consequence of the events of 2003 was the disruption of Saudi Arabia's traditional strategy of balancing Iraq against Iran or vice versa. It quickly became apparent to Abdullah that, with Saddam out of the picture and Iraq in shambles, the path was clear for Iran to seek hegemony. Moreover, Ahmadinejad's election and the pressure over the nuclear programme raised Abdullah's suspicions about Iran's behaviour.[85] Thus, he slowly abandoned his tendency towards appeasing Iran in the name of a collective regional order to incline towards the Sudayri clan's preference for rejecting Iran's regional influence. By the end of 2006, the Sudayri's world view prevailed. With Abudullah's approval, Defence Minister Prince Sultan bin Abdulaziz reoriented foreign policy away from the rapprochement initiatives, particularly after perceiving that Iran was gaining influence among Arab politics, predominantly in Lebanon.[86] When the Lebanese war broke down in 2006, Saudis quickly pointed fingers at Iran; Abdullah even told Iranian Foreign Minister Manouchehr Mottaki that 'you as Persians have no business meddling in Arab matters'.[87]

As already discussed, Abdullah was a pragmatic leader with a remarkable ability to read his surroundings. That permitted him to reassess his preferences to respond to Iran's growing power to best ensure Saudi Arabia's national interest. Therefore, first, the monarchy began to frame Iran as a non-Arab actor interfering in Arab matters in the region. Promoting Saudi Arabia as an influential Arab actor while casting Iran as a foreign interventionist, Abdullah hoped to check Tehran's regional influence while boosting his own. Against this background, the monarchy linked the 'Iranian factor' to a series of events provoking instability in Arab countries.

Second, Abdullah was particularly apprehensive about Iran's nuclear empowerment and how this could ensure its hegemony. Although he supported Iran's right to nuclear autonomy in the 1990s, the level of suspicion towards the nuclear programme, its level of secrecy, and Ahmadinejad's aggressive tone changed the circumstances for the monarch. By 2005, Abdullah started to call for a nuclear-free Persian Gulf, even if that meant heavily sanctioning Iran; he stated that 'Iran's goal is to cause problems'.[88] In a meeting with US Secretary of State Hillary Clinton in 2010, Prince Faisal bin Salman said it was imperative to have 'an immediate resolution [for the Iranian nuclear programme's threat] rather than a gradual solution'.[89] As these leaked cables reveal, they wanted to convince Washington of harsher action against Iran:

> 'The position of the King is very clear on Iran,' al-Jubeir said. King Abdullah believes that only a show of US strength will stop Iran's expansionist policies

and halt its nuclear program, he said, adding that the program is clearly intended to produce nuclear weapons. He noted that the King rejects the argument that military action against Iran will coalesce popular support around President Ahmadinejad.[90]

The King was particularly adamant on this point, and it was echoed by the senior princes as well. Al-Jubeir recalled the King's frequent exhortations to the US to attack Iran and so put an end to its nuclear weapons program. 'He told you to cut off the head of the snake' ... The Foreign Minister, on the other hand, called instead for much more severe US and international sanctions on Iran, including a travel ban and further restrictions on bank lending. Prince Muqrin echoed these views, emphasising that some sanctions could be implemented without UN approval. The Foreign Minister also stated that the use of military pressure against Iran should not be ruled out.[91]

The third step in Abdullah's readjustment concerned a gradual decrease in the pan-Islamist discourse. While Abdullah began his rule stressing the need for constructive bonds between all Islamic sects, he gradually adopted the idea of a Shia crescent of instability. Sectarian discourse advanced further during the Arab Uprisings, as Iran and Saudi Arabia sided with opposition groups in Bahrain, Yemen, and Syria. Under this context, the Saudi monarchy doubled down on its critiques, overstating that Iran had an 'expansionist project in the region' and that its rising influence among the Shias throughout the Arab world was nocive for peace and progress.[92] Abdullah argued that the 'moderate Arabs' should, therefore, build a cohesive block against Iran's role in the region. Unsurprisingly, he promoted Saudi Arabia as a leader among these moderate actors, arguing that they all should oppose Iran's political action in Iraq and Lebanon, its nuclear project, and its alliance with Syria, Hezbollah, and Hamas. Thus, the 2011 events presented an opportunity to expand Saudi Arabia's influence and ensure it had a position of authority among the Arab countries.

His regionalist ambitions became visible in how he proactively attempted to promote the GCC as an instrument of regional stability. In February 2010, Abdullah proposed that the GCC move towards a confederation, which would give Saudi Arabia a position of a significant power broker.[93] In June of the same year, he also proposed that the only two other Sunni monarchies, Jordan and Morocco, join the GCC, expanding the organisation's reach and scope. Abdullah aimed, therefore, to expand Saudi Arabia's ambitions facing the growing Iranian influence. He promoted Riyadh as an Arab regional leader capable of assisting its partners during and after the protests if necessary. In this sense, Abdullah guaranteed his priorities towards regionalism, as described in the last chapter. However, this time, Saudi Arabian regionalism did not include cooperation with Iran but a new set of policies that aimed to contain Tehran's influence.

The rebooted stable marriage triangle

The 2003–2014 period was one of transition, in which relations between Saudi Arabia and Iran advanced towards rivalry, whereas the Saudi–US one got slightly weakened and the Iran–US one shifted from intense confrontation to reduction of animosities. At first glance, the balance of power explains the return to the 'stable marriage' triangle due to Iran's empowerment. Nonetheless, by exploring the intervening variables, one can detect the gradual pace of the change from one triangle to another. Most importantly, it explains how Saudi Arabia's strategic shift resulted from its gradual discontent with the US' and Iran's regional decisions in combination with a power increase. By the end of the period, Saudi Arabia's new regional power ambition, conservative and Arab-centred, became evident.

Hence, the 2003–2014 triangle developed progressively. The two tendencies that define the period – the Iran nuclear impasse and Saudi Arabia's growing regional proactivity – were not an immediate consequence of the 2003 events. Both Saudi Arabia and Iran attempted to maintain the previous coexistence and cooperative spirit from the 1990s despite having different gains with the Iraqi debacle. However, a divergence between how they perceived the environmental restrictiveness drove Saudi Arabia to recalculate. Simultaneously, Iran's growing empowerment did not provoke an automatic confrontation with the US. Instead, the clash between the two over nuclear negotiations evolved throughout the period due to different assessments of threats and opportunities.

Immediately after the Iraqi invasion, Tehran knew it might be the next target and sent appeasement signals to Washington. While Iran's grand bargain indicated its willingness to discuss the nuclear deal openly, the Bush administration showed no interest. The neoconservative lens suggested that negotiating with Iran unnecessarily compromised US values. Reportedly, Vice President Cheney said 'we don't talk to evil' when asked about the decision to ignore Iran's signals.[94] This same level of inflexibility was found in Iran during the Ahmadinejad years. In his words, 'as long as the US remains in the region, it is a foreign object that people in the region will repel. Iran, however, cannot be repelled because it is part of the region and is here to stay'.[95] From 2005 to 2009, hardliners in Iran and neoconservatives in the US escalated antagonism and hostilities.

Iranian hardliners accelerated the nuclear project in line with a nationalist narrative, arguing that those contesting its right to reach a complete enrichment programme were damaging the country's sovereignty and autonomy. It is important to stress that accusations that Iran was hiding uranium enrichment and heavy-water facilities emerged during the Khatami administration. Since 2003, the US has brought accusations to the United Nations and pressured the IAEA to inspect different facilities in Iranian cities and provide reports. For the rest of Khatami's government, the IAEA, Iranian officials, and other European countries negotiated back and forth a resolution concerning the matter. Bush, for his part, continued to refuse to join discussions if Tehran did not halt all of its nuclear activities as a precondition.

However, things escalated with Ahmadinejad, who accused the West of provoking a 'nuclear apartheid' and gradually became less willing to cooperate with the IAEA. On the domestic front, the *Majlis* voted to end IAEA inspections, and Iran stopped negotiations with EU-3, showing less compliance and, thus, reiterating Western suspicions. In January 2006, Iran announced it was resuming its nuclear research, triggering a reaction from many Western actors and neighbouring countries. Neoconservative figures like US Ambassador to the UN John Bolton and Secretary of State Condoleezza Rice would often appear in interviews saying that the US was prepared to use 'political, economic and other measures to dissuade Iran from developing a nuclear weapon' and that 'all options were on the table'.[96] Eventually, the UNSC adopted the Resolution 1996 on 31 July 2006, which demanded the suspension of all uranium enrichment activities. Ahmadinejad doubled down, saying he would 'not bow to threats and ultimatums' and announced opening a new heavy-water plant in Arak.[97] On 25 February 2007, Iran reportedly fired its first rocket into space. Arguing fear of proliferation, the UNSC announced an arms embargo on 24 March 2007 (UNSC Resolution 1747).

Many other bilateral and multilateral sanctions followed. By the end of Bush's presidency, specialists were apprehensive of a possible conflict between Iran and the US as the hostilities had reached an unprecedented level. The more the US pressured, the more headstrong Iran's behaviour became. Obama arrived in power aware of this gridlock. Moreover, he seemed concerned about the limitations of the US international role and aimed to reduce international obligations. Thus, his dual-track strategy began. The first offered carrots were removing the preconditions for negotiations. It is reported that Washington sent letters to Khamenei in early 2009 asked Iran to demonstrate a willingness to negotiate or tougher sanctions would be imposed.[98]

It is important to stress that after the wave of protests after the 2009 presidential elections in Iran in June, the scenario for any cooperation between the West and Tehran became restricted. Simultaneously, domestic tensions intensified factionalism gridlock in Iran, which took priority over foreign policy. Either way, as Ahmadinejad rejected Obama's carrots, the sticks followed, and new sanctions began in the same year. In 9 June 2010, the UNSC 1929 resolution against Iran had more of a bite, imposing harsh controls on oil sector investment. In the same month, the US Congress passed the Comprehensive Iran Sanctions, Accountability, and Divestment Act, targeting several foreign investments. In 2012, an even more severe blow came when Iranian banks were disconnected from SWIFT (Society for Worldwide Interbank Financial Telecommunication), damaging their ability to conduct trade. While previous sanctions targeted Iran's political and military elites more specifically, these financial sanctions affected the population directly and severely.

Rouhani's election tilted Iran back to pragmatism, independentism, and image rehabilitation. Unlike Ahmadinejad, Rouhani saw the environment as restrictive for extreme anti-imperialist discourse and believed isolation endangered Iran's power. Moreover, he had received support within factions against the hardliner candidate and Khamenei's backing to head-start negotiations with the West. Thus, things moved quickly. Secret US–Iranian talks picked up early in August 2013. In October, Rouhani offered 'time-bound and results-oriented talks' over the nuclear question and spoke with Obama on the phone.[99] Right afterwards, Javad Zarif and John Kerry met on the sidelines of the UN General Assembly. Thus, in early November, the P5+1 (United States, China, France, United Kingdom, Russia, and Germany) talks started in Geneva, and after five days, the group announced the Geneva Interim Agreement or the Joint Plan of Action with Iran.

That opened the path to the signature of the JCPOA, adopted on 20 July 2015 and implemented on 16 January 2016. The deal established that all uranium enriched beyond 5 per cent would be diluted, no new uranium at the 3.5 per cent enrichment level would be added, and 50 per cent of the centrifuges at Natanz and 75 per cent at Fordow would be left inoperable. Besides, Iran would allow IAEA inspectors daily access to plants and grant access to uranium mines and centrifuge production facilities. In return, Iran would receive sanctions relief of approximately US$7 billion, and no further sanctions would be imposed. It was the first deal signed by the US and Iran since before the Islamic Revolution.

Nevertheless, many international actors criticised the agreement for not having the ambition to coerce Iran's regional behaviour. Some US partners, like Israel and Saudi Arabia, saw it as international consent to Iran's growing interventionist behaviour. From the viewpoint of Saudi Arabia, the US created another opportunity for Iran to project growing influence and seek regional hegemony. This resonated with the perception among the Saudi leadership that Washington had already beneficiated Iran in the war in Iraq. Back in 2003, Abdullah urged a three-way dialogue to solve the conflict in Baghdad, but Iran and the US repeatedly rejected it.[100]

Throughout the period, Saudi Arabia became gradually more dissatisfied with Tehran's and Washington's decisions in the region. Between 2003 and

2006, both Tehran and Riyadh attempted to maintain their rapprochement. Ahmadinejad visited Saudi Arabia four times, and he and Khamenei often stated that friendship with the Saudis was a priority.[101] Khamenei even reportedly sent a series of letters to Riyadh to improve dialogue and allow ministerial interchanges. Nevertheless, Abdullah drew a line on Arab politics. During the 2006 conflict between Hezbollah and Israel in Lebanon, Saudi Arabia strongly condemned the paramilitary group's actions and blamed its actions on its ties with Iran.[102] In early 2007, Iran and Saudi Arabia even tried to work to solve tensions among the different Lebanese groups they backed. However, that was ill-fated, and Abdullah increasingly blamed Iran for building a network of instability in the Levant.[103]

When Hezbollah took over downtown Beirut in May 2008 and clashed with pro-government Sunnis, the Saudi monarchy quickly accused Iran of being behind it.[104] WikiLeaks cables revealed that Prince Saud al-Faisal attempted to convince sceptical US officials to use NATO to support the creation of an Arab military force to intervene in Beirut.[105] The US, however, remained detached from the issue. In response, Riyadh boosted its support to Lebanese Salafi factions. Perceiving the Iranian interference in Arabian affairs as unprecedented, Abdullah gradually employed sectarianism to tackle the issue. He aimed to equate Iran as an external actor interfering in Arab politics while promoting Saudi Arabia as an Arab-centred leadership alternative.

Thus, when IAEA reports failed to guarantee the international community that Iran's nuclear programme complied with international standards, Saudi Arabia's rapprochement goals were long gone. In Riyadh's perception, if Iran achieved enrichment, it would be heading to regional supremacy. Saudi Arabia began to announce that it was 'okay with nuclear electric power and desalination, but not with enrichment' as 'they [Iran] do not need it!'[106] It insisted that a nuclear-free Persian Gulf was the only option, or else there would be proliferation. This would happen because of a general view among Arab countries that Iran 'could not be trusted'.[107] Obama's choice to sign a nuclear deal without previously informing Riyadh was perceived as a betrayal of trust. An apparent trust deficit emerged despite Obama's attempts to assure his counterparts that their partnership continued to be solid.[108] Showing disbelief, Prince Turki al-Faisal asked, 'how can you build trust when you keep secrets from what are supposed to be your closest allies?'[109]

There was a swelling frustration with Obama's policies in the Middle East. The administration's reticence towards the Syrian conflict and its unwillingness to protect partners such as Egypt and Tunisia from mass protests signalled that the extra-regional power was not protecting the order. Even Obama's Asian Pivot was framed by some as an abandonment of the Carter Doctrine and its commitments towards the Persian Gulf stability. Accordingly, some Saudis said Washington treated its allies 'like it treated the Shah when he was deposed', and Riyadh sent messages advising the US to 'listen to its friends'.[110] That is not to say that the relations between the two were tainted, but there was much more open criticism from then on. In other words, the US–Saudi side of the triangle was not becoming negative but permitting more independent action.

Thus, Saudi foreign policy's evolution is linked to discontent towards the US' *and* Iran's regional policies. The relative empowerment after 2003 gave conditions for Saudi Arabia to develop a new, more proactive regional strategy. Threat perception, status ambition, and Abdullah's grasp of the foreign environment drove the country to promote itself as a candidate for regional leadership that could check Iran. Unlike authors who say Saudi Arabia and Iran returned to a context of rivalry, this book shows that Saudi Arabia did not rival Iran for regional supremacy before 2007. From 1969 to 1979, Saudi Arabia had a secondary role in guaranteeing the conservative order with Iran. From 1979 to 2003, the country resigned to a strategy of balancing Iran or Iraq under the US security umbrella, competing with Iran only in religious matters.

This rivalry has been played through proxy conflict, meaning by influencing, supporting, or intervening in competing actors in different regional conflicts. While some pinpoint Iraq as the stage for Saudi–Iran rivalry, it is important to stress that Abdullah did not engage officially after Iraq's Shia Nuri al-Maliki rose as Prime Minister in 2006. It is reported that Bush attempted to convince Saudi Arabia to engage with the new Iraqi leader, but to no avail.[111] In Abdullah's view, al-Maliki was an Iran agent on Iraqi soil and could not be trusted – even if, symbolically, his first international travel as Prime Minister was to Riyadh in 2006, intending to restore ties with the monarchy.[112] Thus, while it is possible to assume that many Saudi actors had influence in the sectarian conflict in Iraq, on the political level, there was not even a competition for Iran's influence in Baghdad.

Things were different during the Syrian demonstrations that began in March 2011. Traditionally, Iran and Syria have shared an alliance since the 1980s Iran–Iraq war. Hence, Iran strongly supported the Bashar al-Assad government when the first protests began and the extreme violent repression that followed, leading to direct confrontation between rebels and government forces. Saudi Arabia's relations with Syria were never easy and were already tense since the 2006 Lebanon war, as both Arab countries disagreed on their standing. However, Abdullah first attempted to bring Assad to the negotiation table, but as that did not evolve, he gradually began to criticise Syrian policies of repression. By the eve of 2012, Saudi Arabia became the first Arab country to openly call for the end of the Assad regime, condemn Iran's backing, and provide financial and military assistance to the Free Syrian Army.[113] Saudi Arabia was publicly critical of how Washington and the West were handling the Syrian conflict, and, as a gesture of disapproval, it turned down a UNSC non-permanent seat in 2013. The rivalry was evident as the conflict continued, and Saudi Arabia and Iran strengthened their support to different fighting groups.

Saudi Arabia's new-found regional activism became even more evident in the Persian Gulf, with direct intervention. In February 2011, anti-government protests started in Bahrain, led by a Shia majority. The Sunni Al Khalifa monarchy has been in power since the times of the British protectorate and has often been criticised for its segregation policies towards the majority Shia population. Arguing that the Shia protesters had the assistance of Iran, the Bahraini King asked Riyadh for help.[114] Reportedly against US advice, Riyadh sent more than a thousand troops to Bahrain in March to help end the unrest. Supposedly, Abdullah told Obama that 'if the United States interfered in Bahrain, it would provoke a rupture in Saudi-American relations'.[115] After Saudi's intervention, martial law was declared, and the streets were cleared. Accusations from Tehran followed.

Therefore, Saudi Arabia intervened militarily in Bahrain for the first time under the pretext of protecting Sunni regimes from Iranian interference. The case in Yemen is somewhat similar. Protests against economic conditions, political corruption, inflation, and unemployment emerged in many cities in Yemen in 2011, demanding a change in the constitution and President Ali Abdullah Saleh's resignation.[116] Saudi Arabia – together with the other GCC countries – pressured for a political transition, which was reached with Saleh abdicating power for interim President Abdrabbuh Mansour Hadi. That did not ease tensions, and unrest returned around 2014. In the turbulent scenario, a political armed group from the South, the Houthis, entered the capital in September and took Hadi out of power. In response, Saudis launched Operation Decisive Storm in 2015 against the Houthis, whom the monarchy has for long framed as a proxy group of Iran. While most Houthis are not from the same Shia strand as Iranians, the war has been framed as a sectarian conflict, with Saudis protecting the Sunni government against the Shia-linked rebels. The war, which has prolonged itself for more than seven years now, is one of the major humanitarian catastrophes in the Middle East, with massive death tools and few solutions in sight.

By the end of this triangle period, Saudi Arabia's new ambitions were out in the open. Riyadh sought to affirm its regional prominence, driven by the need to secure the Persian Gulf and in a context of escalating Iranian threat and the US' perceived neglect. Thus, the US decision to invade Iraq increased Saudi Arabia's relative power and, at the same time, it set in motion a strategic reassessment process directly related to how Washington and Tehran were behaving in the region – reaffirming, once again, the structure of the strategic triangle.

*

From 2003 until 2014, Iran saw opportunities in Iraq, whereas Saudi Arabia was forced to find a new strategy as the US invasion wrecked its usual one. This triangle stressed the importance of analysing power as fluctuant by breaking down its elements. The moment that Saddam's regime fell, the three actors increased in power. The US expanded its military presence to unforeseeable levels and boosted security ties with the GCC. Iran's influence enhanced in tandem with the enfranchisement of non-hegemonic groups in the Middle East. In its turn, Saudi Arabia was relieved to see Saddam go. The rise of oil prices in the first half of 2000 also served Iran and Saudi Arabia to enhance their economy and increment military capacities. However, by the mid-2000s, US Americans showed signs of war fatigue and were interested in withdrawing from the region, while growing sanctions ceased the Iranian empowerment moment. Only Saudi Arabia retained steady growth and arrived at the end of the period with more power than it started with.

Therefore, while Iran's empowerment and growing regional interference explain the Saudi–Iran rapprochement's discontinuance, Riyadh's new ambition for regional leadership must also account for the US role. The status variable showed their discontent with Washington's commitment to the Carter Doctrine. Riyadh's anxiety only increased with Obama's decision not to support traditional partners. As the leadership variable discussed, Obama's assessment of US power limitations pushed him away from conflicts that did not serve direct national interests. All these aspects shaped the new Saudi Arabia's ambition: proactively guaranteeing the regional order. Nevertheless, this does not make Riyadh a revisionist actor as it wants only to improve its position in the same order – it seeks a promotion.

A closer analysis of the leadership variable is also necessary for understanding how nuclear negotiations came to be when they did and not in any other period. Bush and Ahmadinejad, two leaders who saw their countries' empowerment as a sign that the environment was open to vindicative behaviours, brought tensions to a new, dangerous level. Conversely, a realist-progressive, Obama believed it to be necessary to acknowledge Iran's regional power. Simultaneously, Rouhani had an acute sense of environmental restrictiveness and was aware of the need to fix the nuclear situation, which he saw as the primary source of socioeconomic distress. That enabled negotiations to begin. Nevertheless, Obama's failure to assess Riyadh's dissatisfaction while reaching out to Iran led to increased anxieties in the Arab nation, which responded with proactivity and interventionism. By the time ISIS became a central concern in the Middle East, Iran and Saudi Arabia found themselves in a unique scenario of rivalry, supporting different groups in many regional conflicts.

The 2014 conflict against ISIS, which drove Iran and the US to deploy troops to Iraq, is another systemic change that shifted the power balance.

Soon after, the right-wing Republican President Donald Trump took advantage of this scenario to revise Obama's diplomatic gains with Iran and spike US–Iran tensions once again. At the same time, an emerging powerful Crown Prince, Mohammad bin Salman, was determined to promote Saudi Arabia as the new regional power in the Persian Gulf, rivalling Iran and pushing for a less asymmetrical alliance between Washington and Riyadh.

Notes

1 Toby Dodge, State and society in Iraq ten years after regime change: The rise of a new authoritarianism, *International Affairs* 89: 2, 2013, pp. 241–257, p. 243.
2 Hiro, *Cold War in the Islamic world*, p. 190.
3 Hiro, *Cold War in the Islamic world*, p. 215.
4 World Bank, Military expenditure (current USD) – United States: 1960–2019; World Bank, Military expenditure (% of GDP) – United States: 1960–2019.
5 Fred Lawson, Security dilemmas in the contemporary Persian Gulf, in Kamrava (ed.), *International politics of the Persian Gulf*, pp. 50–71, p. 65.
6 Micah Zenko, US military policy in the Middle East – An appraisal: Research paper (US and Americas Programme, Chatham House: The Royal Institute of International Affairs, October 2018).
7 Degang Sun and Yahia H. Zoubir, From hard military bases to soft military presence: US military deployment in Iraq reassessed, *Journal of Middle Eastern and Islamic Studies (in Asia)* 6: 3, 2012, pp. 85–106.
8 Degang Sun and Yahia H. Zoubir, The eagle's nest in the Gulf: Analysis of US military deployment in the GCC Countries (1991–2014), in Tim Niblock and Steven Hook (eds), *The United States and the Gulf: Shifting pressures, strategies and alignments* (Berlin: Gerlach Press, 2015), pp. 78–97, p. 96.
9 Zenko, US military policy in the Middle East, p. 10.
10 Ali R. Abootalebi, What went wrong in Iraq?, in Lesch and Haas (eds), The Middle East and the United States, pp. 274–289, p. 279.
11 World Bank, GDP growth (annual %) – United States: 1960–2019.
12 Thomas Palley, *The U.S. economy after Bush: Policy brief* (Düsseldorf: Hans Bockler Stiftung, October 2008), p. 3.
13 World Bank, GDP (current US$) – United States: 1960–2019.
14 World Bank, GDP (current US$) – United States: 1960–2019.
15 Yakub Halabi, *US foreign policy in the Middle East: From crises to change* (Farnham: Ashgate, 2009).
16 Steven Kull, Muslim public opinion on US policy, attacks on civilians, and al Qaeda, April 2007.
17 Shibley Telhami, 2008 annual Arab public opinion pool survey.
18 Gregory Gause, Saudi regime stability and challenges, in Madawi Al-Rasheed (ed.), *Salman's legacy: The dilemmas of a new era in Saudi Arabia* (London: Hurst & Company, 2018), pp. 31–45.
19 World Bank, GDP (current US$) – Iran, Islamic Rep.: 1961–2019.

20 Saikal, *Iran rising*, p. 119.
21 World Bank, Military expenditure (current USD) – Iran, Islamic Rep.: 1961–2019.
22 Ben Rich, Gulf War 4.0: Iran, Saudi Arabia and the complexification of the Persian Gulf equation, *Islam and Christian-Muslim Relations* 4, 2012, pp. 471–486, p. 475.
23 Abedin, *Iran Resurgent*, p. 33; Anthony H. Cordesman, *The Gulf military balance in 2010: An overview* (Washington, DC: Center for Strategic and International Studies, April 2010).
24 Ward, *Immortal*, p. 313.
25 Rich, Gulf War 4.0: Iran, Saudi Arabia and the complexification of the Persian Gulf equation, p. 475.
26 Juneau, *Squandered opportunity*, p. 63.
27 Saikal, *Iran rising*, p. 147; Ward, *Immortal*, p. 299.
28 Anthony H. Cordesman, Robert M. Shelala, and Omar Mohamed, *The Gulf military balance: The Gulf and the Arabian Peninsula* (Lanham: Center for Strategic & International Studies, 2014).
29 Juneau, *Squandered opportunity*.
30 Anoushiravan Ehteshami, Domestic politics and foreign policy in contemporary Iran, in Anoushiravan Ehteshami and Reza Molavi (eds), *Iran and the international system* (London, New York: Routledge, 2012), pp. 121–130, p. 126.
31 Shahram Chubin, *Iran and the Arab Spring: Ascendancy frustrated* (GRC Gulf papers, Geneva: Gulf Research Center, 2012); Charles Kurzman, The Arab Spring: Ideals of the Iranian green movement, methods of the Iranian Revolution, *International Journal Middle East Studies* 44: 1, 2012, pp. 162–165.
32 Hiro, *Cold War in the Islamic world*, p. 229.
33 World Bank, GDP (current US$) – Saudi Arabia: 1968–2019.
34 Data from the CEIC database (see: www.ceicdata.com/en/indicator/saudi-arabia/government-debt--of-nominal-gdp).
35 Hertog, The 'rentier mentality'; Krane, *Energy kingdoms*.
36 Joe Barnes and Amy M. Jaffe, The Persian Gulf and the geopolitics of oil, *Survival* 48: 1, 2006, pp. 143–162.
37 World Bank, Military expenditure (current USD) – Saudi Arabia: 1968–2019.
38 World Bank, Military expenditure (% of GDP) – Saudi Arabia: 1968–2019.
39 Rich, Gulf War 4.0: Iran, Saudi Arabia and the complexification of the Persian Gulf equation, p. 478.
40 Richter, *Regional powers in the Middle East*, p. 185.
41 World Bank, Armed forces personnel, total – Saudi Arabia: 1968–2019.
42 Cronin, Tribes, coups and princes, p. 25.
43 James Russell, Saudi Arabia in the 21st century: A new security dilemma, *Middle East Policy* XII, 2005, pp. 64–78, p. 68.
44 Florence Gaub, *The Gulf Moment: Arab Relations since 2011* (Washington, DC: United States Army War College, May 2015).

45 Richter, *Regional powers in the Middle East*; Frederic Wehrey, Saudi Arabia's anxious autocrats, Journal of Democracy 26: 2, 2015, pp. 71–85, p. 72.

46 Gause, *Beyond sectarianism*.

47 White House, The national security strategy of the United States of America, news release, 2002.

48 Mohammed Ayoob, American policy towards the Persian Gulf: Strategies, effectiveness, and consequences, in Kamrava (ed.), *International politics of the Persian Gulf*, pp. 120–143.

49 Keynoush, *Saudi Arabia and Iran*, p. 158.

50 Al-Saud, *Saudi Arabia and the international oil market*.

51 Russell, Saudi Arabia in the 21st century, p. 67.

52 Madawi Al-Rasheed, Sectarianism as counter revolution: Saudi responses to the Arab Spring, *Studies in Ethnicity and Nationalism* 11: 3, 2011, pp. 516–523.

53 Richter, *Regional powers in the Middle East*, p. 173.

54 Monten, The roots of the Bush Doctrine.

55 George W. Bush, President Bush address to a joint session of Congress and the American people United States Capitol Washington, DC, news release, October 2001.

56 Adam D. Morton, The 'failed state' of international relations, *New Political Economy* 10: 3, 2005, pp. 371–379.

57 Andrew Flibbert, The road to Baghdad: Ideas and intellectuals in explanations of the Iraq War, *Security Studies* 15: 2, 2006, pp. 310–352.

58 Onea, Putting the 'classical' in Neoclassical Realism, p. 154.

59 Condoleezza Rice, Remarks at the American University in Cairo, news release, 20 June 2005.

60 Jeffrey Goldberg, The Obama Doctrine, *The Atlantic*, April 2016.

61 Goldberg, The Obama Doctrine.

62 White House, Remarks by President at Cairo University (Cairo, 4 June 2009).

63 Seliktar, *Navigating Iran*, p. 162.

64 Shahram Akbarzadeh (ed.), *Routledge handbook of International Relations of the Middle East* (London and New York: Routledge, 2019), p. 163.

65 White House, Remarks by President at Cairo University.

66 Committee on Foreign Affairs, New beginnings: Foreign policy priorities in the Obama Administration (hearing before the Committee on Foreign Affairs House of Representatives, Serial No. 111–167, Washington, DC, 22 April 2009).

67 Goldberg, The Obama Doctrine.

68 Goldberg, The Obama Doctrine.

69 Shahram Akbarzadeh (ed.), *America's challenges in the greater Middle East: The Obama administration's policies* (Basingstoke: Palgrave Macmillan, 2011), p. 6.

70 PBS Frontline, Showdown with Iran, October 2007.

71 Saikal, *Iran rising*.

72 Arjomand, *After Khomeini*, p. 149.

73 Seliktar, *Navigating Iran*, p. 140.

74 Sadjadpour, *Reading Khamenei*, p. 17.

75 Saikal, *Iran rising*, p. 118.
76 Morgane Colleau, Iran's Janus-faced US foreign policy: Continuity and change, opportunity and constraint, in Shahram Akbarzadeh and Dara Conduit (eds), *Iran in the World: President Rouhani's foreign policy* (Basingstoke: Palgrave Macmillan, 2016), pp. 33–59.
77 Ladane Nasseri, Rouhani tells Iranians economy can't grow with nation isolated, *Bloomberg*, 4 January 2015.
78 BBC Monitoring, Iran election: Hassan Rouhani in his own words, 15 June 2013.
79 Saikal, *Iran rising*, p. 123.
80 Colleau, Iran's Janus-faced US foreign policy, p. 49.
81 Aljazeera, Rouhani urges leaders to engage with Iran, 20 September 2013.
82 The Office of the Supreme Leader, Supreme Leader's response to President Rouhani's letter on nuclear negotiations, news release, 25 November 2013.
83 Riedel, *Kings and presidents*, pp. 140–141.
84 Lydia Georgi, Saudi King slams 'illegitimate occupation' of Iraq, *Agence France Presse*, 28 March 2007.
85 Amiri, Samsu, Ku, and Fereidouni, The Hajj and Iran's foreign policy towards Saudi Arabia, p. 685.
86 Keynoush, *Saudi Arabia and Iran*, p. 167.
87 Saudi Arabia Embassy, Saudi King says talks with Iranian FP 'heated'.
88 Saudi Arabia Embassy, Saudi King says talks with Iranian FP 'heated'.
89 BBC News, Saudi FM al-Faisal doubts Iran sanctions plans, 16 January 2010.
90 Saudi Arabia Embassy, Saudi Ambassador to the US on Iran, Sanctions. Riyadh (07RIYADH2322_a), 2007. Available at https://wikileaks.org/plusd/cables/07RIYADH2322_a.html. Accessed on 23 December 2020.
91 Saudi Arabia Embassy, Saudi King Abdullah and Senior Princes on Saudi Policy toward Iraq' (2008). Available at https://wikileaks.org/plusd/cables/08RIYADH649_a.html. Accessed on 23 December 2020.
92 Al-Rasheed, Sectarianism as counter revolution, p. 541.
93 Rich, Gulf War 4.0, p. 480.
94 Meir Javedanfar, The grand bargain with Tehran, *The Guardian*, 3 March 2009.
95 Keynoush, *Saudi Arabia and Iran*, p. 197.
96 CBS News, Rice: Iran's president is 'dangerous', 12 January 2006.
97 Spiegel, Iran's Ahmadinejad rejects looming UN deadline on nuke program, 29 August 2006.
98 El-Khawas, Obama's engagement strategy with Iran.
99 Shahram Shahram Akbarzadeh and Dara Conduit (eds), *Iran in the World: President Rouhani's foreign policy* (Basingstoke: Palgrave Macmillan, 2016), p. 46.
100 Keynoush, *Saudi Arabia and Iran*, p. 178.
101 Al Toraifi, *Understanding the role of state identity in foreign policy decision-making*, p. 241.
102 Darwich, *Threats and alliances in the Middle East*.
103 Dawn Today Paper, Saudi king says Iran endangering region, 28 January 2007.

104 Aarts and van Duijne, Saudi Arabia after the U.S.–Iranian détente, p. 70.

105 Mohamad Bazzi, Lebanon and the start of Iran and Saudi Arabia's proxy war, *The New Yorker*, 26 May 2015.

106 Saudi Arabia Embassy, Saudi exchange with Russian Ambassador on Iran's nuclear plans (2009). Available at https://wikileaks.org/plusd/cables/09RIYADH181_a.html. Accessed on 23 December 2020.

107 Saudi Arabia Embassy, Saudi king says talks with Iranian FP 'heated'.

108 Gawdat Bahgat and Robert Sharp, Prospects for a new US strategic orientation in the Middle East, *Mediterranean Quarterly* 25 (3), 2014, pp. 27–39, p. 31.

109 Theodore Karasik, Obama's anticipated march to Saudi Arabia, *Al Arabiya*, 3 February 2014.

110 Riedel, *Kings and presidents*, p. 162.

111 Riedel, *Kings and presidents*, p. 162.

112 Katherine Harvey, *A self-fulfilling prophecy: The Saudi struggle for Iraq* (London: Hurst & Company, 2021).

113 Yehuda U. Blanga, Saudi Arabia's motives in the Syrian Civil War, *Middle East Policy* 24: 4, 2017, pp. 45–62.

114 Amr Yossef and Joseph R. Cerami, *The Arab Spring and the geopolitics of the Middle East: Emerging security threats and revolutionary change* (London: Palgrave Macmillan UK, 2015).

115 Riedel, *Kings and presidents*, p. 159.

116 Maria-Louise Clausen, Understanding the crisis in Yemen: Evaluating competing narratives, *The International Spectator* 50: 3, 2015, pp. 16–29.

Conclusion

The ongoing fifth triangle

Historical analyses are not the simple exposition of facts but academic debates about meanings, entailing, therefore, contestation, competing constructions of reality, and different interpretations and claims. Thus, it is not possible to present here the same analysis as in the other chapters, as we cannot define the characteristics of a relationship that is going on – especially in the Middle East, where things change so fast and abruptly. Thus, this section presents the current state of the three dyads, leaving the tendencies of the ongoing fifth triangle open for discussion.

The fourth triangle ended when Mosul fell under ISIS control, shaking, once again, the balance of power. Both the US and Iran were anxious about containing the ISIS threat. They also took the event as an opportunity to boost their direct military engagement in the region and security cooperation with Iraq. Iran broadened its influence considerably over Iraqi and Syrian politics, particularly by IRGC training local forces and militias. The US, on the other hand, returned once again to Iraq with a military advisory role and deployable troops. While the US air campaign and the Iranian ground campaign complemented each other, both actors denied cooperation or military coordination.[1]

In December 2018, US President Donald Trump declared victory over ISIS and announced he would retreat the troops gradually. By then, he had already unilaterally withdrawn the US from the JCPOA, accusing the deal of privileging Iran too much, and the world was already familiar with the Salman leadership in Saudi Arabia, which has been shaking things up in Ryiadh since 2015. The following pages examine these issues and more, presenting a picture of the current US–Iran–Saudi Arabian relations. Afterwards, we delve into the book's theoretical contribution and conclude with some notes on the emerging global multipolarity and its consequences for the IR of the Middle East.

The US–Saudi dyad: a not-so-special partnership?

In January 2015, King Abdullah died, and his brother, Salman bin Abdulaziz Al Saud, took the throne. What has been called the 'Salman era' has shifted the gears in Saudi Arabia, adjusting not only how it is perceived all over the world but, most notably, how it sees itself.[2] The King's son, Mohammad bin Salman – mostly known as MBS – became the image of a massive national transformation. A young, modern prince, MBS promotes himself as a nationalist and a reformist, the leader needed to guarantee Saudi Arabia a position of predominance in a changing world. In charge of the defence and economic policies since the beginning of his father's reign, MBS was the commander-in-chief of the country's first autonomous military intervention, Operation Decisive Storm, in Yemen, which started in March 2015 and evolved into Operation Restoring Hope in April. The intervention aimed to oust the Houthi rebels from Sanaa and restore the government of President Abrabbuh Hadi. Nevertheless, the war in Yemen is often also described as MBS' battle for influence against Iran, which supports the Houthis.

MBS has pursued a much bolder foreign policy, enabled by the country's power growth and the new ambition for regional leadership detected in the previous period. In June 2017, he announced a blockage against Qatar due to its relations with Iran and the Muslim Brotherhood. He has also been linked to the resignation of Lebanese Prime Minister Saad al-Hariri in 2017. Domestically, a set of reforms, particularly concerning women's rights and labour regulations, as well as crackdowns on corruption, were enchanting international audiences. Most importantly, MBS is the spokesperson for the immense national development project, Saudi Vision 2030, announced in April 2016, which aims to transform the country into a financial, techno-logical, and industrial powerhouse in a post-oil future. However, this ben-evolent image was shattered when it became clear that MBS was linked with the gruesome assassination of journalist Jamal Khashoggi in Istanbul on 2 October 2018.

The harsh reaction from the US legislative branch and the ample coverage of the assassination by the Western media was yet another indicator of the deterioration of the US–Saudi 'special' relationship. The Saudis have been frustrated with the US' behaviour towards the region since George W. Bush decided to invade Iraq. They also reproved Obama's response to the 2011 Arab Uprisings, his lack of action on Syria, and the whole JCPOA nego-tiation. While the Obama administration tried to appease the Saudis by calling the 2015 US–GCC meeting at Camp David, the results were ques-tionable and Saudi scepticism remained. Trump's election represented an attempt to rekindle the closeness between the two countries. Indeed, his first international travel as President was to Riyadh, where he was received with all the pomp and glamour that the kingdom had to offer. His harsher stand on Iran most definitely pleased the Saudis, but that was just about it. Throughout his mandate, Trump reinforced the US' discomfort with the excessive engagement in the Middle East, and his 2018 National Defense Strategy made it clear that the Asian Pivot goal was alive and well.

The US–Saudi unique partnership has been labelled as an oil-for-security bargain for decades. This type of interdependency, however, was not attractive to the brand of hyper-nationalism that Trump subscribed to. Pledging to make 'America Great Again', he promised to protect and promote US business and the working class, create jobs and reduce taxes, control immigration, renegotiate trade deals, and remove the country from wayward international commitments. Under these lenses, he saw the Saudi monarchy as a money bag that could invest in the US and, most importantly, buy more armaments. Hence, despite growing concerns towards the prolongation of the Yemen War, the Trump administration approved multiple arms sales to Riyadh. However, Trump also insisted on reducing troops and showed less commitment to the region's security. This was particularly noticeable in his reticence towards a severe missile attack on Saudi oil installations in 2019. It is interesting to note that, by that time, Trump declared that the US was energy-independent and did not need to import oil, which may have influenced him to not honour the US side of the traditional bargain.

Thus, the US–Saudi relationship may be losing its specialness – not because of a particular failure from one side or another but rather due to the pursuit of different national interests. MBS perceives that the international order is rearranging, and he wants to take advantage of that, reorienting Saudi Arabia's goals and partnerships. He assumes that his country is a regional power in the making, geopolitically important enough that it can branch out its strategic ties to other great powers, particularly China and Russia. It is central to stress here that Vision 2030 depends on deepening the economic link between the Persian Gulf and Asia – Saudi's most significant oil export destination – attracting more foreign investments and complex energy cooperation agreements. Excessive reliance on Washington amid increasing US–China competition would go against these objectives.

Contrary to MBS, President Joseph Biden has shown a grasp of the international order that is binary, which is the usual 'with us or against us' stand that was seen many times throughout this book. His 2022 National Security Strategy even argues that the world today is divided into a 'competition of democracies and autocracies'.[3] Thus, when the 2022 Ukrainian–Russian war threatened skyrocketing oil prices, the US President flew to the Persian

Gulf in July to court its partners and address their sense of abandonment. He expected that Riyadh would honour its side of the oil-for-security bargain and stabilise the oil markets. This is despite the fact that Biden criticised Saudi Arabia for its human rights records many times, withdrew the US support in Yemen, chaotically removed troops from Afghanistan, and ended combat involvement in Iraq. Maybe it was too late, or maybe Biden's offer was just not good enough. On 5 October, the OPEC+ countries, under Saudi leadership, announced a heavy cut on oil production, boosting prices and devastating expectations from the US stakeholders.[4]

Therefore, Saudi Arabia is making it clear that it will prioritise its national interests even if it goes against the US interests in the Persian Gulf. That does not mean that Riyadh is interested in harming its relationship with Washington; it is far from that. Instead, its growth in power and new-found confidence has enabled Saudi Arabia to bring the relationship to a more normal level, in which disagreements on geopolitical events are possible and even expected.

US–Iran dyad: maximum pressure, maximum resistance

While the negotiations over the Iranian deal kept advancing during the rest of Obama's years, Trump's election was a cold shower. Since his campaign, Trump has been firmly against the JCPOA, calling it the 'worst deal ever' and an 'embarrassment'. He argued that the deal was 'too soft' on Iran. The other EU signatories made several pleas to the President so that he would stop sabotaging it. Nevertheless, in May 2018, Trump announced that he was unilaterally withdrawing from the JCPOA and imposing a new set of sanctions on Iran. While the other signatories maintained their commitment towards the deal, it is undeniable that its ability to reduce Iran's international isolation and bring economic relief was shattered; few international companies were interested in suffering secondary sanctions from the US.

Trump orchestrated a maximum pressure campaign against Iran, thoroughly discarding Obama's view that Iran needed to be reintegrated into the regional security arrangement. He aimed to pressure Iran into accepting a new, more restrictive nuclear deal that also covered its missile capabilities and limitations on its regional activities. He also designated IRGC as a terrorist organisation and eliminated all waivers over oil sanctions in 2019. As a response, Khamenei and the IRGC advanced their maximum resistant front with low-intensity military actors, sabotage and seizure of tanks, and other deniable attacks in Iraq. It is in this context that Trump ordered the drone strike that killed the leader of the Quds Force, General Qassem

Soleimani, on 3 January 2020. That shut down any open window for nego-tiation between the two countries. Iran responded by targeting US bases in Iraq, unintentionally shooting down the 752 Ukraine Airlines flight, killing all passengers on 8 January 2020. Tensions got extremely high.

In his turn, President Rouhani, who had based his socioeconomic improve-ment promises on ending sanctions, lost credibility and faced public disen-chantment and accusations of mismanagement and corruption. The new sanctions severely inflicted the Iranian population as inflation continued to grow, national currency entered a spiral of devaluation, and unemployment and general impoverishment augmented. Widespread protests took place in several cities until the end of his presidency. The regime not only downplayed the protests' impact but also responded with growing repression, violence, and imprisonment. The situation got even more daunting with the outbreak of the COVID-19 pandemic, which was severely mishandled, making Iran one of the countries with the highest mortality rates in the world.

Under this context, the conservative cleric Ebrahim Raisi was elected President in 2021 in the election with the lowest turnout since the Revolution. With the support of Khamenei, the *Majlis*, and the IRGC, the President promised to overcome Rouhani's chronic problems via smart economic policies and a foreign policy focusing on regional and non-Western part-ners to circumvent sanctions. This has been successful in guaranteeing Iran long-term strategic cooperation agreements with China and Russia as well as a full membership position in the Shanghai Cooperation Organisation (SCO). However, at the domestic level, Raisi did not find alternatives to respond to economic stagnation, widespread political dissatisfaction, and increasing civil contestation. Moreover, since the death of Mahsa Amini on 16 Setember 2022, women have taken the lead in large-scale protests against the mandatory veiling policy and the oppression of the moral police, defyingly calling for the end of the regime.

There were high expectations that Biden would bring the US back into the JCPOA. He had openly criticised Trump's decision to withdraw and promised to work hard to revert the situation to the status quo ante. However, almost reaching the end of Biden's mandate, very little has changed. Negotiations had started and stopped without reaching solutions as the parties are in a deadlock on issues concerning sanctions relief and IAEA inspections. Furthermore, despite his criticism towards Trump's heavier sanctions, Biden maintained all of them. As a result, Iran continued to advance its nuclear programme, and some reports suspect it is closer than ever before to being able to create a nuclear device. This would only endanger regional security and instigate a nuclear race among neighbouring countries.

In short, Trump's decision to unilaterally leave the nuclear deal was catastrophic. As problematic as the JCPOA was, it was groundbreaking and unprecedented. This book showed how hard it has been, since 1979, for Iran and the US to find themselves in a situation where both leaders find international and domestic momentum in improving the relationship. A new nuclear deal may take an even longer negotiation time and higher risk assessments. So far, maximum pressure and maximum resistance have only resulted in stagnation in the best case or inflated tensions and conflict risk in the worst case.

Iran–Saudi Arabia dyad: the new competition normal

By the end of the fourth triangle, Saudi Arabia has assumed for itself the ambition to be a regional power with the means to compete for influence against Iran, the other aspirer of Persian Gulf leadership. Both project very different types of leadership. While Saudi Arabia is the conservative, Arab, Sunni, and status quo protector candidate, Iran is the revolutionary, Persian, Shia, and revisionist one. The arrival of MBS to power heated things further, as he justified the intervention in Yemen to combat Iran's interference in Arab politics, framing Houthis as one of Tehran's many proxy actors. For Saudi Arabia, Iran has no space in Arab politics. Conversely, Iran sees itself as an actor that can construct alliances with different groups that are excluded by traditional political elites, such as Hezbollah, Houthis, or Hamas, and, for these reasons, its regional influence is only natural.

Iran and Saudi Arabia often accused each other of provoking instability, taking advantage of sectarianism and acting out of opportunism. They seek to increase their influence in regional theatres like Syria, Iraq, Yemen, Bahrain, and Lebanon while attempting to contain the other. Caught in this scenario, the influential Shia cleric Sheikh Nimr Baqir al-Nimr was executed in January 2016 by the Saudi government. That drove a series of protesters to ransack the Saudi embassy in Tehran. As a response, Riyadh cut diplomatic ties and recalled all embassy staff. Tensions may have reached their peak in September 2019, when the monarchy accused Iran of assisting the Houthis' ballistic missile attacks on Saudi oil refineries. The Houthis carried out other attacks in 2020 and 2021 – in which Iran has uneagerly denied involvement.

Many factors indicate that Saudi Arabia and Iran will have to learn how to live with one another under a normal level of regional competition. Securitising their rivalry to the level it reached by the eve of the 2020s has not brought any benefits for both. The continuation of the conflict in Yemen and Syria, despite efforts to reach a resolution, exemplifies both Riyadh's and Tehran's limitations in assuring their interests in the region. Especially for Saudi Arabia, the success of its Vision 2030 depends on significant stability in the country and its surroundings – or else investors will continue to over-estimate their risks. Conversely, Iran seeks to improve economic relations with regional actors, something that is also threatened if there are no ties with one of the most influential Arab nations. Additionally, it is possible to say that the COVID-19 pandemic served as a wake-up call for both Riyadh and Tehran, as the oil prices drop echoed strongly in their already struggling economies. In this daring scenario, appeasement signals began to emerge.

It is primarily believed that Iraq and Oman facilitated a direct line of communication between Saudi Arabia and Iran in April 2021. Representatives from both Riyadh and Tehran appeared on their respective national media and announced that they were interested in building good working relations and reopening embassies.[5] Thus, on 10 March 2023, they announced the normalisation of ties brokered by China, releasing a joint trilateral statement that promised not only the reopening of the embassies but also cooperation in areas such as trade, investment, technology, science, sports, and culture. They also indicated the will to advance on a security agreement. The normalisation happened after Chinese President Xi Jinping visited Riyadh in December 2022 and President Raisi visited Beijing in February 2023. It is possible to assume that the topic of the Iran–Saudi hostilities has been presented as a deterring situation for a broad range of Chinese economic and developmental plans in the region.

The Chinese role in this negotiation should not be a surprise to those observing the region closely. In the last decade, China has become an essential actor for both Iran and Saudi Arabia. While a latecomer player in regional affairs, China has extended its weight in the Middle East, first as a trade partner and later as a direct investor in local development and infrastructure. The Persian Gulf is essential for the Chinese development plan as Saudi Arabia, Iran, and other GCC resource-rich countries are the leading suppliers of energy resources to Beijing. Thus, its interest in playing a constructive role in promoting regional stability makes sense, as it sees the region as crucial for its own economic growth. Moreover, the deal sends a message that China can project power into the region beyond economic growth, presenting itself as an effective alternative to the Western order in a growing multipolar international environment. If the Saudi–Iran rapprochement does bear fruits, China will increase its political leverage in the Middle East and improve its own international image.

Both Iran and Saudi Arabia are interested in boosting the Chinese role in the region. For Iran, China is not only an economic partner and source of foreign investment but also an essential strategic partner to rise above the mechanisms of isolation from the West. Beijing seems to agree with the strategic functionality of close ties with Iran vis-à-vis growing competition with the US. It has vetoed many UN sanctions against Iran since

Trump left the JCPOA, for example. In turn, Saudi Arabia is the most significant trade partner and oil supplier of China in the region, and there are already many deals between the two countries – and the two national companies, ARAMCO and Sinopec – covering multiple areas of potential collaboration that go beyond the transactional level. Most importantly, there is remarkable convergence on the architectures of both the Chinese transnational Belt and Road Initiative (BRI) and the Saudi Vision 2030.[6] Thus, the trilateral deal represented a win-win-win situation, as a sense of peace in the Middle East is crucial for China to continue expanding its economic role, which, in turn, is decisive for both Iran's and Saudi Arabia's national interests and long-term development objectives.

In short, the tensions between Iran and Saudi Arabia began to escalate when the Saudi leadership fully grasped its ambition and capability of being a regional leader, which undoubtedly put it on a colliding route with the long-standing Iranian goal of being seen as such. In the process of escalation, the competition, the rivalry, and the war of words took a severe sectarian tone. However, the leaderships of both countries seemed to be aware of their limitations. The 2020s began in a much more restrictive environment and exposed a multitude of crises at the international, regional, and domestic levels. Thus, pragmatism took place, and the de-escalation process began.

It is unlikely that the Iran–Saudi ties will evolve into a rapprochement soon. Their interest now is reaching and maintaining a cold peace in which they can pursue their interests without the threat of a direct attack. Regional power competition between them should be understood as the new normal. They will continue to interact in a mix of containment, competition, and collaboration in different political scenarios, constantly under the risk of taking up different sides in geopolitical conflicts and, therefore, rekindling hostilities once again.

NCR's relevance for the IRME

This book has argued that the IRME defy any theoretical extremes of parsimony or particularism. On the one hand, theories that see the region like any other fall short because they do not consider specific elements such as identity, religion, and transnational ideologies. On the other hand, models judging those domestic elements as the primary sources of international relations ignore the overbearing effect of structural conditions and the distribution of power. This book presented NCR as a rewarding theoretical approach that can find a middle ground between parsimony and particularism, between agency and structure. NCR investigates political events as they are, not how they ought to be. It sustains that international policy is driven first and foremost by a country's place in the systemic distribution of power. Still, it is necessary to look into domestic variables to explain why and how states deliberate policies. In other words, the international system creates conditions but does not have complete control over the outcomes.

Moreover, by determining that independent variables are at the systemic level and intervening variables at the unit level, NCR offers explanatory chains that are synthetical, hierarchical, and reproducible. Hence, the book presents NCR as an upgrade to the analytical eclecticism often employed in the IRME, as it avoids the degeneration and overdetermination pitfalls of patchworking different theoretical approaches and concepts. Thus, NCR is a route to strengthen the IRME's research programme within the discipline by offering scholars a ready-made framework and methodology to theorise about the dynamics of international politics in the region.

In short, NCR allows for research with similar diagnostic precision and political relevancy to analytical eclecticism while not losing theoretical accumulation or methodological rigour. One outtake of this book is bringing forward more profound discussions about advancing the IRME via NCR as well as fleshing out new research trends in the field. Certainly, questions about which are the best types of intervening variables for the Middle East, how to include non-state actors and state-society relations in the analysis, and which complex relational arrangements influence and are influenced by regional order are far from being exhausted – presenting, therefore, an exciting field for future research.

Ideas, identities, and leadership in the Middle East

This book makes a strong case for the inclusion of non-tangible variables like ideas, identities, and leadership in how we understand the international politics of the Middle East. Politics are not done in a vacuum, and different actors with diverse backgrounds, mindsets, and affiliations grasp systemic signals differently. That is not to say that one must abandon a structural understanding of how international relations work. Indeed, units interact at a level that is outside of their domestic limits and permeated by systemic characteristics that condition their action. These characteristics reflect the unequal distribution of power among units, which are imposed upon actors, leading them to act accordingly. The international, therefore, cannot be what states make of it, but that does not mean that they cannot interpret it in several ways. Different perceptions, expectations, ambitions, and identitarian subscriptions will lead those making decisions towards many directions. Thus, agency matters.

In the current international system, states are the primary unit. However, in the Middle East, like many other Global South countries, the state is far from a cohesive unit. As many of them have been outlined by external colonial actors, the ideal-like image of a Westphalian nation-state is almost non-existent. States are permeated by many identities, some of which are transnational, that give the people and leaders different understandings of belonging. Colonial experience and anti-imperialist struggle inform many of the states' ambitions, as well as ideals of solidarity, religious unity, and collective will. Equality, patterns of exclusion, sectarianism, and tribal rivalry orient how states perceive a threat, sometimes as more than military or power distribution assessments. Hence, the state cannot be understood as a black box unit.

This book opened the state's black book by looking into three unit-level variables. First, status satisfaction indicates the ideational factors shaping decision-making, *shifting* parameters towards revisionism or continuity. Status satisfaction relates directly to the systemic distribution of power via perception. Moreover, it shows a country's international ambitions beyond survival. Second, state identity accounts for the cognitive elements that are cohesive to an actor's sense of self, *narrowing* the band of possible actions. This variable shows that every state has a narrative of how it came to be, what it stands for, and what principles should guide the way it positions itself in international matters. Finally, leadership preferences reinforce the importance of those executing policies, thus *tilting* the outcomes to the direction of their interests, fears, and particular interpretations. This shows how policy outcomes are ultimately bound to decision-makers and how they calculate risks, gains, and opportunities.

Thus, by outlining analytical frameworks in which ideas, identities, and preferences help explain distinct steps in the processes of developing a response to systemic inputs, the book demonstrated how opening this black box does not necessarily mean opening Pandora's box. While challenging, the result will always be a much more complex and multifactorial understanding of an international relations phenomenon. Thus, the added value of including ideational, cognitive, and leadership factors is exposing important political patterns that otherwise would remain hidden. Far from being an inoperative task, opening the black box of the state can be a thrilling and stimulating intellectual exercise that is essential to bring progress to the IRME.

NCR and Global IR

IR as a discipline has been marked, since its emergence, by Western centrism. Reproducing the many material, political, and institutional inequalities of our international society, the discipline has developed with a distorted comprehension of what the international is for those on the periphery of the global power distribution. In other words, those in the Global North have primarily determined what knowledge is in IR and what it is not. In contrast, the Global South has been mostly relegated to a consumer of the theories, concepts, and ideas. However, this has been increasingly challenged by scholarly movements that seek to break with Western parochialism and bring in pluralism, diversity, and inclusion. These initiatives map how IR is done *by* and *for* regions outside the Western centre of knowledge production, aiming at de-Westernising or globalising the discipline. Among these initiatives, Global IR presents itself as a collective and reformist moment that aims to subsume all IR paradigms, making them genuinely diverse and capable of having a plural conversation about the most diverse global phenomena.

This book presented how NCR can work as a framework to globalise the Realist tradition. Its paradigmatic flexibility enables the creation of analytical instruments – like the strategic triangle – that dialogue with other fields of knowledge and are shaped by it. Moreover, Global IR instigates a two-way conversation with Area Studies in which specialised scholars from different backgrounds can teach, learn, and expand their knowledge boundaries. In other words, it argues for transformative interaction between different approaches and ways of thinking and intensifying interdisciplinarity within IR.

An appropriate NCR variable selection depends primarily on grasping the history of the study case and building on a proper literature review of the knowledge produced by and for it. Therefore, an NCR framework is only efficient if it interacts with and learns from the specialised literature. Only through this process do the intervening variables that work within the triangle actually work. Thus, by exploring cases outside the traditional centre of knowledge production – like the Persian Gulf – NCR can incorporate often excluded voices, actors, and experiences into its theory-building. That will help reduce NCR's own Western biases and make the tradition of Realism more in touch with realities all around the world.

The value of the NCR strategic triangle

The strategic triangle employed in this book is an analytical construct designed to generate hypotheses and stimulate more systematic thinking about complex relational patterns. It was built based on Dittmer's typology to refer to a complex relational arrangement that includes three countries that share highly interconnected foreign policies and strategies. To be a strategic triangle, each of the three actors must (i) acknowledge that the other two are crucial geopolitical actors, (ii) recognise the other two as autonomous, sovereign players, and (iii) elaborate their policy or strategies with awareness to each other. Thus, each of the three dyads within the triangle is liable to the other two, meaning that a change in one 'side' of the triangle can alter the other two. NCR gave theoretical meaning to this construct, defining that changes happen with an alteration of the balance of power within the system. The ideational, cognitive, and leadership intervening variables, hierarchically arranged, worked to explain the process that drove the characterisation of each triangular period.

This analytical instrument presented itself quite efficiently in exposing tendencies and patterns of relations between Iran, Saudi Arabia, and the US that would remain hidden if one analysed each bilateral relation separately. Now, it should travel to other cases and regions. Good IR theories should be able to expand knowledge beyond their initial empirical boundaries by travelling, adapting, and adjusting to other realities. This book's intention is not to construct and examine a triangle *just* to add it to the list of 'exceptionalities' that ostracise the Middle East from the centre of IR knowledge production. Thus, it is expected that this triangular framework will now be adapted, with the required contextualisation, to other regions. For example, it would be valuable to see whether this framework works for triads like Brazil–Argentina–US, Pakistan–India–China, or Japan–South Korea–US.

However, it is vital to stress the terms *travel* and *adapt*. While ideational, cognitive, and leadership elements were enough to explain the Persian Gulf triangle, that does not mean those are the sole necessary intervening variables for other cases. While this book argues that these variables are broad enough to explore many cases in the Global South, science is not made out of intuition. For applying this NCR framework to other cases, it is first necessary to investigate the dyads in depth by dialoguing with respective specialised literature, as done in Chapter 2. Only then can one confirm if the intervening variables suggested here are enough or not.

Multipolarity and the Persian Gulf

IR is currently in a state of flux. While only some would risk in the 2000s to say that the US unipolarity was beginning to fade, this is now a reality. It took a global financial crisis, a devastating pandemic, waves and waves of protests, clashes and conflicts in the Global South, and war in Ukraine for the term 'multipolarity' to become mainstream. However, how this multipolarity will look is still up for debate. With the rise of actors like China and India as well as non-hegemonic organisations like BRICS+, OPEC+, and SCO, the emerging scenario does not look like classical multilateralism but a contested and deeply plural fractionalism. The West is also changing, facing relative decline and splits that will force some regrouping among their representatives. Thus, the future seems to be moving towards a scenario with multiple and diffuse centres of power, with elevated variations in wealth distribution, divergent ideological authorities, competing norms and institutions, and many powerful non-state actors.[7]

The Middle East is caught in these global transformations. First, the role of the US is shifting as a reflection of great power competition rearrangement. The last three US presidents expressed an inevitable Middle East fatigue and a desire to rearrange efforts towards Asia. The Russia–Ukraine war increased this sense of emergency, with Biden reducing troops from Iraq, Saudi Arabia, and Afghanistan and reorienting expending to NATO and Ukraine. Moreover, supposing the geopolitical competition with Russia and China continues to increase, Washington will be forced to re-evaluate its traditional efforts of imposing political and economic reforms to avoid pushing its own partners closer to its global rivals. For now, the US seems to be still confused about which effective strategy it should take in the Middle East in this emerging multipolar context. In this process, it has alienated traditional partners, arbitrarily reacting to events instead of following a cohesive policy and giving preference to arms sales over building new security partnerships.

Thus, one possible consequence of the global multipolarity in the Middle East is a growing tendency towards self-regulation. Traditional partners will take the lead on guaranteeing the order more independently, answering their scepticism about Washington's willingness to do so. They will pursue their own peace initiatives and regional security accords as well as revitalise and fortify regional organisations, like the GCC and even the Arab League. Signals are already there. For example, since 2021, tensions within the GCC have decreased, with Saudi Arabia lifting the blockage against Qatar in 2021 and Mohamed bin Zayed, the Emir of the UAE, visiting Doha during the 2022 World Cup. Iraq and Saudi Arabia accelerated their political normalisation and have been boosting economic cooperation. Likewise, the UAE has re-established its embassy in Tehran. Beyond the Persian Gulf, Turkey and Egypt are back at the negotiation table to discuss security issues. However, the most astonishing event was the normalisation of relations between Israel and Morocco, Bahrain and the UAE. Although these changes go in line with the US interest in burden-sharing in the region, a byproduct will be a more endogenous regional security system – one that Washington may not have so much leverage on to intervene as before.

This autogenous process is also possible because other external actors are increasing their influence in the region, offering alternatives to the West-dominant order. Global multipolarity means that actors like China, Russia, and India are becoming new spheres of influence in international society, enabling many Global South countries to build different types of partnerships, alliances, and institutions. For example, Moscow's role in the Middle East expanded instead of reducing after the Ukrainian invasion. Russia has maintained its troops in Libya and Syria, is mediating Assad's regime out of isolation, and has boosted its economic ties with most of the Middle Eastern countries. That is because the region is critical for Russian reorientation to non-European markets. The Middle East is not only a receptor of oil, arms, and agricultural products but also a transit hub for the flow of Russian products towards African markets.

Furthermore, it would be naïve to ignore the role of India, the fastest-growing economy in the world, in this shifting multipolarity. In fact, particularly the GCC countries are proactively seeking to expand their ties with India and take advantage of its gigantic market. India has long-standing relations with many Middle Eastern countries, but those have been overshadowed in the past by tensions with Pakistan. Things are on a changing course now, with elaborate trade agreements and investment partnerships being signed with India across the region. Particular attention must be given to the intensification of technological and securitarian collaboration between India and Israel. Moreover, India has compromised itself to build, together with the EU countries, the India–Middle East–Europe Economic Corridor (IMEC), an ambitious transport passageway linking energy-rich countries with hungrier markets.

A final word on the Chinese role is necessary. As already mentioned, China has upscaled its position in the Middle East to unforeseen levels. While its links have initiated as economic ones, they are no longer only transactional, having gained a long-standing strategic connotation that merges the Chinese development goals and the ones from regional actors. Chinese foreign policy doctrine is non-interventionist and based on the principle of coexistence, seeking to establish working relations without taking a side in regional conflicts. Thus, its negotiations with the Global South, much differently from Washington or Europe, do not impose political or human rights preconditions on partners. This has been taken as increasingly more attractive by Middle Eastern leaders, particularly in those regimes in which there was a resurgence of the robust and staunch state after the lamentable failure of the widespread protests of 2011 to increase democratic standards and political accountability.

However, it is crucial to stress that while it is taking advantage of the US' declining power, China is not interested in replacing its position as the sole superpower, let alone the Middle East's order guarantor. First, it is far from having a comparable military footprint as the US in the region. Second, China is highly dependent on the US security umbrella there, remarkably in the Persian Gulf and the Fifth Fleet's security of the Strait of Hormuz, from where the oil flows. Thirdly, one must not forget that China's own economic growth is highly interdependent on the US' economy. Thus,

President Xi Jinping's vision of a global security order does not benefit from a direct zero-sum rivalry, à la Cold War, with the US.

The emergent global multipolarity will have profound effects on the Middle East, altering some geopolitical patterns while maintaining others. What it is possible to say now is that it will bring more autonomy for regional leaders to leverage their policy options and negotiate their interests. The alliances will become even more pragmatic and multilayered than ever before. Contrary to accounts that see a future in which the Middle East is less important to international relations, this book argues that its importance will only grow. In the upcoming age of climate change mitigation, energy transition, environmental catastrophes, and expanding extractivism, the Middle East will not only be a stage in which geopolitics conundrums will take place but also from where many global decisions will have to be made. An example of that was the inclusion of not one but four Middle Eastern countries into the BRICS+ in August 2023. Predicting the necessity of reshifting alliances in the region and beyond, Brazil, Russia, India, China, and South Africa invited Saudi Arabia, Iran, the UAE, and Egypt, together with Argentina and Ethiopia, to join the most famous non-hegemonic bloc of nations.

*

This book argued that the Persian Gulf, since it emerged as a regional system in the 1970s, has been marked by a strategic triangulation between the US, Saudi Arabia, and Iran. It showed how this triangulation was formed and evolved throughout time, constantly influencing not only how these three actors behave but also having a spillover effect on other actors and the regional balance of power. This triangulation emerged as a product of insecurity. Back in 1969, Tehran, Washington, and Riyadh struggled to conceptualise an endogenous regional system in which stability would reign. Since 1979, Iran's conception of regional security arrangement became a threat to Saudi Arabia and the US, a threat they needed to handle together. It seems that now both Saudi and US American leaders are on the brink of grasping that their threat perception has changed, as well as their preferences for regional order. Growing global multipolarity, together with the increasing endogeneity of finding Middle Eastern solutions to Middle Eastern problems, may be leading to the final triangulation. History will tell.

Notes

1 Colleau, Iran's Janus-faced US foreign policy, p. 47.
2 Madawi Al-Rasheed, King Salman and his son: Winning the USA, losing the rest, in Madawi Al-Rasheed (ed.), *Salman's legacy: The dilemmas of a new era in Saudi Arabia* (London: Hurst & Company, 2018), pp. 235–251; Ben Hubbard,

MBS: The rise to power of Mohammed bin Salman (New York: William Collins, 2020); Mohammed Nurzzzaman, Chasing the dream: The Salman Doctrine and Saudi Arabia's bid for regional dominance, *Insight Turkey* 21: 3, 2019, pp. 41–52.

3 White House, National security strategy. Washington, DC, 12 October 2022. Available at www.whitehouse.gov/wp-content/uploads/2022/10/Biden-Harris-Administrations-National-Security-Strategy-10.2022.pdf. Accessed on 4 June 2024.

4 The '+' represents the collaboration between OPEC and other non-OPEC oil producing countries, particularly Russia. Saudi Arabia was very influential in forming this collaboration back in 2016 as a response to high fluctuation on prices and changing market dynamics. Since 2016, the group has met regularly to decide on collective action and influence prices.

5 Simon Mabon, Samira Nasirzadeh, and Eyad Alrefai, De-securitisation and pragmatism in the Persian Gulf: The future of Saudi–Iranian relations, *The International Spectator* 56: 4, 2021, pp. 66–83.

6 Jonathan Fulton, Situating Saudi Arabia in China's Belt and Road Initiative, *Asian Politics & Policy* 12: 3, 2020, pp. 362–383.

7 See, for example: Barry Buzan and Robert Falkner (eds), *Great powers, climate change, and global environmental responsibilities* (Oxford: Oxford University Press, 2022); Peter J. Katzenstein, Many wests and polymorphic globalism, in Peter J. Katzenstein (ed.), *Anglo-America and its discontents: Civilizational identities beyond west and east* (London and New York: Routledge, 2012), pp. 207–247; Trine Flockhart, The coming multi-order world, *Contemporary Security Policy* 37: 1, 2016, pp. 3–30.

Bibliography

Aarts, Paul; van Duijne, Joris (2009): Saudi Arabia after the U.S.–Iranian détente: Left in the lurch? *Middle East Policy* XVI (3), pp. 64–78.

Abedin, Mahan (2019): *Iran resurgent: The rise and rise of the Shia state.* London: Hurst & Company.

Abir, Mordechai (1993): *Saudi Arabia: Government, society, and the Gulf crisis.* London: Routledge.

Abootalebi, Ali R. (2018): What went wrong in Iraq? In David Lesch; Mark Haas (eds), *The Middle East and the United States: History, politics, and ideologies.* New York: Taylor & Francis, pp. 274–289.

Abrahamian, Ervand (1982): Ali Shari'ati: Ideologue of the Iranian Revolution. *MERIP Reports* 102, pp. 24–28.

Abrahamian, Ervand (1993): *Khomeinism: Essays on the Islamic Republic.* Berkeley, CA: University of California Press, p. 3.

Abrahamian, Ervand (2008): *A history of modern Iran.* New York: Cambridge University Press.

Acharya, Amitav (2014): Global International Relations (IR) and regional worlds. *International Studies Quarterly* 58 (4), pp. 647–659.

Acharya, Amitav; Buzan, Barry (2007): Why is there no non-Western international relations theory? An introduction. *International Relations of the Asia-Pacific* 7 (4), 287–312.

Adib-Moghaddam, Arshin (2006): *The international politics of the Persian Gulf: A cultural genealogy.* London: Routledge.

Adib-Moghaddam, Arshin (2012): Discourse and violence: The friend–enemy conjunction in contemporary Iranian–American relations. In Anoushiravan Ehteshami; Reza Molavi (eds), *Iran and the international system.* London: Routledge, pp. 150–163.

Agnew, John (2001): The new global economy: Time–space compression, geopolitics, and global uneven development. *Journal of World Systems Research* 7 (2), pp. 133–154.

Ahmadian, Hassan (2018): Iran and Saudi Arabia in the age of trump. *Survival* 60 (2), pp. 133–150.

Akbarzadeh, Shahram (ed.) (2011): *America's challenges in the greater Middle East: The Obama administration's policies.* London: Palgrave Macmillan.

Akbarzadeh, Shahram (ed.) (2019): *Routledge handbook of International Relations of the Middle East.* London: Routledge.

Al Oboudi, Sharifah M. (2015): Najd, the heart of Arabia. *Arab Studies Quarterly* 37 (3), pp. 282–299.

Al-Rasheed, Madawi (2010): *A history of Saudi Arabia.* New York: Cambridge University Press.

Al-Rasheed, Madawi (2011): Sectarianism as counter revolution: Saudi responses to the Arab Spring. *Studies in Ethnicity and Nationalism* 11 (3), pp. 516–523.

Al-Rasheed, Madawi (2013): *A most masculine state: Gender, politics and religion in Saudi Arabia.* London: Cambridge University Press.

Al-Rasheed, Madawi (2018): King Salman and his son: Winning the USA, losing the rest. In Madawi Al-Rasheed (ed.), *Salman's legacy: The dilemmas of a new era in Saudi Arabia.* London: Hurst & Company, pp. 235–251.

Al-Saud, Saud al Faisal bin Abdulaziz (2003): *Iran, Saudi Arabia and the Gulf: Power politics in transition.* London: I.B. Tauris.

Al-Saud, Saud al Faisal bin Abdulaziz (2005): *Saudi Arabia and the international oil market: An executive summary of the special presentation.* Houston, TX: James Baker III Institute for Public Policy, Rice University.

Al Toraifi, Adel (2012): Understanding the role of state identity in foreign policy decision-making: The rise of Saudi–Iranian rapprochement (1997–2009). PhD thesis. London: London School of Economics and Political Science.

Aljazeera (2013, 20 September): Rouhani urges leaders to engage with Iran. News Agency. Available at www.aljazeera.com/news/2013/9/20/rouhani-urges-leaders-to-engage-with-iran. Accessed on 25 September 2013.

Alsultan, Fahad; Saeid, Pedram (2016): *The development of Saudi–Iranian relations since the 1990s: Between conflict and accommodation.* New York: Routledge.

Alvandi, Roham (2010): Muhammad Reza Pahlavi and the Bahrain question, 1968–1970. *British Journal of Middle Eastern Studies* 37 (2), pp. 159–177.

Alvandi, Roham (2012): Nixon, Kissinger, and the Shah: The origins of Iranian primacy in the Persian Gulf. *Diplomatic History* 36 (2), pp. 337–372.

Amanpour, Christine (1998, 1 July): Transcript of interview with Iranian President Mohammad Khatami. CNN. Available at http://edition.cnn.com/WORLD/9801/07/iran/interview.html. Accessed on 2 March 2019.

Amiri, Reza Ekhtiari; Samsu, Ku; Ku, Hasnita Binti; Fereidouni, Hassan Gholipour (2011): The Hajj and Iran's foreign policy towards Saudi Arabia. *Journal of Asian and African Studies* 46 (6), pp. 678–690.

Anievas, Alexander; Nişancıoğlu, Kerem (2015): *How the West came to rule: The geopolitical origins of capitalism.* London: Pluto Press.

Ansari, Ali (1998): Shah Mohammad Reza Pahlavi and the myth of imperial authority. PhD thesis. London: School of Oriental and African Studies.

Ansari, Ali (2001): The myth of the white revolution: Mohammad Reza Shah, 'modernization' and the consolidation of power. *Middle Eastern Studies* 37 (3), pp. 1–24.

Aris, Stephen (2020): International vs. area? The disciplinary-politics of knowledge-exchange between IR and Area Studies. *International Theory* 13 (3), pp. 1–32.

Arjomand, Said Amir (2009): *After Khomeini: Iran under his successors.* Oxford: Oxford University Press.

Ayoob, Mohammed (2002): Inequality and theorizing in International Relations: The case for subaltern Realism. *International Studies Review* 4 (3), pp. 27–48.

Ayoob, Mohammed (2011): American policy towards the Persian Gulf: Strategies, effectiveness, and consequences. In Mehran Kamrava (ed.), *International politics of the Persian Gulf.* Syracuse, NY: Syracuse University Press, pp. 120–143.

Azdinli, Ersel; Biltekin, Gonca (2018): A typology of homegrown theorizing. In Ersel Aydınlı; Gonca Biltekin (eds), *Widening the world of International Relations.* London: Routledge, pp. 15–40.

Badeeb, Saeed M. (1993): *Saudi–Iranian relations 1932–1982*. London: Centre for Arab and Iranian Studies and Echoes.

Bahgat, Gawdat (2000): Iranian–Saudi rapprochement: Prospects and implications. *World Affairs* 162 (3), pp. 108–115.

Bahgat, Gawdat; Sharp, Robert (2014): Prospects for a new US strategic orientation in the Middle East. *Mediterranean Quarterly* 25 (3), pp. 27–39.

Barnes, Joe; Jaffe, Amy Myers (2006): The Persian Gulf and the geopolitics of oil. *Survival* 48 (1), pp. 143–162.

Barnett, Michael (1998): *Dialogues in Arab Politics: Negotiations in the regional order*. New York: Columbia University Press.

Bazzi, Mohamad (2015): Lebanon and the start of Iran and Saudi Arabia's proxy war. In The New Yorker, 26 May 2015. Available at www.newyorker.com/news/news-desk/lebanon-and-the-start-of-iran-and-saudi-arabias-proxy-war. Accessed on 2 February 2020.

BBC Monitoring (2013): Iran election: Hassan Rouhani in his own words. BBC News, 6 June 2013. Available at www.bbc.com/news/world-middle-east-22921680. Accessed on 16 November 2022.

BBC News (2010): Saudi FM al-Faisal doubts Iran sanctions plans, 16 January 2010. Available at http://news.bbc.co.uk/2/hi/middle_east/8517308.stm. Accessed on 26 June 2021.

Beck, Martin (2014): The concept of regional power as applied to the Middle East. In Henner Fürtig (ed.), *Regional powers in the Middle East: New constellations after the Arab revolts*. New York: Palgrave Macmillan, pp. 1–23.

Beeman, William (2005): *The 'Great Satan' vs. the 'Mad Mullahs': How the United States and Iran demonize each other*. London: Greenwood Press.

Bilgin, Pinar (2008): Thinking past Western IR. *Third World Quarterly* 29 (1), pp. 5–23.

Bilgin, Pinar (2015): One model of engagement between MES and IR. In *International Relations theory and a changing Middle East*. Washington, DC: Project on Middle East Political Science, pp. 6–12.

Bill, James (1998): *The eagle and the lion: The tragedy of American–Iranian relations*. London: Yale University Press.

Bill, James (2001): The politics of hegemony: the United States and Iran. *Middle East Policy*, 8 (3), pp. 89–100.

Blanchard, Christopher (2008): *The Islamic traditions of Wahhabism and Salafiyya*. Washington, DC: The Library of Congress: Congressional Research Service.

Blaney, David; Tickner, Arlene B. (2017): International relations in the prison of colonial modernity. *International Relations* 31 (1), pp. 71–75.

Blanga, Yehuda U. (2017): Saudi Arabia's motives in the Syrian Civil War. *Middle East Policy* 24 (4), pp. 45–62.

Blight, James; Lang, Janet; Hussain, Banai; Byrne, Malcon; Tirman, John (2012): *Becoming enemies: US–Iran relations and the Iran–Iraq War, 1979–1988*. Plymouth: Rowman & Littlefield.

Bowman, Bradley (2005): Realism and idealism: US policy towards Saudi Arabia from the Cold War to today. *Parameters* 35 (4), pp. 91–106.

Brands, Hal (2004): George Bush and the Gulf War of 1991. *Presidential Studies Quarterly* 34 (1), pp. 113–131.

Brands, Hal (2016): *Making the unipolar moment: U.S. foreign policy and the rise of the post-Cold War order*. New York: Cornell University Press.

Bronson, Rachel (2006): *Thicker than oil: America's uneasy partnership with Saudi Arabia*. Oxford: Oxford University Press.

Brown, Anthony Cave (1999): *Oil, God and gold: The story of Aramco and the Saudi kings*. Boston, MA: Houghton Mifflin Harcourt.

Bueger, Christian (2012): From epistemology to practice: A sociology of science for international relations. *Journal of International Relations and Development* 15 (1), pp. 97–109.

Buzan, Barry; Acharya, Amitav (2019): *The making of global international relations: Origins and evolution of IR at its centenary*. Cambridge: Cambridge University Press.

Buzan, Barry; Waever, Ole (2003): *Regions and powers: The structure of international security*. Cambridge: Cambridge University Press.

Buzan, Barry; Falkner, Robert (eds) (2022): *Great powers, climate change, and global environmental responsibilities*. Oxford: Oxford University Press.

Buzan, Barry; Lawson, George (2015): *The global transformation: History, modernity and the making of international relations*. Cambridge: Cambridge University Press.

Caldwell, Dan (2009): The legitimation of the Nixon–Kissinger grand design and grand strategy. *Diplomatic History* 33 (4), pp. 633–652.

Carter, Jimmy (1989, 23 January): State of Union Address 1980. Washington, DC. Available at www.jimmycarterlibrary.gov/assets/documents/speeches/su80jec.phtml. Accessed on 10 October 2018.

CBS News (2006): Rice: Iran's president is 'dangerous', 12 January 2006. Available at www.cbsnews.com/news/rice-irans-president-is-dangerous/. Accessed on 5 October 2019.

Chafetz, Glenn; Spirtas, Michael; Frankel, Benjamin (1998): Introduction: Tracing the influence of identity on foreign policy. *Security Studies* 8 (2–3), pp. 7–22.

Chollet, Derek; Goldgeier, James (2008): *America between the wars: From 11/9 to 9/11*. New York: Public Affairs.

Chubin, Shahram (2012): *Iran and the Arab Spring: Ascendancy frustrated*. GRC Gulf papers. Geneva: Gulf Research Center.

Chubin, Shahram; Tripp, Charles (1996): *Iran–Saudi Arabia relations and regional order*. London: Oxford University Press.

Citino, Nathan (2002): *From Arab nationalism to OPEC: Eisenhower, King Saud, and the making of US–Saudi relations*. Indianapolis, IN: Indiana University Press.

Clausen, Maria-Louise (2015): Understanding the crisis in Yemen: Evaluating competing narratives. *International Spectator* 50 (3), pp. 16–29.

Cohen, Danielle F. S. (2005): *Retracing the triangle: China's strategic perceptions of Japan in the post-Cold War Era* (Contemporary Asian Studies No. 2). Baltimore, MD: School of Law.

Colleau, Morgane (2016): Iran's Janus-faced US foreign policy: Continuity and change, opportunity and constraint. In Shahram Akbarzadeh; Dara Conduit (eds), *Iran in the World: President Rouhani's foreign policy*. Basingstoke: Palgrave Macmillan, pp. 33–59.

Committee on Foreign Affairs (2009): New beginnings: Foreign policy priorities in the Obama Administration. Hearing before the Committee on Foreign Affairs House of Representatives. Washington, DC: US Government Printing Office (Serial No. 111–167).

Cook, Alethia H.; Rawshandil, Jalīl (2009): *The United States and Iran: Policy challenges and opportunities*. New York: Palgrave Macmillan.

Cooper, Andrew Scott (2012): *The oil kings: How the U.S., Iran and Saudi Arabia changed the balance of power in the Middle East.* New York: Simon & Schuster Paperbacks.

Cordesman, Anthony H. (1997): *Saudi Arabia: Guarding the desert kingdom.* Boulder, CO: Westview Press.

Cordesman, Anthony H. (2002): *Saudi Arabia enters the 21st century: The military and internal security dimension. IV. The Saudi army.* Washington, DC: Center for Strategic and International Studies.

Cordesman, Anthony H. (2010): *The Gulf military balance in 2010: An overview.* Washington, DC: Center for Strategic and International Studies.

Cordesman, Anthony H. (2016): *Saudi Arabia and the United States: Common interests and continuing sources of tension.* Washington, DC: Center for Strategic and International Studies.

Cordesman, Anthony H.; Shelala, Robert M.; Mohamed, Omar (2014): *The Gulf military balance: The Gulf and the Arabian Peninsula.* Washington, DC: Center for Strategic and International Studies.

Cronin, Stephanie (2013): Tribes, coups and princes: Building a modern army in Saudi Arabia. *Middle Eastern Studies* 49 (1), pp. 2–28. DOI: 10.1080/00263206.2012.743892.

Crystal, Jill (1989): Coalitions in oil monarchies: Kuwait and Qatar. *Comparative Politics* 32 (4), pp. 427–443.

Darwich, May (2014): The ontological (in)security of similarity: Wahhabism versus Islamism in Saudi foreign policy, no. 263. Hamburg: German Institute of Global and Area Studies.

Darwich, May (2019): *Threats and alliances in the Middle East.* Cambridge: Cambridge University Press.

Darwich, May; Kaarbo, Juliet (2020): IR in the Middle East: Foreign policy analysis in theoretical approaches. *International Relations* 34 (2), pp. 225–245.

Dawn Today's Paper (2007): Saudi king says Iran endangering region. Available at www.dawn.com/news/230232/saudi-king-says-iran-endangering-region. Accessed on 23 June 2021.

DeLong-Bas, Natana (2004): *Wahhabi Islam: From revival and reform to global Jihad.* New York: Oxford University Press.

Dittmer, Lowell (1981): The strategic triangle: An elementary game-theoretical analysis. *World Politics* 33 (4), pp. 485–515.

Dittmer, Lowell (2014): Japan, China and the American pivot: A triangular analysis. Singapore: EAI working papers, no. 163.

Dodge, Toby (2013): State and society in Iraq ten years after regime change: The rise of a new authoritarianism. *International Affairs* 89 (2), pp. 241–257.

Dueck, Colin (2006): *Reluctant crusaders: Power, culture, and change in American grand strategy.* Princeton, NJ: Princeton University Press.

Edwards, Alex (2013): A neoclassical realist analysis of American 'dual containment' policy in the Persian Gulf: 1991–2001. PhD thesis. London: London School of Economics and Political Science.

Ehteshami, Anoushiravan (1995): *After Khomeini: The Iranian Second Republic.* London: Routledge.

Ehteshami, Anoushiravan (2008): Iran and its immediate neighbourhood. In Anoushiravan Ehteshami; Mahjoob Zweiri (eds), *Iran's foreign policy from Khatami to Ahmadinejad.* New York: Ithaca Press, pp. 129–130.

Ehteshami, Anoushiravan (2012): Domestic politics and foreign policy in contemporary Iran. In Anoushiravan Ehteshami; Reza Molavi (eds), *Iran and the international system*. London: Routledge, pp. 121–130.

El-Khawas, Mohamed (2011): Obama's engagement strategy with Iran: Limited results. *Mediterranean Quarterly* 22 (1), pp. 93–113.

Escudé, Carlos (1992): *Realismo periférico*. Buenos Aires: Planeta.

Esfahani, Hadi Salehi; Pesaran, M. Hasem (2009): Iranian economy in the twentieth century: A global perspective. *Iranian Studies* 42 (2), pp. 177–211.

Esfahani, Hadi Salehi; Squire, Lyn (2007): Explaining trade policy in the Middle East and North Africa. *Quarterly Review of Economics and Finance* 46 (5), pp. 660–684.

Fain, William Taylor (2008): *American ascendance and British retreat in the Persian Gulf region*. New York: Palgrave Macmillan.

Fawcett, Louise (ed.) (2016): *International Relations of the Middle East*. London: Oxford University Press.

Fawcett, Louise (2020): International Relations and the Middle East: Bringing Area Studies (back) in. In Contributor introduction: Does International Relations need Area Studies? *St Antony's International Review (STAIR)* 16, pp. 8–14.

Flibbert, Andrew (2006): The road to Baghdad: Ideas and intellectuals in explanations of the Iraq War. *Security Studies* 15 (2), pp. 310–352.

Flockhart, Trine (2016): The coming multi-order world. *Contemporary Security Policy* 37 (1), pp. 3–30.

Fonseca, Melody (2019): Global IR and Western dominance: Moving forward or Eurocentric entrapment? *Millennium* 48 (1), pp. 45–59.

Foreign Relations of the United States (1967, 29 July): Address by Richard M. Nixon to the Bohemian Club. San Francisco (Foundations of Foreign Policy, 2). Available at https://history.state.gov/historicaldocuments/frus1969–76v01/d2. Accessed on 5 June 2018.

Foreign Relations of the United States (1969, 21 November): Memorandum from the Chairman of the Interdepartmental Group for Near East and South Asia (Sisco) to the Chairman of the Review Group (Kissinger). 1969–1976. Washington, DC (Middle East Region and Arabian Peninsula, 133). Available at https://history.state.gov/historicaldocuments/frus1969–76v24/d133. Accessed on 17 May 2018.

Foreign Relations of the United States (1969, 30 January): Memorandum from the Executive Secretary of the Department of State (Read) to the President's Assistant for National Security Affairs (Kissinger). 1969–1976. Washington, DC (Documents on Iran and Iraq). Available at https://history.state.gov/historical documents/frus1969–76ve04/d2. Accessed on 5 June 2018.

Foreign Relations of the United States (1969, 20 October): Memorandum from the President's Assistant for National Security Affairs (Kissinger) to President Nixon. 1969–1972 (Foundations of Foreign Policy, 41). Available at https://history.state.gov/historicaldocuments/frus1969–76v01/d41. Accessed on 1 September 2018.

Foreign Relations of the United States (1969, 1 April): Memorandum of conversation. 1969–1976 (Documents on Iran and Iraq). Available at https://history.state.gov/historicaldocuments/frus1969–76ve04/d9. Accessed on 10 July 2018.

Foreign Relations of the United States (1969, 14 October): Memorandum of conversation. 1969–1976 (Middle East Region and Arabian Peninsula, 132). Available at https://history.state.gov/historicaldocuments/frus1969–76v24/d132. Accessed on 25 May 2018.

Foreign Relations of the United States (1969, 30 January): Paper prepared by the Interdepartmental Group for Near East and South Asia. Washington DC. (Middle East Region and Arabian Peninsula, 2). Available at https://history.state. gov/historicaldocuments/frus1969–76v24/d2. Accessed on 25 May 2018.

Foreign Relations of the United States (1969, 11 March): Memorandum of conversation. 1969–1976 (Middle East Region and Arabian Peninsula, 72). Available at https://history.state.gov/historicaldocuments/frus1969–76v24/d72. Accessed on 28 September 2018.

Foreign Relations of the United States (1970, 22 October): Memorandum from the President's Assistant for National Security Affairs (Kissinger) to President Nixon (Middle East Region and Arabian Peninsula, 89). Available at https://history.state. gov/historicaldocuments/frus1969–76v24/d89. Accessed on 11 August 2018.

Foreign Relations of the United States (1970, 15 May): Memorandum of conversation. Washington, DC (Middle East Region and Arabian Peninsula, 21). Available at https://2001–2009.state.gov/r/pa/ho/frus/nixon/e4/72077.htm. Accessed on 15 August 2018.

Foreign Relations of the United States (1970, 20 February): Telegram from the Department of State to the Consulate General in Dhahran (Middle East Region and Arabian Peninsula, 79). Available at https://history.state.gov/historical documents/frus1969–76v24/d79. Accessed on 3 September 2018.

Foreign Relations of the United States (1970, 4 November): Letter from the Under Secretary of State for Political Affairs (Johnson) to the Deputy Secretary of Defense (Packard). Middle East Region and Arabian Peninsula. Jordan (13). Available at https://history.state.gov/historicaldocuments/frus1969–76v24/d13. Accessed on 17 June 2018.

Foreign Relations of the United States (1972, 21 September): Intelligence memorandum prepared in the Central Intelligence Agency (Middle East Region and Arabian Peninsula, 122). Available at https://history.state.gov/historicaldocuments/ frus1969–76v24/d122. Accessed on 14 July 2018.

Foreign Relations of the United States (1973, 24 July): Memorandum of conversation. Washington, DC (Iran; Iraq, 1973–1976, 27). Available at https://history.state. gov/historicaldocuments/frus1969–76v27/d27. Accessed on 14 August 2018.

Foreign Relations of the United States (1974, 26 June): Telegram from the Embassy in Iran to the Department of State. Tehran (Iran; Iraq, 1973–1976, 62). Available at https://history.state.gov/historicaldocuments/frus1969–76v27/d62. Accessed on 31 May 2018.

Foreign Relations of the United States (1977, 2 February): Memorandum from William Quandt and Gary Sick of the National Security Council Staff to the President's Assistant for National Security Affairs (Brzezinski). 1977–1980 (Middle East Region and Arabian Peninsula, 1). Available at https://history.state. gov/historicaldocuments/frus1977–80v18/d1. Accessed on 1 July 2018.

Foreign Relations of the United States (1979, 19 June): Memorandum from Gary Sick and Fritz Ermarth of the National Security Council Staff to the President's Assistant for National Security Affairs (Brzezinski). Washington, DC (1977–1980, volume XVIII, 24). Available at https://history.state.gov/historicaldocuments/ frus1977–80v18/d24. Accessed on 5 October 2018.

Foreign Relations of the United States (1979, 17 March): Memorandum of conversation. 1977–1980, Volume XVIII. Riyadh (Middle East Region and Arabian Peninsula, 188). Available at https://history.state.gov/historicaldocuments/ frus1977–80v18/d188. Accessed on 12 May 2018.

Foreign Relations of the United States (1979, 5 June): Telegram from the Embassy in Saudi Arabia to the Department of State. Jidda (1977–1980, volume XVIII, 193). Available at https://history.state.gov/historicaldocuments/frus1977–80v18/d193. Accessed on 10 December 2018.

Foreign Relations of the United States (1979, 9 February): Letter from President Carter to Secretary of Defense Brown. Washington, DC (1977–1980, volume XVIII, 19). Available at https://history.state.gov/historicaldocuments/frus1977–80v18/d19. Accessed on 10 December 2018.

Foreign Relations of the United States (1979, 11 May): Minutes of a special co-ordination committee meeting. Washington, DC (1977–1980, volume XVIII). Available at https://history.state.gov/historicaldocuments/frus1977–80v18/d23. Accessed on 10 December 2018.

Foreign Relations of the United States (1978, 9 September): Telegram from the Embassy in Saudi Arabia to the Department of State and the Department of Defense. Jidda (1977–1980, volume XVIII, 215). Available at https://history.state.gov/historicaldocuments/frus1977–80v18/d255. Accessed on 10 October 2018.

Fouad, Alaa (1998): The OIC summit in Tehran: Herald of a new beginning? *Insight Turkey* 12, pp. 121–128.

Foulon, Michiel (2015): Neoclassical Realism: Challengers and bridging identities. *International Studies Review* 17, pp. 635–661.

Foulon, Michiel; Meibauer, Gustav (2020): Realist avenues to global International Relations. *European Journal of International Relations* 26 (4), 1203–1229.

Freedman, Lawrence (2009): *A choice of enemies: America confronts the Middle East.* New York: Public Affairs.

Freyberg-Inan, Annette; Harrison, Ewan; James, Patrick (2009): *Rethinking Realism in International Relations.* Baltimore, MD: Johns Hopkins University Press.

Fulton, Jonathan (2020): Situating Saudi Arabia in China's Belt and Road Initiative, *Asian Politics & Policy* 12 (3), pp. 362–383.

Fürtig, Henner (2002): *Iran's rivalry with Saudi Arabia between the Gulf Wars.* Reading: Ithaca Press.

Ganji, Babak (2006): *Politics of confrontation: The foreign policy of the USA and revolutionary Iran.* New York: Palgrave Macmillan.

Gaub, Florence (2015): *The Gulf moment: Arab relations since 2011. SSI.* Washington, DC: United States Army War College.

Gause, Gregory (1990): *Saudi–Yemeni relations: Domestic structures and foreign influence.* New York: Columbia University Press.

Gause, Gregory (1994): *Oil monarchies: Domestic and security challenges in the Arab Gulf states.* New York: Council on Foreign Relations Press.

Gause, Gregory (1999): Systemic approaches to Middle East International Relations. *International Studies Review* 1, pp. 11–31.

Gause, Gregory (2003): Balancing what? Threat perception and alliance choice in the Gulf. *Security Studies* 13 (2), pp. 273–305.

Gause, Gregory (2010): *The international relations of the Persian Gulf.* Cambridge: Cambridge University Press.

Gause, Gregory (2011): Saudi Arabia's regional security strategy. In Mehran Kamrava (ed.), *International politics of the Persian Gulf.* Syracuse, NY: Syracuse University Press, pp. 169–183.

Gause, Gregory (2014): *Beyond sectarianism: The new Middle East Cold War.* Washington, DC: Brookings Doha Center.

Gause, Gregory (2018): Saudi regime stability and challenges. In Madawi Al-Rasheed (ed.), *Salman's legacy: The dilemmas of a new era in Saudi Arabia*. London: Hurst & Company, pp. 31–45.

Gelardi, Maiken (2020): Moving Global IR forward: A road map. *International Studies Review* 22 (4), pp. 830–852.

Georgi, Lydia (2007): Saudi King slams 'illegitimate occupation' of Iraq. *Agence France Presse*, 28 March. Available at https://archive.globalpolicy.org/security/issues/iraq/attack/statement/2007/0328saudiking.htm. Accessed on 26 June 2021.

Gerges, Fawaz (1991): The study of Middle East International Relations: A critique. *British Journal of Middle Eastern Studies* 18 (2), pp. 208–220.

Ghaneabassiri, Kamyar (2002): U.S. foreign policy and Persia, 1856–1921. *Iranian Studies* 35 (1), pp. 145–175.

Ghattas, Kim (2020): *Black wave: Saudi Arabia, Iran, and the forty-year rivalry that unravelled culture, religion, and collective memory in the Middle East.* New York: Henry Holt and Company.

Giddens, Anthony (1991): *Modernity and self-identity*. New York: Polity Press.

Goldberg, Jeffrey (2016): The Obama Doctrine. *The Atlantic*, April. Available at www.theatlantic.com/magazine/archive/2016/04/the-obama-doctrine/471525/. Accessed on 12 November 2018.

Gray, Colin; Barlow, Jeffrey (1985): Inexcusable restraint: The decline of American military power in the 1970s. *International Security* 10, pp. 27–69.

Grey, Felicia (2017): How oil twists the hegemon's arm: The case of the United States and Saudi Arabia and their ambivalent partnership. *Digest of Middle East Studies* 26 (2), pp. 320–339.

Halabi, Yakub (2009): *US foreign policy in the Middle East: From crises to change.* Farnham: Ashgate.

Halliday, Fred (1994): *Rethinking international relations*. New York: Red Globe Press.

Halliday, Fred (2005): *The Middle East in international relations: Power, politics and ideology*. Cambridge: Cambridge University Press.

Halliday, Fred (2009): The Middle East and conceptions of 'international society'. In Barry Buzan; Ana Gonzales-Pelaez (eds), *International society and the Middle East: English school theory at the regional level*. New York: Palgrave Macmillan, pp. 1–24.

Hart, Parker (1998): *Saudi Arabia and the United States: Birth of a security partnership*. Bloomington, IN: Indiana University Press.

Harvey, Katherine (2021): *A self-fulfilling prophecy: The Saudi struggle for Iraq*. London: Hurst & Company.

Heisey, D.; Trebing, David (1983): A comparison of the rhetorical visions and strategies of the Shah's white revolution and the Ayatollah's Islamic revolution. *Communication Monographs* 50 (2), pp. 158–174.

Hellmann, Gunther; Valbjørn, Morten (2017): Problematizing global challenges: Recalibrating the 'inter' in IR-theory inter alia. *International Studies Review* 19 (2), pp. 279–309.

Hertog, Steffen (2020): The 'rentier mentality', 30 years on: Evidence from survey data. *British Journal of Middle Eastern Studies* 47 (1), pp. 6–23.

Hinnebusch, Raymond (2003): *The international politics of the Middle East*. New York: Manchester University Press.

Hinnebusch, Raymond; Ehteshami, Anousharivan (eds) (2014): *The foreign policies of the Middle East states*. Boulder, CO: Lynne Rienner.

Hiro, Dilip (2018): *Cold War in the Islamic world: Saudi Arabia, Iran and the struggle for supremacy*. New York: Oxford University Press.

Hoffman, Stanley (1977): An American social science: International relations, *Daedalus* 106 (3), pp. 41–60.

Holsti, Kalevi (1996): *The state, war and the state of war*. Cambridge: Cambridge University Press.

Hook, Steven (2015): Hegemonic stability and American power. In Tim Niblock; Steven Hook (eds), *The United States and the Gulf: Shifting pressures, strategies and alignments*. Berlin: Gerlach Press, pp. 23–41.

Hopf, Ted (1998): The promise of constructivism in International Relations theory. *International Security* 23 (1), pp. 171–200.

Hubbard, Ben (2020): *MBS: The rise to power of Mohammed bin Salman*. New York: William Collins.

Huntington, Samuel P. (1996): *The clash of civilizations and the remaking of world order*. New York: Simon & Schuster.

Spiegel (2006): Iran's Ahmadinejad rejects looming UN deadline on nuke program, 29 August 2006. Available at www.spiegel.de/international/defiance-in-tehran-iran-s-ahmadinejad-rejects-looming-un-deadline-on-nuke-program-a-434190.html. Accessed on 5 October 2019.

Isemberg, David (1984): *The rapid deployment force: The few, the futile, the expendable*. Policy analysis, 44. Washington, DC: Cato Institute.

Ismael, Tareq (1986): *International relations of the Contemporary Middle East: A study in world politics*. Syracuse, NY: Syracuse University Press.

Javedanfar, Meir (2009): The grand bargain with Tehran. The Guardian, 3 March. Available at www.theguardian.com/commentisfree/2009/mar/03/iran-nuclear-weapons. Accessed on 20 December 2020.

Jones, Jason (2011): *American rhetorical construction of the Iranian nuclear threat*. London: Continuum International Publishing Group.

Jones, Toby (2010): *Desert kingdom: How oil and water forged modern Saudi Arabia*. Cambridge, MA: Harvard University Press.

Juneau, Thomas (2014): U.S. power in the Middle East: Not declining. *Middle East Policy* 21 (2), pp. 40–52.

Juneau, Thomas (2015): *Squandered opportunity: Neoclassical Realism and Iranian foreign policy*. Stanford, CA: Stanford University Press.

Kamrava, Mehran (ed.) (2011): *International politics of the Persian Gulf*. Syracuse, NY: Syracuse University Press.

Karanjia, Ruston Kurshedji (1997): *The mind of a monarch*. London: Allen & Unwin.

Karasik, Theodore (2014): Obama's anticipated march to Saudi Arabia. *Al Arabiya*, 2 March. Available at https://english.alarabiya.net/en/views/news/middle-east/2014/02/03/On-President-Obama-s-anticipated-march-to-Saudi-Arabia. Accessed on 21 December 2020.

Katouzian, Homa (2010): The Iranian Revolution at 30: The dialectic of state and society, *Middle East Critique* 1, pp. 35–53.

Katzenstein, Peter J. (2012): Many wests and polymorphic globalism. In Peter J. Katzenstein (ed.), *Anglo-America and its discontents: Civilizational identities beyond west and east*. London: Routledge, pp. 207–247.

Kayaoglu, Turan (2010): Westphalian Eurocentrism in International Relations theory. *International Studies Review* 12 (2), pp. 193–217.

Kechichian, Joseph (2000): Saudi Arabia will to power. *Middle East Policy* 7 (2), pp. 47–59.

Kechichian, Josoph (2008): *Faysal: Saudi Arabia's king for all seasons.* Gainesville, FL: University Press of Florida.

Keynoush, Banafsheh (2016): *Saudi Arabia and Iran: Friends or foes?* New York: Palgrave Macmillan.

Khomeini, Ruhollah (1981): *Islam and revolution: Writings and declarations of Imam Khomeini.* Contemporary Islamic Thought. Berkeley, CA: Library of Congress Cataloguing in Publication Data (Persian Series).

Khomeini, Ruhollah al-Mousavi (1983): Imam Khomeini's last will and testament. Unknown. Available at www.al-islam.org/printpdf/book/export/html/39086. Accessed on 7 August 2018.

Kinch, Penelope (2016): *The US–Iran relationship: The impact of political identity on foreign policy.* London: I.B. Tauris.

Kitchen, Nicholas (2020): Neoclassical Realism and a theory of international politics. In Gustav Meibauer; Linde Desmaele; Tudor Onea; Nicholas Kitchen; Michiel Foulon; Alexander Reichwein; Jennifer Sterling-Folker (eds), Forum: Rethinking Neoclassical Realism at theory's end. *International Studies Review* 23 (1), pp. 268–295.

Koppes, Clayton R. (1972): Captain Mahan, General Gordon, and the origins of the term 'Middle East'. *Middle Eastern Studies* 12 (1), pp. 95–98.

Korany, Bahgat; Dessouki, Hillah (2008): *The foreign policies of Arab states: The challenge of globalization.* Cairo: American University of Cairo Press.

Kramer, Martin (1987): Behind the riot in Mecca. *Washington Institute for Near East Policy* 5, pp. 1–10.

Krane, Jim (2019): *Energy kingdoms: Oil and political survival in the Persian Gulf.* New York: Columbia University Press.

Kull, Steven (2007): Muslim public opinion on US policy, attacks on civilians, and al Qaeda. World Public Opinion. Available at www.worldpublicopinion.org/pipa/pdf/apr07/START_Apr07_rpt.pdf. Accessed on 14 August 2018.

Kumar, Deepa (2018): The right kind of 'Islam'. *Journalism Studies* 19 (8), pp. 1079–1097.

Kurzman, Charles (2012): The Arab Spring: Ideals of the Iranian green movement, methods of the Iranian Revolution. *International Journal Middle East Studies* 44 (1), pp. 162–165.

Lake, Anthony (1994): Confronting backlash states. *Foreign Affairs*, March/April. Available at www.foreignaffairs.com/articles/iran/1994–03–01/confronting-backlash-states. Accessed on 10 August 2018.

Lauer, Matt (1998): Interview with Secretary of State Madeleine K. Albright, NBC-TV 'The Today Show', 19 February 1998. Columbus, OH. Office of the Spokesman, US Department of State.

Lawson, Fred (2011): Security dilemmas in the contemporary Persian Gulf. In Mehran Kamrava (ed.), *International politics of the Persian Gulf.* Syracuse, NY: Syracuse University Press, pp. 50–71.

Layne, Christopher (2006): *The peace of illusions: American grand strategy from 1940 to the present.* Ithaca, NY: Cornell University Press.

Lemke, Douglas (2002): *Regions of war and peace.* Cambridge: Cambridge University Press.

Levran, Aharon (2019): Major Middle East armed forces. In Aharon Levran (ed.), *The Middle East military balance 1986,* New York: Routledge, pp. 123–205.

Lobell, Steven; Taliaferro, Jeffrey; Ripsman, Norrin (2009a): Introduction: Neo-classical Realism, the state, and foreign policy. In Steven Lobell; Jeffrey Taliaferro;

Norrin Ripsman (eds), *Neoclassical Realism, the State, and foreign policy*. New York: Cambridge University Press, pp. 1–42.

Lobell, Steven; Taliaferro, Jeffrey; Ripsman, Norrin (eds) (2009b): *Neoclassical Realism, the State, and Foreign Policy*. New York: Cambridge University Press.

Long, David (1985): *The United States and Saudi Arabia: Ambivalent allies*. Boulder, CO: Westview Press.

Long, David (2004): US–Saudi relations: Evolution, current conditions, and future prospects. *Mediterranean Quarterly* 15 (3), pp. 24–37.

Luke, Timothy (1985): Dependent development and the OPEC states: State formation in Saudi Arabia and Iran under the international energy regime. *Studies in Comparative International Development* 20, pp. 31–54.

Lynch, Marc (1999): *State interests and public spheres: The international politics of Jordan's identity*. New York: Columbia University Press.

Mabon, Simon (2015): *Saudi Arabia and Iran: Power and rivalry in the Middle East*. London: I.B. Tauris.

Mabon, Simon (2023): *The struggle for supremacy in the Middle East*. Cambridge: Cambridge University Press.

Mabon, Simon; Nasirzadeh, Samira; Alrefai, Eyad (2021): De-securitisation and pragmatism in the Persian Gulf: The future of Saudi–Iranian relations. *The International Spectator* 56 (4), pp. 66–83.

Mahdavy, Hossein (1970): Patterns and problems of economic development in rentier states: The case of Iran. In M. A. Cook (ed.), *Studies in the economic history of the Middle East: From the rise of Islam to the present day*. New York: Oxford University Press, pp. 428–468.

Majin, Shokrollah K. (2017): Iranian and Saudi cultural and religious identities: Constructivist perspective, *Open Journal of Political Science* 7 (1), pp. 65–81.

Mason, Robert (2014): Back to realism for an enduring US–Saudi relationship. *Middle East Policy* 21, pp. 32–44.

McGlinchey, Stephen (2012): Arming the Shah: U.S. arms policies towards Iran, 1950–1979. Doctor of Philosophy in International Relations thesis. Cardiff: Cardiff University.

Mearsheimer, John (2001): *The tragedy of great power politics*. New York: Norton.

Meibauer, Gustav (2020): Interests, ideas, and the study of state behaviour in neoclassical realism. *Review of International Studies* 46 (1), pp. 20–36.

Meibauer, Gustav; Desmaele, Linde; Onea, Tudor; Kitchen, Nicholas; Foulon, Michiel; Reichwein, Alexander; Sterling-Folker, Jennifer (eds) (2020): Forum: Rethinking Neoclassical Realism at theory's end. *International Studies Review* 23 (1), pp. 268–295.

Meneshari, David (1988): Khomeini's policy toward ethnic and religious minorities. In Milton Esman; Ilamar Rabinovich (eds), *Ethnicity, pluralism, and the state in the Middle East*. New York: Ithaca Press, pp. 215–230.

Mitzen, Jennifer (2006): Ontological security in world politics: State identity and the security dilemma. *European Journal of International Relations* 12 (3), pp. 341–370.

Moazami, Behrooz (2013): *State, religion, and revolution in Iran, 1796 to the present*. New York: Palgrave Macmillan US.

Mohammadi, Manouchehr (2012): The Islamic republic of Iran and the international system: Clash with the domination paradigm. In Anoushiravan Ehteshami; Reza Molavi (eds), *Iran and the international system*. London: Routledge, pp. 71–90.

Monten, Jonathan (2005): The roots of the Bush Doctrine: Power, nationalism, and democracy promotion in US strategy. *International Security* 29 (4), pp. 112–156.

Morgenthau, Hans J. (1954): *Politics among nations*. Chicago, IL: University of Chicago Press.

Morton, A. (2005): The 'failed state' of international relations. *New Political Economy* 10 (3), pp. 371–379.

Musavian, Hossein (2014): *Iran and the United States: An insider's view on the failed past and the road to peace*. New York: Bloomsbury.

Nasr, Vali (2007): *The Shia revival: How conflicts within Islam will shape the future*. New York: W.W. Norton & Company.

Nasseri, Ladane (2015): Rouhani tells Iranians economy can't growth with nation isolated. Bloomberg, 1 April. Available at www.bloomberg.com/news/articles/2015–01–04/iran-s-economy-can-t-grow-while-nation-isolated-rouhani-says. Accessed on 5 March 2019.

National Security Advisor (1980): Text of Khomeyni's message on hostage situation. Collection JC-NSA (Records of the Office of the National Security Advisor (Carter Administration)). Available at www.docsteach.org/documents/document/text-of-khomeynis-message-on-hostage-situation. Accessed on 14 August 2020.

New York Times (1987): Excerpts from Khomeini speeches. *New York Times*, 8 April, Times Machine. Available at www.nytimes.com/1987/08/04/world/excerpts-from-khomeini-speeches.html. Accessed on 10 October 2019.

New York Times (1995): Burned by loss of Conoco deal, Iran says U.S. betrays free trade. *New York Times*, 20 March. Available at www.nytimes.com/1995/03/20/business/burned-by-loss-of-conoco-deal-iran-says-us-betrays-free-trade.html. Accessed on 30 July 2023.

Niblock, Tim (2006): *Saudi Arabia: Power, legitimacy and survival*. London: Routledge.

Nixon, Richard (1969): Address by President Richard Nixon to the UN General Assembly. United States Department of State. Available at https://2009–2017.state.gov/p/io/potusunga/207305.htm. Accessed on 20 September 2018.

Nixon, Richard (1978): *RN: The memoirs of Richard Nixon*. New York: Simon & Schuster Paperbacks.

Nonemman, Gerd (2005): *Analyzing Middle East foreign policies: The relationship with Europe*. New York: Routledge.

Nurzzaman, Mohammed (2019): Chasing the dream: The Salman Doctrine and Saudi Arabia's bid for regional dominance. *Insight Turkey* 21 (3), pp. 41–52.

Office of the Chief of Staff Files (n.d.): Hamilton Jordan's Confidential Files, Iran. 11/79, Container 34b declassified on 20 August 1997.

Office of Staff Secretary (n.d.): Folder 10/13/80 Container 180 (Presidential Files). Available at www.jimmycarterlibrary.gov/library/findingaids/Staff_Secretary.pdf. Accessed 17 September 2018.

The Office of the Supreme Leader (2013, 25 November): Supreme Leader's response to President Rouhani's letter on nuclear negotiations. Tehran. Available at www.leader.ir/en/content/11329/Supreme-Leader's-Response-to-President-Rouhani's-Letter-on-Nuclear-Negotiations. Accessed on 20 December 2020.

Okruhlik, Gwenn (2003): Saudi Arabian–Iranian relations: External rapprochement and internal consolidation. *Middle East Policy* 10 (2), pp. 113–125.

Onea, Tudor (2012): Putting the 'classical' in Neoclassical Realism: Neoclassical Realist theories and US expansion in the post-Cold War. *International Relations* 26 (2), pp. 139–164.

Oren, Michael B. (2007): *Power, faith and fantasy: America in the Middle East, 1779 to the present.* New York: W. W. Norton & Company.

Palley, Thomas (2008): *The U.S. economy after Bush. Policy Brief, IMK: Institut fur Makrookonomie und Konjunkturforschung.* Düsseldorf: Hans Bockler Stiftung.

Parsi, Trita (2007): *Treacherous alliance: The secret dealings of Israel, Iran, and the United States.* New Haven, CT: Yale University Press.

Partrick, Neil (2016): *Saudi Arabian foreign policy? Conflict and cooperation.* New York: I.B. Tauris.

Paul, T. V.; Larson, Deborah Welch; Wohlforth, William (2014): Status and world order. In T. V. Paul; Deborah Welch Larson; William Wohlforth (eds), *Status in world politics.* New York: Cambridge University Press, pp. 3–32.

PBS Frontline (2007): Showdown with Iran, 25 October 2007. Available at www.pbs.org/wgbh/pages/frontline/showdown/etc/synopsis.html. Accessed on 20 December 2020.

Petersen, Tore (2011): *Richard Nixon, Great Britain and the Anglo-American alignment in the Persian Gulf and Arabian Peninsula: Making allies out of clients.* Brighton: Sussex Academic Press.

Pollack, Josh (2002): Saudi Arabia and the United States, 1931–2002. *Middle East Review of International Affairs* 6 (3), pp. 77–102.

Pollack, Kenneth (2005): *The Persian puzzle: The conflict between Iran and America.* Munich: Random House.

Potter, Lawrence (2009a): Introduction. In Lawrence Potter (ed.), *The Persian Gulf in History.* New York: Palgrave Macmillan, pp. 1–26.

Potter, Lawrence (ed.) (2009b): *The Persian Gulf in history.* New York: Palgrave Macmillan.

Presidential Library and Museum (1985): Remarks at the welcoming ceremony for King Fahd bin Abdulaziz Al Saud of Saudi Arabia. Washington, DC. Available at www.reaganlibrary.gov/research/speeches/21185a. Accessed on 5 October 2018.

Presidential Library and Museum (1986): Statement by Principal Deputy Press Secretary speakers on the Congressional disapproval of the United States Arms Sale to Saudi Arabia. Available at www.reaganlibrary.gov/research/speeches/50786d. Accessed on 5 October 2018.

Pressman, Jeremy (2009): Power without influence: The Bush Administration's foreign policy failure in the Middle East. *International Security* 33 (4), pp. 149–179.

Prosser, Andrew (2017): Much ado about nothing? Status ambitions and Iranian nuclear reversal. *Strategic Studies Quarterly* 11 (3), pp. 26–81.

Rakel, Eva Patricia (2008): Power, Islam, and political elite in Iran: A study on the Iranian political elite from Khomeini to Ahmadinejad. PhD thesis. Amsterdam: Amsterdam Institute for Social Science Research, Faculty of Social and Behavioural Sciences.

Ramazani, R. K. (1997): ARAB v. Arab–Iranian relations in modern times. In Ehsah Yarshater (ed.), *Encyclopaedia Iranica.* Costa Mesa: Mazda Publishers, 8, pp. 220–224.

Rathbun, Brian (2008): A rose by any other name: Neoclassical Realism as the logical and necessary extension of structural realism. *Security Studies* 17 (2), pp. 294–321.

Renshon, Jonathan (2017): *Fighting for status: Hierarchy and conflict in world politics.* Princeton, NJ: Princeton University Press.

Rich, Ben (2012): Gulf War 4.0: Iran, Saudi Arabia and the complexification of the Persian Gulf equation. *Islam and Christian-Muslim Relations* 23 (4), pp. 471–486.

Richter, Thomas (2014): Saudi Arabia: A conservative p(l)ayer on the retreat? In Henner Fürtig (eds), *Regional powers in the Middle East: New constellations after the Arab revolts*. New York: Palgrave Macmillan.

Riedel, Bruce (2018): *Kings and presidents: Saudi Arabia and the United States since FDR*. Washington, DC: Brookings Institution.

Ripsman, Norrin; Taliaferro, Jeffrey; Lobell, Steven (2016): *Neoclassical Realist theory of international politics*. New York: Oxford University Press.

Ronald Reagan Presidential Library (n.d.a): Collection: Roberts, John G/ Box. Available at www.reaganlibrary.gov/sites/default/files/digitallibrary/smof/counsel/roberts/box-008/40–485–6908381–008–002–2017.pdf. Accessed on 5 October 2018.

Ronald Reagan Presidential Library (n.d.b): Folder: Saudi Arabia: King Khalid. (8100189–8102956) Box 29. Executive Secretariat, NSC (Digital Library Collections). Accessed on 5 October 2018.

Ross, Michael L. (2012): *The oil curse: How petroleum wealth shapes the development of nations*. Princeton, NJ: Princeton University Press.

Rubin, Lawrence (2017): *Islam in the balance: Ideational threats in Arab politics*. Stanford, CA: Stanford University Press.

Russell, James (2005): Saudi Arabia in the 21st century: A new security dilemma. *Middle East Policy* 12 (3), pp. 64–78.

Ryan, Curtis (2019): *Shifting alliances and shifting theories in the Middle East: Shifting global politics and the Middle East*, Project on Middle East Political Science Studies (34).

Sadegui, Hossein; Ahmadian, Hassan (2011): Iran–Saudi relations: Past pattern, future outlook. *Iranian Review of Foreign Affairs* 1 (4), pp. 115–148.

Sadjadpour, Karim (2009): *Reading Khamenei: The world view of Iran's most powerful leader*. Washington, DC: Carnegie Endowment of International Peace.

Safran, Nadav (1998): *Saudi Arabia: The ceaseless quest for security*. Ithaca, NY: Cornell University Press.

Said, Edward (1978): *Orientalism*. New York: Vintage Books.

Saikal, Amin (2019): *Iran rising: The survival and future of the Islamic Republic*. Princeton, NJ: Princeton University Press.

Salimi, Hossein (2012): Foreign policy as a social construction. In Anoushiravan Ehteshami; Reza Molavi (eds), *Iran and the international system*. London: Routledge, pp. 130–150.

Saudi Arabia Embassy (2008): Saudi King Abdullah and senior princes on Saudi policy toward Iraq. Riyadh (08RIYADH649_a). Available at https://wikileaks.org/plusd/cables/08RIYADH649_a.html. Accessed on 23 December 2020.

Saudi Arabia Embassy (2009a): Saudi Exchange with Russian Ambassador on Iran's nuclear plans. Riyadh (09RIYADH181_a). Available at https://wikileaks.org/plusd/cables/09RIYADH181_a.html. Accessed on 23 December 2020.

Saudi Arabia Embassy (2009b): Saudi King says talks with Iranian FP 'heated'. Riyadh (09RIYADH427_a). Available at https://wikileaks.org/plusd/cables/09RIYADH427_a.html. Accessed on 23 December 2020.

Schmidt, Brian (2007): Realism and facets of power in international relations. In Felix Berenskoetter; M. K. Williams (eds), *Power in world politics*. New York: Routledge, pp. 43–64.

Seliktar, Ofira (2012): *Navigating Iran: From Carter to Obama*. New York: Palgrave Macmillan.

Shami, Seteney Khalid; Miller-Idriss, Cynthia (eds) (2016): *Middle East Studies for the new millennium: Infrastructures of knowledge*. New York: New York University Press.

Sick, Gary (2018): The United States in the Persian Gulf: From twin pillars to dual containment. In David Lesch; Mark Haas (eds), *The Middle East and the United States: History, politics, and ideologies*. New York: Taylor & Francis, pp. 237–253.

Simes, Dimitri K. (2002): Learning to lead: President George W. The National Interest, 10 September 2002. Available at https://nationalinterest.org/article/learning-to-lead-2143. Accessed on 17 June 2021.

Sindi, Abdullah M. (1980): King Faisal and Pan-Islamism. In Willard A. Beling (ed.), *King Faisal and the modernisation of Saudi Arabia*. New York: Routledge, pp. 171–189.

Singer, J. David; Bremer, Stuart; Stuckeym, John (1972): Capability distribution, uncertainty, and major power war, 1820–1965. Version 5.0. In Bruce Russet (ed.), *Peace, war, and numbers*. Beverly Hills, CA: SAGE, pp. 19–48.

Sobek, David; Clare, Joe (2013): Me, myself, and allies: Understanding the external sources of power. *Journal of Peace Research* 50 (4), pp. 469–478.

Stein, Janice Gross (1989): The wrong strategy in the right place: The United States in the Gulf. *International Security* 13 (3), pp. 142–167.

Sterling-Folker, Jennifer (2009a): Forward is as forward does: Assessing Neoclassical Realism from a traditions perspective. In Annette Freyberg-Inan; Ewan Harrison; Patrick James (eds), *Rethinking Realism in international relations*. Baltimore, MD: Johns Hopkins University Press, pp. 192–218.

Sterling-Folker, Jennifer (2009b): Neoclassical Realism and identity: Peril despite profit across the Taiwan Strait. In Steven Lobell; Jeffrey Taliaferro; Norrin Ripsman (eds), *Neoclassical Realism, the state, and foreign policy*. New York: Cambridge University Press, pp. 99–139.

St. Marie, Joseph; Naghshpour, Shahdad (2011): *Revolutionary Iran and the United States: Low-intensity conflict in the Persian Gulf*. Farnham: Ashgate.

Sun, Degang; Zoubir, Yahia H. (2012): From hard military bases to soft military presence: US military deployment in Iraq reassessed. *Journal of Middle Eastern and Islamic Studies (in Asia)* 6 (3), pp. 85–106.

Sun, Degang; Zoubir, Yahia H. (2015): The eagle's nest in the Gulf: Analysis of US military deployment in the GCC Countries (1991–2014). In Tim Niblock; Steven Hook (eds), *The United States and the Gulf: Shifting pressures, strategies and alignments*. Berlin: Gerlach Press, pp. 78–97.

Takeyh, Ray (2009): *Guardians of the Revolution: Iran and the world in the age of the Ayatollahs*. Oxford: Oxford University Press.

Taliaferro, Jeffrey (2004): *Balancing risks: Great power intervention in the periphery*. Ithaca, NY: Cornell University Press.

Telhami, Shibley (1992): *Power and leadership in international bargaining: The path to the Camp David Accords*. New York: Columbia University Press.

Telhami, Shibley (2008): 2008 annual Arab public opinion pool survey. Available at www.brookings.edu/wp-content/uploads/2012/04/0414_middle_east_telhami.pdf. Accessed on 20 December 2020.

Telhami, Shibley; Barnett, Michael (2002): *Identity and foreign policy in the Middle East*. London: Cornell University Press.

Terrill, Andrew W. (2011): *The Saudi–Iranian rivalry and the future of Middle East security*. Carlisle: Strategic Studies Institute, US Army War College.

Tessler, Mark (ed.) (1999): *Area Studies and social science: Strategies for understanding Middle East politics*. Bloomington, IN: Indiana University Press.

Teti, Andrea (2007): Bridging the Gap: IR, Middle East Studies and the disciplinary politics of the Area Studies controversy. *European Journal of International Relations* 13 (1), pp. 117–145. DOI: 10.1177/1354066107074291.

Tickner, Arlene B.; Wæver, Ole (2009): Introduction. In Arlene B. Tickner; Ole Wæver (eds), *International relations scholarship around the world*. New York: Routledge, pp. 1–18.

Time magazine (1974, 4 November): *Time* magazine cover. Available at https://content.time.com/time/covers/0,16641,19741104,00.html.

Turton, Helen Louise; Freire, Lucas G. (2016): Peripheral possibilities: Revealing originality and encouraging dialogue through a reconsideration of 'marginal' IR scholarship. *Journal of International Relations and Development* 19 (4), pp. 534–557.

Ulrichsen, Kristian Coateias (2015): *Insecure Gulf: The end of certainty and the transition to the post-oil era*. New York: Oxford University Press.

United Nations (1987): General Assembly: Provisional verbatim record of the fifteenth meeting. New York. Available at https://digitallibrary.un.org/record/144904. Accessed on 10 April 2018.

United Nations, General Assembly (1986): Forty-first session: Provisional verbatim record of the 19th meeting. New York. Available at https://undocs.org/en/A/41/PV.19. Accessed on 4 October 2018.

United States, Presidency (1989): *Public papers of the presidents of the United States*, George H. W. Bush. Washington, DC: Volume 1A, Part 1.

United States, Presidency (1994): *Public papers of the presidents, William J. Clinton*. Washington, DC: Book II – 1 August to 31 December.

United States, Presidency (1999): *Public papers of the presidents of the United States, William J Clinton. Book I*. Washington, DC: United States Government Printing Office.

US Department of State (2000, 17 March): Remarks before the American-Iranian Council. As released by the Office of the Spokesman. Washington. Available at: https://1997–2001.state.gov/statements/2000/000317.html. Accessed on 7 August 2018.

US Department of State (2005, 20 June): Remarks at the American University in Cairo. Available at https://2001–2009.state.gov/secretary/rm/2005/48328.htm. Accessed on 21 June 2021.

US Diplomatic Mission to Germany (2001, October): President Bush address to a joint session of Congress and the American People United States Capitol Washington, DC. Available at https://usa.usembassy.de/etexts/docs/ga1–010920.htm. Accessed on 23 June 2021.

Valbjørn, Morten (2004a): 'Culture blind and culture blinded': Images of Middle Eastern conflicts in international relations. In Dietrich Jung (ed.), *The Middle East and Palestine: Global politics and regional conflict*. New York: Palgrave Macmillan US, pp. 39–78.

Valbjørn, Morten (2004b): Toward a 'Mesopotamian turn': Disciplinarily and the study of the International Relations of the Middle East, *Journal of Mediterranean Studies* 14 (1/2), pp. 47–75.

Van Evera, Stephen (1999): *Causes of war: Power and the roots of conflict*. Ithaca, NY: Cornell University Press.

Vitalis, Robert (2007): *America's kingdom: Mythmaking on the Saudi oil frontier.* Stanford, CA: Stanford University Press.

Volgy, Thomas J.; Corbetta, Renato; Grant, Keith; Baird, Ryan G. (eds) (2011): *Major powers and the quest for status in international politics: Global and regional perspectives.* New York: Palgrave Macmillan.

Walt, Stephen (1987): *The origin of alliances.* New York: Cornell University Press.

Walt, Stephen M.; Mearsheimer, John (2007): *The Israel lobby and U.S. foreign policy.* New York: Farrar, Straus, and Giroux.

Waltz, Kenneth (1979): *A theory of international politics.* New York: Random House.

Ward, Steven R. (2009): *Immortal: A military history of Iran and its armed forces.* Washington, DC: Georgetown University Press.

Wastnidge, Edward; Mabon, Simon (eds) (2022): *Saudi Arabia and Iran: The struggle to shape the Middle East.* Manchester: Manchester University Press.

Wedeen, Lisa (2016): Scientific knowledge, liberalism, and empire: American political science in the modern Middle East. In Seteney Khalid Shami; Cynthia Miller-Idriss (eds), *Middle East Studies for the new millennium: Infrastructures of knowledge.* New York: New York University Press, pp. 31–82.

Wehrey, Frederic (2015): Saudi Arabia's anxious autocrats. *Journal of Democracy* 26 (2), pp. 71–85.

Wehrey, Frederic M.; Karasik, Theodore; Nader, Alireza; Ghez, Jeremy; Hansell, Lydia; Guffey, Robert (2009): *Saudi–Iranian relations since the fall of Saddam: Rivalry, cooperation, and implications for U.S. policy.* Santa Monica, CA: RAND Security Research Division.

Weiss, Stanley (2015): It's time to talk about Saudi Arabia. *The Huffpost*, 23 October. Available at www.huffpost.com/entry/its-time-to-talk-about-sa_b_8363936. Accessed on 23 June 2021.

Wendt, Alexander (1992): Anarchy is what states make of it: The social construction of power politics. *International Organization* 46, pp. 391–425.

White House (1984): National Security Decision Directive 139: Measures to improve U.S. posture and readiness to respond to developments in the Iran–Iraq War, 5 April. Washington, DC, Declassified – 90423. Available at https://irp.fas.org/offdocs/nsdd/nsdd-139.pdf. Accessed on 14 July 2018.

White House (2002): The national security strategy of the United States of America. Washington, DC. Available at http://georgewbush-whitehouse.archives.gove/nsc/nss/2002. Accessed on 21 June 2021.

White House (2009): Remarks by President at Cairo University. Cairo. Available at https://obamawhitehouse.archives.gov/the-press-office/remarks-president-cairo-university-6–04–09. Accessed on 21 April 2018.

White House (2022): National security strategy. Washington, DC, 12 October. Available at www.whitehouse.gov/wp-content/uploads/2022/10/Biden-Harris-Administrations-National-Security-Strategy-10.2022.pdf. Accessed on 4 June 2024.

Williams, Phil (1987): The limits of American power: From Nixon to Reagan. *International Affairs* 63 (4), pp. 575–587.

Williams, Willian (1972): *The tragedy of American diplomacy.* New York: Dell.

Wohlforth, William (1993): *The elusive balance: Power and perceptions during the Cold War.* Ithaca, NY: Cornell University Press.

World Bank (n.d.a): Armed forces personnel, total – Iran. 1984–2018. Available at https://data.worldbank.org/indicator/MS.MIL.TOTL.P1?locations=IR. Accessed on 15 June 2021.

World Bank (n.d.b): Armed forces personnel, total – Saudi Arabia. 1985–2018. Available at https://data.worldbank.org/indicator/MS.MIL.TOTL.P1?locations=SA. Accessed on 15 June 2021.

World Bank (n.d.c): Armed forces personnel, total – United States. 1984–2018. Available at https://data.worldbank.org/indicator/MS.MIL.TOTL.P1?locations=US. Accessed on 15 June 2021.

World Bank (n.d.d): Fertility rate, total (births per woman) – Iran. from 1960 to 2019. Available at https://data.worldbank.org/indicator/SP.DYN.TFRT.IN?locations=IR. Accessed on 6 September 2021.

World Bank (n.d.e): Fertility rate, total (births per woman) – Saudi Arabia from 1960 to 2019. Available at https://data.worldbank.org/indicator/SP.DYN.TFRT.IN?locations=SA. Accessed on 6 September 2021.

World Bank (n.d.f): GDP (current US$) – Iran, Islamic Rep. 1960–2018. Available at https://data.worldbank.org/indicator/NY.GDP.MKTP.CD?locations=IR. Accessed on 21 May 2021.

World Bank (n.d.g): GDP (current US$) – Saudi Arabia. 1968–2019. Available at https://data.worldbank.org/indicator/NY.GDP.MKTP.CD?locations=SA. Accessed on 21 May 2021.

World Bank (n.d.h): GDP (current US$) – United States. 1960–2019. Available at https://data.worldbank.org/indicator/NY.GDP.MKTP.CD?locations=US. Accessed on 21 May 2021.

World Bank (n.d.i): GDP growth (annual %) – Iran, Islamic Rep. 1961–2019. Available at https://data.worldbank.org/indicator/NY.GDP.MKTP.KD.ZG?locations=IR. Accessed on 21 May 2021.

World Bank (n.d.j): GDP growth (annual %) – Saudi Arabia. 1969–2019. Available at https://data.worldbank.org/indicator/NY.GDP.MKTP.KD.ZG?locations=SA. Accessed on 21 February 2021.

World Bank (n.d.k): GDP growth (annual %) – United States. 1961–2019. Available at https://data.worldbank.org/indicator/NY.GDP.MKTP.KD.ZG?locations=US. Accessed on 21 May 2021.

World Bank (n.d.l): GDP per capita (current US$) – Iran, Islamic Rep. 1960–2019. Available at https://data.worldbank.org/indicator/NY.GDP.PCAP.CD?locations=IR. Accessed on 21 May 2021.

World Bank (n.d.m): GDP per capita (current US$) – Saudi Arabia, Islamic Rep. 1960–2019. Available at https://data.worldbank.org/indicator/NY.GDP.PCAP.CD?locations=IR. Accessed on 21 May 2021.

World Bank (n.d.n): GDP per capita (current US$) – United States. 1960–2019. Available at https://data.worldbank.org/indicator/NY.GDP.PCAP.CD?locations=US. Accessed on 21 May 2021.

World Bank (n.d.o): Inflation, consumer prices (annual %) – Iran, Islamic Rep. 1960–2019. Available at https://data.worldbank.org/indicator/FP.CPI.TOTL.ZG?locations=IR. Accessed on 21 June 2021.

World Bank (n.d.p): Military expenditure (% of GDP) – Iran, Islamic Rep. 1960–2019. Available at https://data.worldbank.org/indicator/SP.POP.GROW?locations=IR. Accessed on 21 May 2021.

World Bank (n.d.q): Military expenditure (% of GDP) – Saudi Arabia. 1963–2019. Available at https://data.worldbank.org/indicator/MS.MIL.XPND.GD.ZS?locations=SA. Accessed on 21 May 2021.

World Bank (n.d.r): Military expenditure (% of GDP) – United States. 1960–2019. Available at https://data.worldbank.org/indicator/MS.MIL.XPND.GD.ZS?locations=US. Accessed on 21 May 2021.

World Bank (n.d.s): Military expenditure (current USD) – Iran, Islamic Rep. 1960–2019. Available at https://data.worldbank.org/indicator/MS.MIL.XPND.CD?locations=IR. Accessed on 21 May 2021.

World Bank (n.d.t): Military expenditure (current USD) – Saudi Arabia. 1960–2019. Available at https://data.worldbank.org/indicator/MS.MIL.XPND.CD?locations=SA. Accessed on 21 May 2021.

World Bank (n.d.u): Military expenditure (current USD) – United States. 1960–2019. Available at https://data.worldbank.org/indicator/MS.MIL.XPND.CD?locations=US. Accessed on 21 May 2021.

World Bank (n.d.v): Population growth (annual %) – Iran. 1961–2019. Available at https://data.worldbank.org/indicator/SP.POP.GROW?locations=IR. Accessed on 21 May 2021.

World Bank (n.d.w): Population growth (annual %) – Saudi Arabia. 1961–2019. Available at https://data.worldbank.org/indicator/SP.POP.GROW?locations=SA. Accessed on 21 May 2021.

World Bank (n.d.x): Population growth (annual %) – United States. 1961–2019. Available at https://data.worldbank.org/indicator/SP.POP.GROW?locations=US. Accessed on 21 May 2021.

World Bank (n.d.y): Population, total – Iran, Islamic Rep. 1960–2019. Available at https://data.worldbank.org/indicator/SP.POP.TOTL?locations=IR. Accessed on 21 May 2021.

World Bank (n.d.z): Population, total – Saudi Arabia. 1960–2019. Available at https://data.worldbank.org/indicator/SP.POP.TOTL?locations=SA. Accessed on 21 May 2021.

World Bank (n.d.aa): Population, total – United States. 1960–2019. Available at https://data.worldbank.org/indicator/SP.POP.TOTL?locations=US. Accessed on 21 May 2021.

World Bank (2021): GDP per capita (current US$) – Saudi Arabia. 1968–2019. Available at https://data.worldbank.org/indicator/NY.GDP.PCAP.CD?locations=SA. Accessed on 21 May 2021.

Wynbrandt, James. (2004): *Brief history of Saudi Arabia*. New York: Facts on File.

Yetiv, Steven A. (1999): The evolving Persian Gulf (1979–97): A comparative analysis. *Defense Analysis* 15 (2), pp. 147–166.

Yetiv, Steven A. (2008): *The absence of grand strategy: The United States in the Persian Gulf, 1972–2005*. Baltimore, MD: Johns Hopkins University Press.

Yetiv, Steven A. (2018): The Iraq War of 2003: Why the United States decided to invade. In David Lesch; Mark Haas (eds), *The Middle East and the United States: History, politics, and ideologies*. New York: Taylor & Francis, pp. 53–274.

Yossef, Amr; Cerami, Joseph R. (2015): *The Arab Spring and the geopolitics of the Middle East: Emerging security threats and revolutionary change*. London: Palgrave Macmillan UK.

Zenko, Micah (2018): *US military policy in the Middle East – An appraisal: Research Paper*. US and Americas Programme. London: Royal Institute of International Affairs.

Index

EU authorised representative for GPSR:
Easy Access System Europe, Mustamäe tee 50,
10621 Tallinn, Estonia
gpsr.requests@easproject.com

www.ingramcontent.com/pod-product-compliance
Ingram Content Group UK Ltd.
Pitfield, Milton Keynes, MK11 3LW, UK
UKHW021948130625
459659UK00007B/80